OTES

DANGER

405088   403667   500891

Questions
pour un
Champion
Le jeu officiel
ÉDITION
SPÉCIALE
20 ANS
MINDSCAPE
3+
www.pegi.info

RG
A REG GRUNDY PRODUCTION
FOR TVS TELEVISION
© U.K. TVS TELEVISION LIMITED 1986
WORLDWIDE REG GRUNDY PRODUCTION (G.B.) LTD. 1986

GET READY TO MATCH THE STARS!
BLANKETY
BLANKS
VOLUME ONE 4 DVD SET

ELLES
&
ELLS

Tanamera
Starring
Christopher
Bowen
Ed Devereaux
Khym Lam

CELEBRITY
SQUARES

Distributed by

Ruck
Zuck

RG
REG GRUNDY
PRODUCTIONS, INC.

Surf
Rescue

SCRABBLE
RG

PRISONER
CELL BLOCK
THE CULT PHENOMENON FROM DOWN UN

ER

GRUNDY PRODUCTION

REG GRUNDY

By Reg Grundy

PIER 9

Published in 2010 by Pier 9, an imprint of Murdoch Books Pty Limited.

Murdoch Books Australia
Pier 8/9
23 Hickson Road
Millers Point NSW 2000
Phone: +61 (0) 2 8220 2000
Fax: +61 (0) 2 8220 2558
www.murdochbooks.com.au

Murdoch Books UK Limited
Erico House, 6th Floor
93–99 Upper Richmond Road
Putney, London SW15 2TG
Phone: +44 (0) 20 8785 5995
Fax: +44 (0) 20 8785 5985
www.murdochbooks.co.uk

Publisher: Colette Vella
Editor: Desney King
Designer: Jo Byrne

National Library of Australia Cataloguing-in-Publication entry

Author: Grundy, Reg, 1923-
Title: Reg Grundy / Reg Grundy.
ISBN: 978-1-74266-034-9 (hbk.)
Subjects: Grundy, Reg, 1923---Biography.
                Television producers and directors--Australia--Biography.
                Motion picture producers and directors--Australia--Biography.
                Documentary films--Production and direction--Australia.
Dewey Number: 791.45233092

Printed and bound in Australia by Griffin Press

The paper this book is printed on is certified by the © 1996 Forest Stewardship Council A.C. (FSC). Griffin Press holds FSC chain of custody SGS–COC–005088. FSC promotes environmentally responsible, socially beneficial and economically viable management of the world's forests.

FSC
Mixed Sources
Product group from well-managed forests, controlled sources and recycled wood or fibre
Cert no. SGS-COC-005088
www.fsc.org
© 1996 Forest Stewardship Council

For Joy—
'I'll be loving you always'

Acknowledgements

There are thousands who helped me on my way.

Actors, audio guys, autocue operators, cameramen, caterers, directors, directors' assistants, floor managers, graphic artists, grips, lighting directors, make-up artists, musicians, prop buyers, producers, producers' assistants, production managers, production secretaries, script and story editors, script typists, set carpenters, set designers, set dressers, stagehands, video editors, vision switchers and mixers and writers. Wherever you are, in Australasia, America, Britain or Europe, thank you for so many great shows.

And the thousands of people who made up the studio audiences. Without you, there would have been no applause.

And of course the millions who watched our shows around the world. Without you, there would have been nothing at all.

And thanks to all those relatives, friends and colleagues who so generously shared their thoughts and memories with me as I sifted through my life these last three years.

RG

And special credit goes to ...

In 1957 I was hosting *Wheel of Fortune* on radio and John O'Grady was feeding me the questions.

Then he left.

In 1959 I got my break in television and asked John to join me.

He said, 'You can't afford me.'

I said, 'Yes I can.'

He was right, I was wrong.

Years later he walked out on me again to work for ABC TV comedy where he was involved in many successful shows including *Mother and Son*.

Forty years passed by.

I decided to tell my story.

Jog was back.

Guide, mentor, friend.

THIS IS MY LIFE

Somehow or other, I'm eighty-five years old. I'm told I don't look it, and I certainly don't feel it.

I look in my passport to make sure.

Yep, eighty-five.

Joy and I are about to leave our suite at the Sheraton on the Park in Sydney and move down to the ballroom for the party. Not a celebration of my birthday, you understand; Joy won't have a bar of that. But a celebration just the same.

It was earlier in the year when I realised something was going on. Something I knew nothing about. We were in Bermuda, working our usual seven-day week and living in our beautiful house. It faced onto a quiet harbour that wrapped around an inlet, giving us our own saltwater lagoon. Perfect. What a great place to spend most of our waking hours staring into a computer screen.

We'd moved from Australia to Bermuda when my ambitions stretched from America to our west, to the United Kingdom and Europe on our northeast. We return to Australia whenever we can but Bermuda is the place where we still spend most of each year.

Our first Bermuda home had been on a cliff facing the Atlantic with longtails, the national emblem of Bermuda, wheeling and diving into the crevices. Then we built our current home to accommodate our ever-increasing collection of clothes, shoes and accessories, as well as our books and my photographic gear. A perfect solution, if a tad on the expensive side.

Of course there were more valid reasons for the move. Our shetland sheep dog Caliope loved the lagoon and decided she would become the first sheltie to learn to swim. She beats me most days, but between you and me she cuts corners. But don't tell her I told you so.

Joy and I have the perfect marriage. She's my pride and joy, a very talented writer and a smart businesswoman with strongly held views on important matters and a tendency to speak to her rather older husband as if she were his mother.

And me? Well, I tend to agree with everything she says.

We are in perfect sync. But suddenly the connection seemed to have dropped out. People were quietly closing doors, speaking softly. Avoiding me. I'd had enough.

'Okay, Perce, what's going on?'

Perce is one of the many pet names I have for my wife. Don't ask me why. She was looking sheepish.

'It's nothing, really.'

'Come on, out with it!'

'It's a surprise.'

'I hate surprises.'

She sighed, accepting defeat gracefully.

'It's no big deal, Reg ...'

When she called me Reg I knew it was pretty serious.

'A bit of a show, that's all. I think it's time we celebrated your long, amazing career with a few friends.'

'How many friends?'

'Oh, a couple of hundred, I suppose.'

No big deal indeed.

So here we are in Sydney and this is the night. Joy is in teal, wearing velvet and lace and looking as if she'd stepped out of a palace in the eighteenth century. Me? Well, I'm in a favourite old tux.

The ballroom looks stunning; it is bathed in blue light. The guests are all in black tie and glamorous long dresses. It is a glittering, sparkling occasion and there is a magical feeling in the air. As we enter, our 200 guests turn and applaud. Our MC, the inimitable Alan Jones, resplendent in an elegant evening jacket, is on the stage and ready to go.

The band is playing a tune I know well, but no one else could possibly recognise. David Campbell, one of Australia's best, is singing 'Blue Night', my song, which came third in a national radio contest during the Second World War. The audience seems to like it, especially when they're told I wrote it. I hadn't thought of it in decades but a few weeks ago I'd stumbled my way through it for Grundy producer/composer Peter Pinne and asked him to write an arrangement for me. He gave it a Latin feel and it sounds great—I'm wondering if I'll be able to get through the night without breaking up.

'A bit of a show', Joy had said. Was that ever the understatement of the decade!

So how did I get to be here at this fancy hotel on this amazing night? How did I become someone known not just for my undies—my 'Reg Grundies'—but for the entertainment I created both in Australia and throughout the world? How did I manage to do it all?

That's what this book is about: a young man who once earned a pound a week at David Jones, who not only realised most of his dreams but hopefully helped others dream some of theirs as well.

WHEN ROY MET LILLIAN

I picked up the mandolin. It was covered in dust and the strings needed tightening. It lay on top of an old suitcase and a medley of boxes and discarded objects on the verandah looking out on the backyard, which embraced a chicken coop set among straggling grass and weeds.

My grandparents' house in Blacktown.

I plucked at the strings. I loved the sound but put it down carefully, dreaming of the day when Grandpa might give it to me.

Maybe I would be a musician when I grew up.

I had just turned five and loved to wander through the old weatherboard house. There in the dining room were Grandpa and Grandma in uniform, staring out of their picture frames at me. My father had explained that earlier in their lives they had been in the Salvation Army. Soldiers? It was exciting to imagine the wars they must have fought.

In the kitchen, which housed an old wood-burning stove, I sometimes performed for them, and they always praised me. 'Danny Boy' was my best number and no matter how many times I sang it, I always got a big hand. It was a hit in the kitchen.

Maybe I'd be an entertainer one day.

My mother said, 'Bubby, darling, it's nice for you to dream about being a grown-up, but first you've got to get an education'.

I wasn't sure that was so important.

My mother, Lillian Josephine Lees, had grown up in Newcastle and moved to Sydney when she was old enough to get a job. She was gorgeous— a flapper. In 1919, at age twenty, she became a cashier for Ernest Hillier, a chocolatier whose confectioneries were all the rage.

Two years later my father, Roy Harold Grundy, came to the city from the country roads of Albury. He walked the streets of Sydney and found a room in Woolloomooloo. There were no lights, so he couldn't see the bed bugs that flourished there. He rubbed his aching feet, sore from the unforgiving pavements.

Work was hard to find so he stood in line for a job as a 'useful'. The man behind him in the queue told of the wife and kids he was trying to support.

Dad said, 'Your need is greater than mine, mate. Here—stand in front of me.'

The stranger got the job, but Roy was called in to meet the great man, Ernest Hillier, resplendent in a handmade suit with striking pink shirt and matching tie.

'Roy, I was only looking for one man, but you did the right thing for that fella so I'm taking you on as well.'

Roy Grundy moved quickly through the ranks until he became manager of the store, then overall manager of all twenty Hillier chocolate shops in Sydney.

He had an eye for the girls, particularly Lillian Josephine Lees. They were a striking couple. Lillian, beautiful with chorus girl legs so well suited to the short flapper dresses of the time and Roy, handsome in a flashy way, his hat set jauntily on his head, a cigarette dangling from his mouth. They were the perfect pair, and soon married.

In 1923, I was born. I was to be their one and only child, the son they loved and adored.

But soon the Depression was hitting hard and Hillier was forced to close his stores. In 1929, the small Grundy family moved to Adelaide, where Roy had been offered the job of running the food areas of Myers, one of Adelaide's biggest department stores. And so it was in Adelaide that my formal education began.

And ended.

SONG AND DANCE IN ADELAIDE

Apart from my early triumph with 'Danny Boy', my only contact with show business was when I appeared on stage at the Port Adelaide Town Hall in 'a High Class Variety Concert featuring pupils of the Emma Hamnet Elocution School with Accompaniment by the Port Adelaide Municipal Band'. I was eight years old. Dressed in tails with a ballet of little girls behind me, I strolled across the stage singing: 'There ought to be a Moonlight Saving Time, so I could love that gal of mine, until the birdies wake and shine, good morning'.

The words had no meaning for me because I was concentrating on my footwork. Fred Astaire had nothing to worry about.

Before the concert my father had taken a snapshot of me in tails and top hat at the back of the house in which we were living in the Adelaide suburb of Unley—that very same lawn where I was later to fall and break my left arm. 'Look, Mum, Bonzo tripped me,' I lied, displaying my arm, which sagged in the middle between wrist and elbow. I had jumped off a stack of boxes and overbalanced onto the jagged stones that bordered the pockets of grass. A small deception. Better to blame the dog.

By age ten all thoughts of show business had been forgotten. For now.

I was a quiet boy who liked his own company. I had a couple of friends my own age at the local school at the end of the street in Westbourne Park where we had moved from Unley. I was content with my life and content with my mother and father. The three of us seemed just right to me.

Days at Westbourne Park public were mainly uneventful as I vied with my friend Alan Cox to be top of the class. I never succeeded, always finishing second. One day, a teacher sent me on an errand to a neighbouring suburb and before returning I stopped by a pond in a small public garden and imagined what it must be like to have whole days when only I would decide what I might do. A tingle ran through me. What wonderful things I could achieve.

Apart from school, the days were a blissful mix of cricket in Alan's backyard, where almonds fell from the trees to be eaten during the game, and bike rides to faraway places with Alan and my second-best friend, Harold Hamblyn. And if not all that far away then at least two or three blocks from the street in which we all lived.

And then it was time for high school.

But before I could settle in at Adelaide High my life was to change. My father was now a departmental manager at John Martins, the up-market department store in Rundle Street owned by the Hayward family.

'Ian Hayward says you should go to St Peters,' my father told me. 'He's spoken to the headmaster and if he's satisfied with your grades, you can move over.'

I'm not sure what I thought of that. The Collegiate School of St Peters— Saints—was the very best of the independent schools in Adelaide, and close to the best in Australia.

My friend Alan Cox had finished up at Prince Alfred College on the other side of Adelaide. Princes and Saints were archrivals, but it was the distance between them that meant the end of the friendship.

In spite of the glorious setting and the specialist teachers at Saints, I lost my way academically and became an average student. Maybe it was the burgeoning friendship with Max Short and my love of art which were the distractions. Whenever we could, Max and I worked on impersonations of English radio comics of the time: Flanagan and Allen, George Formby, Clapham and Dwyer, and the Scotsmen Sandy Stewart and Harry Lauder all got a go—what we lacked in talent, we made up for in enthusiasm. Show business was calling me again.

Sadly, Max didn't survive the Second World War. He was killed while flying a Martin Baltimore light bomber with the RAF Middle East Command in North Africa. He was twenty years old.

Considering I was soon to earn my living as a sports commentator, I played sport with little interest during my high school years. I wanted to be doing creative things, and art master Joseph Choate encouraged me in my efforts to express myself graphically. My woodcuts and etch-ings appeared in the school magazine and I contributed set designs to the school's theatrical productions.

But in 1938, when I was fifteen years old, Dad was appointed manager of all the food departments at Grace Bros, Broadway in Sydney, including the huge Grace auditorium.

Rather than become a boarder, I left Saints. I was going to the Big Smoke. It was exciting, and not a little frightening.

TRUE LOVE AT DJs

I was sixteen.

In Sydney the family seemed to want for nothing, even though the lifestyle was simple, homely.

I got a job at David Jones, Sydney's premier department store. I was part of the Junior Executive Training Scheme but, in reality, I was a well-dressed office boy. I was assigned to Frank Cox, nephew of the artist Elioth Gruner. Cox was merchandising manager of DJs' women's fashion departments, which covered the whole of the second floor and much of the third. The fact that I was not uncomfortable in this environment said much for my gentle nature.

And love was just around the corner. Or, at least, just across the corridor from my cubbyhole on the second floor. Love in the exclusive model department. Love in the form of Beverly Watson, an ethereal figure who haunted my dreams. She was a salesgirl but in my dreams she could have been a model. For a long while I was too shy to do anything about it, and was tentative when perhaps I should have been more direct.

On Friday nights the store closed at nine. One Friday evening, plucking up my courage and barely able to breathe, I asked her to go out with me during our tea break and so found myself sitting opposite this vision at a table in the balcony café at Farmers, the other major Sydney department store. It was only a block or so away from DJs and yet the walk there and back—having her by my side—filled me with untold delicious anguish. And then she was sitting across the table from me as, in a fever of indecision, I somehow managed to order our meals.

How sophisticated I was. What a man of the world. If only I'd had the courage to develop matters. I did not.

It was not long after that wonderful dinner date that I was appointed assistant buyer for ladies sportswear, and the connection with Beverly was loosened. Now she was on the second floor and I was on the third.

Ten years later I was working as an announcer at radio station 2SM. Beverly called me. She told me she was married with two kids. Obviously someone had made the moves that I had failed to make.

'I'd love to see you again', she said. 'Why don't we have coffee sometime?'

I made an excuse and that was the last I heard of her.

The buyer for ladies sportswear was Margaret Phillips, an energetic young woman who took me on the rounds of the manufacturers as she placed her orders for the new season. I enjoyed making my own decisions based on what I thought women would wear. My judgments were made on instinct and from watching Margaret go through the process.

And I was introduced to the mysteries of, and differences between, mark-ups and profit margins. Margaret would say:

Suppose we buy a line of swimsuits at, say, 12 shillings a piece and we mark them up 100 per cent. That means we sell them for 24 shillings, and what do we say is our profit margin? Well, it's certainly not 100 per cent. It's 12 shillings divided by 24 shillings times one hundred. That's right. Our profit margin is 50 per cent. That's high but it gets eroded when we have a sale to clear out old stock. In reality, we aim for a profit margin overall of about a third.

It was all news to me but I took it in, even though money matters bored me. I was more interested in what colours, patterns and styles to order from the manufacturer's range. I started to be good at it after a while.

But as time went by the creative urge was working away at me. I had met the head of the display department, Henry Birdwood, an imposing man with a booming voice. Birdwood had seen some of the sketches I'd made during my lunch hours.

'You've got talent, Reg. Just needs developing.'

Suddenly I was transferred to the top floor where the creative people lived. I was told that 'shoes' were moving to the fourth floor and I was to come up with some designs. The job was beyond me, although some of my ideas managed to be incorporated into the final layout.

One day the chairman of David Jones, Sir Charles Lloyd-Jones, sent for me. As the escalator moved me relentlessly towards his floor, I frantically tried to think of what sins I might have committed. Was it about that affair with Beverly? Well, hardly an affair … but maybe DJs didn't like members of staff fraternising … or … It was too late. I was announcing myself to the great man's secretary. In my panic, I was even having trouble remembering my name.

Sir Charles was standing, moving around his desk to shake my hand. He was even smiling.

'Sit down, sit down.'

He pointed to a chair in front of his desk.

I waited for him to pronounce sentence.

I held my breath.

'Reg, I believe you're interested in the arts. Is that right?'

I squeaked that it was.

'Well, we'd like to offer you something. David Jones is prepared to pay your fees at the Julian Ashton Art School. Could be useful to us. Part-time, of course. After hours. What do you say?'

I mumbled my acceptance and backed out of the presence.

It was quite an offer. People like Elioth Gruner, George Lambert and William Dobell had been students there. Every Tuesday night after work I found myself standing at an easel with a charcoal stick in my hand, drawing outlines of a plaster cast head. It was slow and exacting work and my instructor, Henry Gibbons, was relentless in seeking perfection in proportion and line.

Gibbons would look at my charcoal study and ask, 'Do you believe the proportions are correct?'

Invariably and reluctantly, I would admit that they were not.

'Then, my dear Grundy, do it again. Do it again.'

I lasted thirteen weeks.

Those visits to art school were about the extent of my social life at the time, for I was a solitary young man and except for a brief friendship with Maurice Heckenberg, another young David Jones hopeful, my time was spent at home with my parents in our small flat in Double Bay.

And then the war came.

I was with my mother and father driving up William Street towards Kings Cross in Sydney when Prime Minister Menzies came on the radio and told the Australian people they were at war with Germany. It was 3 September 1939.

WHAT I DID IN THE WAR

Two days before Christmas 1941, at the age of eighteen, I was called up and travelled to Waverley Park with my two cut lunches. From there I was taken with other young men to Central Station and on to the army camp at Kurrajong.

I spent my first night in the army sharing a tent with several others and sleeping on a palliasse, which was a canvas bag two metres long and half a metre wide, stuffed with straw and protected from rising damp by a groundsheet. The only light was from a kerosene lamp suspended from the tent pole. It was a strange experience for a quiet young man.

Next day I was medically examined and given inoculations and a vaccination, then sent to the parade ground to learn how to slope arms. As the days went by and the vaccination site grew angry, it was hard to handle the old heavy rifle without it landing on my throbbing arm, not to mention the route marches up the winding road to Kurrajong Heights.

I was Signalman Grundy, a private in the 1st Cavalry (5A) Signals.

The Corps was transferred to Greta Army Camp near Maitland. I was homesick enough in the first few weeks to run the gauntlet by going AWL and heading home to Sydney, risking arrest at Central Station and injury on the return trip as I leapt off the train when it slowed passing the camp.

I suppose the first few months in the army weren't the happiest days of my life but I learned a few things, including how to smoke. My father had even given me tobacco on that clandestine visit. We just didn't know back then the damage it caused.

On 1 November 1943, I was promoted to Corporal. My rapid rise from the ranks had taken only two years, and I'd jumped the intermediate rank of Lance Corporal. Soon after that, camp conditions brought on serious skin problems and I was sent to 113th Australian General Hospital at Concord in the Sydney suburbs where I spent a quiet three months before being classified B2, meaning the Army thought I was 'fit for sedentary duties only'.

When I was discharged from hospital I was allowed to live at home in Double Bay. Each morning I travelled by tram to Rose Hill racecourse, arriving by 0600 to sit in the stand that encircled the track. Eventually I would be called before an officer, my name would be marked off and I'd be dismissed until the following morning at 0600. This pointless routine lasted for about ten days until, at last, I was sent to the Sydney Showground where I slept on concrete in the cattle and pig building.

After a few nights, I returned to our flat in Double Bay.

Some time later, I was assigned to the District Finance Office (DFO) at the Sydney Showground where I found myself acting as pay sergeant to the thousand odd soldiers—accountants in uniform—who worked in the Hordern Pavilion. I had no idea what I was doing there; I had no accounting or bookkeeping experience at all. But I was in the army, and went where I was told.

I found a new friend, Valdemar Smith, who played jazz piano in the florid style of Erroll Garner, and I was soon staging weekly lunchtime concerts in a small hall across from the Hordern Pavilion. I did comedy monologues, performed sketches, sang and was the MC—pretty much a one-man band really, with Vald at the piano.

On Saturdays, Vald and I would listen to recordings of the jazz greats in my flat at Double Bay. With only one track on each side of those old 78s, we got to know the performances very well.

'Vald, why don't we cut a record? You on piano and me singing.'

He liked the idea. We booked a small studio at Palings music store in George Street. Vald played confidently. I sang on key. I thought we sounded pretty good. We walked out of the studio with the precious acetate. Two songs, one on each side: 'Pennies from Heaven' and 'I'm Confessing that I Love You'.

Some weeks later I invited a few guys and gals around to our flat in Double Bay. I slipped the acetate on the turntable, and there I was singing 'I'm Confessing'. I hadn't got past the first couple of lines when one of the girls said, 'Oh my God'. I smiled. I had my first fan. 'He sounds as if he'll die before he finishes the song.'

That night I put the acetate away; it was never again to see the light of day.

Despite that early setback I do still sing, using special DVD backings. I think I must have improved because my friends usually applaud quite enthusiastically these days. I even sing duets on regular occasions with Australia's most listened-to broadcaster, Alan Jones. We call ourselves the Southern Highlanders, so there's no argument about who gets top billing. What an opportunity—if only I still owned a record label.

Meanwhile, back at the DFO I was ordered to read all the official announcements into a microphone set up in the great hall. My voice echoed throughout the building as a thousand or so soldier-clerks listened or ignored me.

'You've got a marvellous voice. You should be in radio,' was a common opinion. It sounded like a great idea to me.

I decided that when I was out of the army I would give myself one year to try and make it happen.

GETTING STARTED

I was demobbed on 1 August 1946. It was time to start a new life, but it took a while.

It was almost Easter before I heard that 2GZ in Orange was looking for an assistant to the program manager for its coverage of the 1947 Royal Easter Show. It was enterprising for a country radio station to have a facility in Sydney and, as it turned out, it was lucky for me. I found myself in a small studio in Angel Place, off Pitt Street.

Ian Samuels, the program manager, shook my hand. 'Okay, Reg. What experience have you had in radio?'

'None,' I said. 'How do I get experience if no one will give me a chance?'

He laughed and handed me two sheets of paper. 'Here's a list of country towns. Just read the list out loud, then follow up with the news item on the other page.'

When the audition was over, Ian Samuels said mildly, 'You pronounced *Canowindra* ... Can-o-win-dra.'

I made a mental note of the pronunciation, *Can-oun-dra*.

'I'll get it right next time.'

He looked at me speculatively.

'Reckon you might. Okay. It's not much of a job, just reading cattle and pig results. But it's yours if you want it.'

Of course I wanted it. I'd be talking into a microphone again, only this time it would be on radio. I floated out of the building.

I was going back to the Showground where I'd spent two years in the army's Pay Corps. And how different it was now. This was the first Show since before the war, and the great building where I'd worked was full of stands and happy families collecting sample bags.

My job was to collect the results of the livestock judging each day, and occasionally read them into a microphone. Although the broadcasts were coming from Sydney, they were heard only in Orange and the surrounding area covered by 2GZ. My parents were beside themselves trying to pick up the signal in Double Bay.

It was hardly demanding work and after a couple of days I made the first of what was to become a lifetime of pitches.

'Mr Samuels. Err, Ian,' I said. 'Seems to me that people in Orange might like to hear from some of their local competitors. I could bring them here for you to interview, if you like.'

'Not a bad idea. Have you talked to any of them? Do you know what questions I should ask?'

'Oh, yes. Here's a list.'

'Well, then, wouldn't it be better if you did the interviews yourself?'

Ian had given me my break.

When the Show ended I was offered a job at 2GZ. I badly wanted to accept but reasoned that I should stay put and try to crack Sydney radio rather than be consigned to the bush. In the end, I bought an acetate recording of one of my interviews, hoping it would be my passport into the big time. I had no idea how I was going to get started, and yet the answer lay very close to home.

Our flat was just up the hill from the Double Bay shopping centre. The entrance to the building was on New South Head Road, down a ramp and through a small foyer to number 1 and number 2 flats. We had flat number 2, which was away from the noise of the trams that trundled up the hill day and night, the only respite being the two hours between 2.19 and 4.19 in the morning.

Our neighbours were the Mahers, in flat number 1. The two back doors faced onto a small concrete landing which contained garbage chutes and which allowed for accidental meetings between Mrs Maher and my mother. Mrs Maher soon learned that the Grundys' one and only son was trying to get into Sydney radio.

'My husband knows John Harper at 2KY. Maybe he can help.'

Presumably Mr Maher made the call, because I remember being at 2KY, upstairs in Dymocks Arcade, George Street.

John Harper was the voice of 2KY and while the station didn't command high ratings, everyone in Sydney knew and had listened to him at one time or another. Harper beckoned through the glass for me to come in, pointed to a chair and held up a warning finger as the music faded and he opened his microphone.

'Well, that's it for another day. To those of you celebrating your birthday my best advice is, if it's a big number, either forget about it,' he paused, 'or tell a lie.' He chuckled. 'And so, ladies and gentlemen, boys and girls, have a wonderful day, and take Uncle John's advice and keep smiling.'

He switched off his mike and swung his chair round to face me.

'Well, what have you got for me, son?'

I tentatively handed over my acetate.

'It's not much, but I've only had one job in radio. It's an interview for 2GZ with some sheaf-tossers. But if you haven't got time …'

Harper put up his hand. 'That's enough. Let your work speak for itself. And never apologise.' He brandished the disc. 'This is your contribution, so don't be afraid—be proud,' he paused. 'Even if it is lousy.'

He grinned at me and slapped the disk onto a turntable. He leaned back in his chair and listened intently.

'My God, it's terrible,' I thought.

At the end of the playback the big man carefully picked the disc off the turntable and handed it back to me.

'I've heard worse,' he said.

I could have died with relief.

'Tell you what, call this man tomorrow.'

He wrote on a pad. 'Bernie Stapleton, Gen Man, 2SM.'

'There might be an opening at 2SM. I'll see if I can talk him into giving you a go.'

The next day my call to Bernie Stapleton was diverted to Tom Jacobs, 2SM's news director.

'Come in next Tuesday at ten, Reg. Just pick any sport and we'll try you out.'

Sport? I didn't know anything about sport. I was hoping for a job as a disc jockey. But now I knew the job had nothing to do with music. They were up to Nellie's garter with disc jockeys. What they needed was someone to describe sporting events. Could I do that? I had no idea, but I thought I might as well give it a shot.

Not long before, my Dad had taken me to Sydney Stadium to watch a fight. It was the first time I'd seen one. I'll write an account of that fight and learn it by heart, I decided. But how to come up with the right phrases?

I went down to Herefords, the newsagent in the Double Bay shopping centre, and bought a book called *How to Box* and a compilation of the comic strip *Joe Palooka, Heavyweight Champion of the World*. I read them over and over.

Jacobs lead me into a small studio with a stand microphone and a dinner gong on a desk.

'Okay, Reg. Let's hear what you've got.'

I hit the gong and gave it my best.

But my best wasn't good enough, apparently.

'Thanks. We'll be in touch.'

Not exactly 'Don't call us, we'll call you', but close enough. He ushered me out of the studio to the lift.

But—miracle of miracles—he did call me.

'Go along to the Stadium on Monday night, Reg. Do your best to describe a round of the fight and keep your fingers crossed. It won't be going to air, just back to the studio by landline to see how you go under fire.'

AT THE HOUSE OF STOUSH

I stepped off the tram at Rushcutters Bay and walked up to one of the Stadium windows. I told the bloke behind the window who I was and what I was there for. Less than impressed, he told me to step away from the window while he called the front office.

'What's your name again?' He looked down at the pass I'd handed him. I told him.

'All right, mate, stand out of the way so I can deal with the paying customers. It's a quiet night so we don't want to let any of the punters get away. If you're fair dinkum, I reckon you'll be in on a freebie. Won't be making much out of you tonight.'

I had passed the Stadium hundreds of times while going into town on the tram but never really taken much notice of it. It certainly wasn't any architectural masterpiece: a great barn seating about 12,000 people, with roof and walls of unlined and uninsulated corrugated iron that turned the place into an oven in the hot Sydney summer.

The one and only entrance was across the apex of New South Head Road and Neild Avenue. It was as if the corner of the two sides had been lopped off to create a wide entrance. I remembered that inside there was a ramp, which dipped down to the start of the ringside section and then levelled out until it stopped at the edge of the ring. There was a narrower aisle, which bordered the four sides.

'Okay, you can go in. Harry Miller wants to see yer. First door on the right.'

The door was wide open. Inside I could see a plain wooden counter and not much else. A rotund man with the remains of a cigar clenched in his mouth appeared from an inner office, walked round the counter and put out his hand.

'Reg Grundy? Harry Miller. I run this house of stoush.'

There were two Harry Millers. This was the other one—not the show business Harry M. Miller who was soon to be representing many of our biggest stars. This Harry Miller managed to talk while never loosening his grip on the stub of an unlit cigar.

'Let's go down to ringside.'

Halfway down he stopped to speak quietly, in an almost conspiratorial fashion, to a man sporting a massive diamond ring on his right hand. Wonder what they're saying to each other, I thought.

We moved on. 'That's Tom Powell. You know, Australia's number one bookmaker.'

I didn't know.

'He's here in the same seat every Monday night. Of course, betting on the fights is illegal and what with the police commissioner being here for all the big fights, well, it just wouldn't be right.'

Harry took the stub out of his mouth, waved it around the way George Burns might have done, winked, and jammed it back between his teeth. I had entered a foreign country, a new world. It was all very confusing, but at least it had stopped me worrying about the audition.

Miller slowed down a bit.

'Bernie Stapleton says you don't know much about the business. Well, you're not the only one and you'll be surrounded by experts. Least they think they are.'

He pointed to the far side of the ring.

'All you've got to do is climb that ladder into that crow's-nest over the number two corner, and then it's up to you. Don't suffer from vertigo, do you?'

I knew I did, but it was too late to turn back.

'I'll be okay, Mr Miller.'

'And call me Harry. Everybody does.'

I don't know which was more frightening—the climb to the crow's-nest or the requirement to call what was happening in the ring below.

On Wednesday, the torture continued. It was not one audition but two. I now had to describe a wrestling match.

I had bought a new book illustrating myriad wrestling holds and backed that up with notes from the daily press on the two gladiators.

When I couldn't recognise a hold, which was more often than not, I fell back on the 'colour pieces' I'd collected from the newspapers.

At last it was over. I'd done my best but I knew it wasn't going to be good enough.

IN THE NUMBER TWO CORNER

Within days I got the call.

'Mr Stapleton will see you at ten tomorrow.'

I was there in plenty of time.

'Reg, half the sports journos in Sydney and quite a few experienced announcers have auditioned for us.' He paused. 'But you've got the job.'

I thought this was the most miraculous event of my life, but wondered if they didn't have me confused with someone else.

'Mr Stapleton, that's wonderful, but I think I should tell you I don't know much about sport.'

Stapleton leaned forward.

'That's bloody obvious. But you sounded okay and we think you'll improve. Report to Tom Jacobs, and good luck.'

He shook my hand.

The year was 1947. My first broadcast was to be Monday 14 July. Bastille Day. A good day for a fight.

It was just four days away. Four days!

I went to 2SM the next day. Why would I stay at home? That Friday, I heard that a VIP was flying in—we radio people knew what was going on. I jumped in the back of an open truck and travelled to Mascot to see the arrival, in a York plane, of Field Marshal Viscount Montgomery, Chief of the Imperial General Staff who had led the Allies in North Africa and defeated Rommel during the Second World War. 2SM was out there to cover the scene.

At one point I got very close to the great man and he looked just the same as on the newsreels. How glamorous and exciting it was, working in radio. And all I was doing was sitting in the back of a truck!

There was good news and bad news when I got to the Stadium on Monday night. The good news: I no longer had to climb up into the birdcage and could take my new position at ringside next to number two corner. The bad news: the seconds of the fighter and some of Sydney's most experienced sports writers who sat beside me could all hear every word I uttered.

The fight was between Australian Ken Bailey and Cuban Orestes Diago. The studio crossed to me a few minutes before the start. No advertising had been sold for the breaks between the rounds and I had not been briefed. So I just kept talking for sixty-five minutes non-stop, then signed off.

Bailey won the twelve-round fight easily on points—Orestes Diago was only about eighteen, and really out of his depth against a man of Bailey's class. I don't know about Diago, but it had been one of the most terrifying nights of my life.

My father had listened to every word and was alarmed when I said over and over again that Bailey threw a left, another left and then another left. Had his son forgotten that Ken had a right hand? So Dad was relieved when he read the *Sydney Morning Herald*'s 15 July 1947 account of the fight: 'Bailey's left jab beat a continuous tattoo on the bobbing head of Diago.'

It was the first of many nights of nervous excitement for me. After each session, my relief at getting through it was coloured by my fear of the next broadcast I had to make. It was especially embarrassing on bad nights when the fights were slow and there was no cheering; then a deathly silence filled the Stadium and people at ringside could hear every word I said.

At every match, sitting next to me on my right was journalist Jack Read, a man with a battered nose, cauliflower ears and the suggestion of a slur in his speech. He'd been a fighter in the 1920s and had gone to America to be overmatched and beaten. He was very helpful, giving me advice and teaching me to see more clearly what was going on right before my eyes. Read's reports appeared in the weekly magazine, the *Bulletin*, and his on-the-spot reviews of my commentary were delivered in whispered tones after each round.

'That was good, Reg, but remember when a fighter throws a righthand punch over a straight left, that's a cross, not a hook. The fight looks close but I reckon the Eyetie is a touch in front.'

He did not have to help me, but he was that sort of a man, and I was very grateful.

My skills improved as I visited the gyms and listened to the old hands. I was blotting paper. And soon another great journalist was to help me widen my vocabulary. Jim Donald, a legend in sports journalism, wrote in a colourful style full of similes and metaphors. The juxtaposition of biblical references with slang descriptions made Donald's review of a fight worth reading. Ken Archer wrote the more orthodox account of the stoush, but Jim did the feature colour pieces. It was said that Jim's work had not been edited for years. What he wrote was what was printed, and it ran in pride of place on the back page of the *Mirror*.

There was a story doing the rounds about how that had come to pass. It went something like this. Ezra Norton, who owned the *Mirror* in those days, was tough and cynical. He ruled the people who worked on the paper with an iron hand. Jim Donald rankled under this editorial dictatorship, so when he saw Ezra Norton in Pitt Street one day, he decided to have it out with him.

'Glad I've run into you,' said Jim. 'Chance to give you a piece of my mind. I'm sick and tired of you chopping up my pieces. If I thought you knew what you were doing, maybe I wouldn't mind, but you wouldn't know decent journalism as long as you've got a hole in your bum.'

'You're sacked!' exploded Norton.

'You're not sacking me. Here's my resignation,' said the reporter, and he nailed Norton with a left hook. Norton went down. Rubbing his chin, he looked up at Donald: 'You know, nobody's ever stood up to me before. And the way you delivered that left, maybe you do know what you're talking about.'

Norton got to his feet. 'I like a man who's a man. Don't seem like there's too many around these days. I tell you what, I'll give you a 20 per cent raise and, in future, leave your stuff alone.' He grinned. 'That's if you don't throw one at me if we ever meet again.'

True? Well, probably apocryphal. But they say Jim's work was never edited after that.

When I first met Jim Donald he was living in what amounted to a closed-in verandah of an old, tired tenement building at the back of Kings Cross.

'Mr Donald, I know I don't have the experience of Cyril Angles or Keith Dunbier and I know that 2GB and 2UW have bigger audiences, so I've got to find a way to get people's attention. I want to make my fight calls different, more colourful. More like the way you write.'

'Tell you what I'll do,' said Donald. 'I won't be there next Monday watching those double-bill deadbeats shuffle round the ring, so I'll listen to your call. Not much of a card. Feel sorry for you. Come round at ten on Tuesday and we'll talk.'

When I walked in on Tuesday morning, Jim was sitting at his table.

'You did all right last night; at least you kept talking instead of dozing off. You know, if Stadiums Limited can't come up with a better bill than that, they should close down. Only open when they've got a decent card. They're killing the game with that stuff.'

I agreed with him. It had been hard work making something out of practically nothing.

'Anyway, you did okay but you've got to vary things. You don't always have to say "stomach". Try solar plexus, belly, maybe even blue plate special. Say "breadbasket". Say "downstairs". Think about it. Try anything to stop your call from getting predictable and boring.'

With Jim Donald's help I started to stand out from the crowd, but I was on a station that had a small audience and so it was an uphill battle. I needed people to start paying attention to me. But I was still the new kid on the block.

Our favourite fighter at the time was Vic Patrick, lightweight champion of Australia, a southpaw with an explosive left hand. His vicious style was at odds with his gentle nature. He had held the title since 1941 and for five of those years had held the welterweight title as well.

On 1 September 1947, I met Patrick at the two o'clock weigh-in on the day he was to fight Chicago's great Freddie Dawson, number two lightweight in the world. He was five years younger than Patrick, who was just a little past his prime in 1947. The weigh-in was a quiet affair with no hype and little media attention. I approached Patrick.

'Mr Patrick, I'm calling the fights for 2SM. I have to admit I don't know much about boxing but I'm trying to learn as fast as I can. But I need an edge. It's a bit of a bunfight when we all jump into the ring at the end of a bout and I was hoping you'd give me a few words tonight after you've spoken to the others.'

'Reg, let's get one thing straight. The name's Vic, don't answer to anything else. I'll help you if I can.'

It was my eighth night calling fights. Ollie Stubbs, chief engineer at 2SM, sat beside me as my on-site engineer. He never had before and never would again. But hell, it was the fight of the century as far as Australia was concerned, and Ollie wasn't going to miss out.

By the eleventh round Patrick was ahead on points, having put Dawson down in the ninth. But it was close. Dawson kept poking his tongue out at Patrick, which may not have been the smartest thing to do. Patrick let go his trademark left hook and knocked Dawson back against the ropes and partly through them. Freddie slid sideways on the middle rope towards me. If he had kept coming he'd have landed in my lap. He scrambled to his feet and managed to see out the round.

In the twelfth round Dawson came back strongly and knocked Patrick down and out.

Vic didn't give me an interview because he was carried from the ring on a stretcher in front of a silent crowd and taken to St Vincent's Hospital. Later that night, I walked into his room. It was strange looking down at the sleeping man, an Australian legend, not knowing if he would ever wake up. No doubt others had visited him earlier but it was all quiet when I was there.

Patrick did wake up, and some weeks later Dawson and Vic shared a microphone in the small studio at 2SM.

'Freddie,' I said, 'it was nearly all over in the eleventh when Vic clobbered you. Yet you came back fresh in the next round and put Vic in hospital. How do you explain that?'

'I guess I recuperate fast.'

This phrase has entered the Grundy household over the years and Joy and I say it to one another if one of us is off colour, simply to get a smile.

Vic had two more fights at Sydney Stadium, beating Roy Treasure on a TKO and Tommy Stenhouse on points, and after each fight he answered my questions in the middle of the ring. Shortly afterwards, he retired and became referee in the same ring where he had made his name.

In 2005, Ron Gwilliams, the husband of Vic's daughter Vicki, brought him to the opening of my photographic exhibition at the Art Gallery of NSW. We hugged and shaped up to each other. Photographers got the shot. Exactly one year after Vic and I posed for that picture, Joy and I went to the South Chapel of the Rookwood Garden Crematorium to say goodbye to Vic. There was a big crowd—old fighters, young fighters and people from every walk of life.

Across the aisle in the chapel sat Tommy Burns, who had fought Vic in a brutal fight in which Vic knocked Tommy out in the ninth round. Even so, when Vic and Tommy retired, they travelled together doing shows, telling their stories, screening films of their fights. Vic didn't need the money but Tommy did. Boxing is a sport where gladiators meet and embrace after the final bell, no matter how tough the contest has been. They respect one another and often become firm friends at the end of their careers.

The women used to flock to Tommy's fights—he was so good looking. Tommy—Geoff Murphy is his real name—is still handsome, even in his eighties.

At Vic's funeral, Nat King Cole's voice filled the chapel, singing 'Unforgettable'. An apt choice, I thought.

The media were present and, for once, I talked to them. They asked me the same old question: had I, as Vic had once said, pushed Dawson back into the ring near the end of the eleventh round, allowing Freddie to come back and knock Patrick out in the twelfth and final round?

Vic's version, as told to Grantlee Kieza, boxing reporter for Sydney's *Daily Telegraph*, went like this: 'I knocked Freddie down in the eleventh round and he went through the ropes and landed on the microphone of Reg Grundy. Reg pushed him back into the ring and if it wasn't for that I'd have probably won on a KO.'

A great story, but it isn't true.

I wish it were. If Freddie had landed in my lap I wouldn't have pushed him back into the ring. I'd have held onto him, and Vic Patrick would have won that fight.

It was a moving service and when I got back to our apartment I wrote down my impressions of the day. That night by chance we had dinner with Alan Jones. He'd been 'on air' and missed the service so I handed him a copy of what I had written.

Alan made it his feature piece next morning on radio and television.

RADIO DAYS

I was in Sydney radio at last, but it was tough going. As well as covering the fights and the wrestling, I was expected to read a fifteen-minute news bulletin at 7.45 am each weekday, present the 8.30 to 10.00 morning show Monday to Friday, and be the late-night DJ from 9.30 to midnight on Saturdays.

Well, I'd wanted to be a disc jockey—but it was a lot of work for 7 pounds 10 shillings a week.

From the time I'd arrived at 2SM I had received no briefing, not on anything. No one had told me how to operate the turntables. There was no discussion regarding the format of the station or the type of music I should play. I was given my roster and left to my own devices.

The day before I was to read my first fifteen-minute news bulletin I approached the news director, Tom Jacobs.

'Tom, where do I get the news bulletin?'

'No worries,' smiled Tom. 'Just go through the morning papers and pick out the main items, change 'em a bit and read 'em.'

It was a twenty-minute tram ride from Double Bay, then a brisk walk to 2SM in Wynyard Street, between George and York. As the tram rattled along I prepared my bulletin. I carried a small pair of scissors to cut out items, and stuffed them in a paper bag. I arrived about 7.20, in time to put my cuttings in some sort of order, then headed into the studio to 'do the news'.

It was a good system except for the day when the cuttings flew from my hand and out of the tram. I got another *Telegraph* from the paperboy in Queens Square but the news was probably a bit rough that day.

The morning shift was a blank sheet onto which I projected my program ideas. I spent hours in the record library finding discs that suited my vision, and called one of my shows *The Stardust Road*, which featured music from the Great American Songbook, fading between versions and linking it all with my commentary on the history of the piece.

There was no tape recording then, no editing. I drew chalk cue marks on each disc. I had only two turntables and it was a test of dexterity swapping discs: queuing them, holding them in place as the heavy turntables spun beneath them, then releasing each disc at the crucial moment to add to the melodic patterns I was weaving.

Who knows how it sounded going to air, but there were no listener complaints; perhaps that was because I had so few listeners.

As the station had no defined format, I played the music I loved— mostly big bands and pop singers. This was the era of Artie Shaw, Benny Goodman, Ella Fitzgerald, Billie Holiday, Bing Crosby, Frank Sinatra and many more. I played them all.

The word got around and my morning show caught the attention of the musicians of Sydney. Soon I found a way to bring in the latest discs from America: things like the Stan Kenton Band, and the multitrack recording by Les Paul and Mary Ford of the jazz standard 'How High the Moon'— everything that was new in music. Many of Sydney's top musicians wanted to hear more so I arranged off-air disc jockey shows, with the musicians sitting in the big 'audience' studio and me spinning the discs from the same tiny studio where I had done that first phantom fight description.

Life was great. Ideas were flowing, but I was just an unknown announcer on a station with a minuscule audience. So I did what I could to get attention. I packed my shift with ideas such as offering myself as a babysitter to the female listener who sent me the best letter. I had myself photographed with Vic Patrick's twin baby daughters, and babysitting a voluptuous showgirl who was sitting on my knee. In those days, Matron Shaw of Crown Street Women's Hospital was a media celebrity. Everyone in Sydney knew her name, so I persuaded her to show me how to fold nappies. The shots appeared in the 2SM staff newsletter and a few suburban throwaway rags, but nowhere else. I was a new voice on a low-rated station, and the media couldn't care less.

I would have stood on my head for a paragraph in one of the papers— a bit different from the way I've been these past thirty years, after I decided to drop off the radar.

* * *

John Sherwood was an actor who had appeared in the Australian movies *Forty Thousand Horsemen* and *Rats of Tobruk*. He was also 2SM's prime time announcer and generous enough to put work my way at Chas E. Blanks, the company that recorded the soundtracks for the advertising slides played in movie theatres between the B support and the main attraction. Chas E. Blanks has long gone, and so have the B supports.

Announcers were required to read anywhere from six to twenty one-paragraph commercials for the local retailers in each town. The copy was often badly written and full of clichés. Scripts of twelve or fewer ads earned the reader 7 shillings and sixpence, and scripts with more than twelve ads were worth 12 shillings. It was tedious, boring work as each script had to be read twice, and an announcer might be required to read twenty scripts in a shift.

The name of the game was to persuade Charlie, the recording engineer, to hand out scripts which had fewer than twelve ads, or those which were just over twelve.

'Come on, Charlie, you know I've got a big fight to call tonight. You stuck me with all those nineteen- and twenty-ad scripts last week. About time you gave me a break.'

Sometimes it worked. It was always worth a try.

The shifts lasted two to three hours and, as the ads were recorded straight to acetate, they often contained mispronunciations and fluffs. There was no way to edit them, and nothing was wasted. All discs were distributed. Heaven help those people who stayed in the theatre instead of going outside during the interval.

Thanks to the work of the National Film and Sound Archive, some of those old acetates have survived. I heard one of mine recently, and I offer my sincere apologies to any of you who may have suffered through it at the Broadway Theatre in Parkes.

It was also through John Sherwood that I got to work on the Cinesound newsreels. Television was still a long way off, and the only way people could see the news was through the Cinesound and Movietone newsreels shown in cinemas. John persuaded Ken G. Hall to give me the job of doing the voiceover when a big fight was included in the reel.

Ken Hall, whom everyone called KG, had been the most successful director of Australian movies ever, making seventeen features and never losing money on any of them. When the Second World War came along, local production of feature films ended. From then on, KG's efforts were concentrated on the weekly Cinesound newsreel.

He directed the items sitting outside the booth with his assistant while we announcers sat looking through the glass at the screen where the item was being projected in black and white. Although a cue light was used I found it was better to watch the action on the screen. KG wanted the sports items read with great gusto, which didn't really suit my style. But that's what he wanted, so that's what he got.

I'd have a go at anything. As Sydney radio veteran Gary O'Callaghan once said, 'If there was a bob in it, Reg would be right onto it'.

By the middle of 1949 I'd been calling fights for eighteen months and people were beginning to take notice. If I were ever going to get my head up above the crowd, maybe sport was the way to do it. After all, I was sports director for the station, so why not exploit it?

I set a pattern which was to continue throughout my life.

Churchill once said, 'Bite off more than you can chew and chew like buggery.' That sounded like good advice to me, so I decided to take on as many sports as I could, even if I knew nothing about them. I had a go at everything that came along.

Nobody stopped me, so I set up coverage for the NSW tennis titles at White City in Sydney, with former Davis Cup player J.O. Anderson at my side. Again, there were no commercials, so I talked for four hours non-stop.

The McWilliams Wines golf tournament was played at Royal Sydney, Rose Bay, where a sound engineer and myself set up on a verandah of the clubhouse. There were no runners, no monitors, no feedback, nothing to indicate what was going on. I ran all over the course making notes of the scores, waited until I caught my breath, then broke into the regular program with an update on the golf.

But I had my eye on Rugby League. At that stage, horse racing attracted the biggest radio audience on Saturday afternoons. The second most popular sport was Rugby League, and only snatches of the *Match of the Day* were broadcast between races. I reckoned that if I could get the okay to broadcast the *Match of the Day* from start to finish, with no interruptions, we'd pull in the majority of the people who loved football. Management was lukewarm about my proposal but eventually let me go to the Sydney Cricket Ground on Saturday afternoons and give it a try.

I think management had given up trying to stop me doing anything.

The season was nearly over. I had only seven weeks to make a go of it.

Well, we set up right on the sideline, four of us in a row perched on four chairs like birds on a telegraph wire. There was Reg, the caller; then the announcer—that was me; engineer Jack Griffin; and Jack Coyne, the resident expert.

GARY O'CALLAGHAN

There was one problem. I had played Australian Rules at school in Adelaide and had never seen a game of Rugby League. It was hard enough for me to identify the twenty-six players on the field, let alone understand the rules of the game, so I relied on Jack Coyne, former South Sydney player, to hold up cards with 'forward pass' or 'knock on' during the play.

Somehow I got through that first broadcast and soon I was giving an adequate commentary of the *Match of the Day*.

As Ron Casey later said, 'Reg knew as much about League as I do about French impressionism. Bugger all, really. But he learned quickly.'

By the end of the season, 2SM had received hundreds of letters and the station's ratings had leapt. As usual, no advertising had been sold, so I went to management and declared that I could sell the football coverage for the next season. Permission was granted. I was placed on commission and promptly found four advertisers to pick up the tab. Each paid 7 pounds 10 shillings. I had sold out the coverage of the *Match of the Day* for 30 pounds a week. I wonder what it's worth now.

My two needs were now being marginally met: I was building a career in radio, and I was earning a living—just. The football coverage had helped me become a little better known. The station paid me nothing as a football commentator but I did get the commission from the advertising. And I was to have the privilege of describing Australia playing Rugby League test matches against England, France and New Zealand.

And then there were the talkie slides and Cinesound money.

So my total weekly take-home pay was more than the 7 pounds 10 shillings a week I had started on. But not much more. And I was working day and night, six days a week.

I added a little more by creating the *Parramatta Hour* on Saturday mornings. Spots were 2 pounds 10 shillings for a sixty-second commercial. I sold all the advertising time, put the show together and did the commercials. Again, I got nothing for doing the show, but I did get a commission on the advertising. My technique was to look for a clue that told me something about the prospective advertiser. It might be a photograph of a yacht on the wall behind him.

I'd say, 'We must have the same interests.'

'You mean sailing?'

'She's a beauty. You work her single handed?'

Then he'd tell me all about his adventures. How could he turn me down? After all, it was only 2 pounds 10 shillings.

I was so successful as a salesman that 2SM lowered my commission rate. It was a setback but, what the heck; I was having a great time.

Gary was right—I'd have a go at anything. Even things I don't remember.

The great radio serial *Dad and Dave* finished in 1952 after 2276 episodes. I remember calling the Snake Gully Cup for them one year but didn't believe I was in the final episode until radio historian Bruce Leonard sent me a copy. That's me all right, playing Mr Ellis, the local announcer, saying goodbye to all the characters.

It was all grist to the mill.

Gary O'Callaghan was an office boy at 2SM until I managed to sneak him on air a few times. He was later to make a name for himself as 2UE's breakfast announcer.

In 1952, Gary found himself in the army. Doing his best to make national service as comfortable as possible, he decided to test our friendship. I'll let him tell the story:

I was doing National Service and I wasn't happy. The Brigadier who ran the 12th National Service Training Battalion at Holsworthy was asking for suggestions to raise money for Legacy. I fronted up and said we ought to have a Sports Show Night and charge 10 shillings to get in. The Brigadier thought that was pretty good, but didn't think people would want to shell out just to see a couple of army blokes knock each other about.

'Course not,' I said. 'But what if we had people like Dave Sands and Vic Patrick and Chief Little Wolf?'

'You're not going to get people like that.'

'I reckon I can. Of course, it would take a lot of work. And I couldn't do it all from here. I'd need to go to town a bit.'

'Well, we could arrange that I suppose.'

I was on a roll, so I kept going.

'I'll need a car.'

'Okay, we can lay on a jeep.'

'I don't actually drive.'

'And a driver. But you'd better pull it off.'

So I went to Sydney and to 2SM twice a week for about two months. First thing I did when I got to SM was to find Reg and remind him that he'd promised to help me out in any way he could. Reg did the lot and organised this terrific night, and MC'd it as well. It was a huge success and raised a lot of money. Reg fought Tommy Burns, who was the Australian welterweight champion, and knocked him out in the third round.

I reckon it was a set-up myself.

GARY O'CALLAGHAN

Don't know where you got that idea, Gary.

CHAMPION OF THE WORLD

Things were going well at 2SM.

And then the big break came.

Jimmy Carruthers, the bantamweight champion of Australia, was going to South Africa to fight the World Champion, Vic Toweel, for the title.

If only I could get over there and call the fight, I thought. I'd never been outside Australia and the idea took my breath away. I went to work organising myself to get to South Africa.

I booked the only radiotelephone link between Johannesburg and Sydney. Because of the notoriously unreliable transmissions there was every chance that the broadcast wouldn't get through to Australia, at least not straight away, so I booked the only radio link from Johannesburg to London as well. And then the link from London to Sydney.

Now, as long as the BBC would record my coverage and forward it to Sydney when conditions made it possible, I had a scoop. I talked to Qantas and organised a free return flight to Johannesburg in exchange for mentions throughout the broadcast.

And then I told 2SM's general manager, Bernie Stapleton, what I'd done.

'You mean you've committed us without any authority from me or the management of this radio station?'

I looked straight at him: 'The PMG department has accepted the booking but we can get out of it if you won't let me go.'

Stapleton studied me. 'Well, I must say you've got balls. What if our competitors want to send one of their commentators over?'

'They can try but there's no way they can get their live coverage back to Australia. There's only one radiotelephone to Australia out of Johannesburg and I've … errm … you've … I mean … 2SM's got it. We've stymied them.'

'You know, you're bloody amazing. Ollie Stubbs tells me you've been taking out the Pyrox wire recorder to do interviews in the gym. Slipping them into the evening schedule. No authorisation from anyone. That'll have to stop. And now you come up with this. It's a wonder you don't want to come in here and take over from me.'

I kept my mouth shut and my head down.

'Now get out. Go and worry someone else with your bright ideas.'

The next morning I fronted up again.

Stapleton opened the batting. 'I've looked into your idea and yes, you're right: we do seem to have it locked up. Amazing that there's only one radiotelephone line between here and Johannesburg and you were right to have a stand-by arrangement. Or have you? Have you spoken to the BBC? Why do I ask? I suppose that's all in the bag.'

'Well, yes, sir. The BBC has said they'll be happy to record my call just in case. The atmospherics could make it impossible to get through for hours, but then no one else will get through either. And even if it's delayed, I reckon there'll be a lot of Aussies listening.'

Stapleton spoke quietly. 'Yes, I guess there will be.'

I jumped on the opening. 'Does that mean I can go? It won't cost much. I wouldn't want anything for doing the broadcast and the flights are free. There'll be my accommodation of course, but that's about all and ...'

'All right, all right. You can go if they'll let you into the Stadium.'

'No problem. I'll confirm with you as soon as I know.'

I moved to the door. I wanted to get out of the office before he changed his mind.

But there was bad news. Julius Martin, chairman of the Transvaal National Sporting Club, had refused me permission to broadcast from the Stadium.

I was back in Bernie's office.

'Everything's set. But they won't let me in.'

'Then I guess that's that.'

'It doesn't have to be. I've got a free flight there and back, and you always tell us to go another round. If I could meet this man, I reckon I could swing it.'

Stapleton sighed, swung his chair away from me and stared at the photograph of Girandole, his racehorse, on the wall behind him.

He stood and walked round his desk, looking down at me.

'Talk to John Dunne and Dom Harnett about your shifts while you're away.'

The word got around fast.

'Reggie, it's Joe Taylor. I run the Celebrity Club in York Street. Congratulations. Great move. Why don't you call in and see me before you fly out? Might be able to help you. How about tomorrow when you come off air?'

I didn't know Joe Taylor but I'd heard things, so I asked the news editor, Tom Jacobs, to fill me in.

'Joe owns and runs Thommo's, the biggest two-up school in Sydney. And nobody cares. In fact most people, even if they've never been there, are proud of Thommo's. Funny people, us Aussies.'

After that, I had to meet him. I walked down the steps to the basement club. Chairs were neatly upturned on tables. Nobody was there except Taylor, who stood leaning on the bar.

'G'day, Reg, I've caught your calls a coupla times. Not bad. You know I get a lot of the ringside crowd in here Monday nights after the fights.'

I returned the compliment. 'And if I get home in time I listen to Lyle Richardson on 2KY interviewing from here.'

Joe nodded.

'Well, most of them will be tuned in to you on November the eighth. Now listen, I don't know how you're fixed, but if you could do with a little extra cash to cover expenses, I'm your man. No strings. I'm a bit of a sportsman and life has dealt me some good hands and I like your style, young Reg. Not frightened to have a go. And knowing Bernie Stapleton as I do, mean bugger that he is, I reckon you could do with some extra spending money.'

I was uneasy. It was hard to say no to such a powerful man but everything inside me said I should cut and run.

'I appreciate that, Joe. I wouldn't want there to be any hard feelings, but I'm sort of independent. I'd rather get there under my own steam, if you know what I mean.'

Joe put his arm round my shoulder.

'Yeah, you do it your way. No hard feelings and good luck. I reckon you'll kill 'em. You reckon Jimmy's got a chance?'

We talked fights and then I walked up the stairs into the sunlight of York Street.

Here I go again, I thought. Flying to Johannesburg not knowing if they'd even let me in to see the fight, let alone broadcast it. And knocking back Joe Taylor.

The international terminal at Mascot airport was little more than a shed, but I was excited just the same. I hadn't been on an aircraft since I was a little boy at Parafield Airport in Adelaide. My dad told me that Charles Kingsford Smith was taking people for a joyride. Dad would have loved to have gone up himself but he couldn't afford to pay for two tickets so he let me have the experience. Smithy held many records, including flying solo from England to Australia, and was raising money for his next international flight. Now, I was about to make my first, and the Qantas Constellation VH-EAF looked immense.

It was night-time as I sat in my window seat. Wow! I was leaving Australia, going out into the world.

The flight was anything but non-stop, a once-a-fortnight service that put down in Melbourne, Perth, the Cocos Islands and Mauritius before finally landing in Johannesburg, where a Qantas official gave me the news.

'Reg, the fight's been put back a week. Jimmy's in hospital.'

I got there as soon as I could.

Carruthers smiled up at me. 'It's nothing much, Reg. Just cut my foot and it got infected. Be out of here pretty quick. By the way, Bill's been talking to Julius Martin about getting you into the Stadium and I reckon everything will be okay.'

Bill McConnell, Jim's manager and trainer, had caught the interest of the press. They loved him. He told them he'd been a useful bantamweight battler himself but he was no world-beater. As he said, 'They called me Kid Candle. One blow and I'm out.' McConnell never let his audience down, and always gave them good copy. He never stopped talking—the journos dubbed him 'Silent Bill'.

He got me a lunch meeting with Julius Martin, chairman of the Transvaal National Sporting Club. We got on well and all barriers were swept away.

'Where do you sit at ringside in Sydney?'

'Well, I'm right beside the number two corner. But wherever you can put me is fine.'

'No, no. You'll sit in exactly the same position as you do in Sydney. It's the least we can do.'

If ever there was an example of the merit of going an extra round, this was it.

With the fight still a week off, I had time to spare. Australian Bill Austin, whom I had met on the flight, had the answer.

'You know Boyd Varty, that South African businessman I've been telling you about? Well, he wants me to visit his farm near Kruger Park, and see the wildlife. Want to come along?'

We travelled in Boyd's Chevrolet about 240 kilometres from Johannesburg to the veldt, and stayed in three of the four huts, called rondavels, that stood alone in the middle of the wilderness. There was no cultivation on the farm. It was simply the unspoiled land adjoining Kruger Park over which the animals roamed.

The farm fronted onto the Sand River. There were no four-wheel-drives, no roads, not even tracks. So we walked along the dry riverbed carrying firearms through terrain that reminded me of the Australian outback. Fifty-nine years later, I still go back to visit. The same four rondavels are there, but now their interiors have all the comforts of a first-class bedroom. Crazy paving leads from the huts to a swimming pool and a five star game lodge, Londolozi. Joy goes with me these days.

Reg and I were on our first trip to Africa together. It was 1992 and we went for a three-day train journey on Rovos Rail from Pretoria up to the Mozambique border and back. One of the nights we spent at a game lodge and we went out in the late afternoon on our first game drive. Afterwards, as the sun set, we all gathered in the palisaded 'boma' around the fire. That was when Reg announced to the ranger who had accompanied us on the drive that he had been in the country at a farm somewhere in South Africa in 1952.

'I don't know where I was, but it belonged to a man named Boyd Varty,' RG said, and the ranger replied, 'Mr Grundy, you are standing on the

very same ground. This game lodge belongs to the Varty family! This is
where you were.'

Reg looked at me and exclaimed, 'Forty years later and magically I
return to the same place. Joy, I better sit down.'

And he handed me his beer and sat.

JOY CHAMBERS-GRUNDY

I killed an impala on that first trip and as I knelt beside the lifeless body I wished I could breathe life back into it. Never again. Now I carry a camera, not a rifle.

The Rand Stadium was open to the night. The stars were brilliant in the black sky. The Stadium was packed.

I made my way to ringside. Karl, the engineer from the South African Broadcasting Corporation, was already there. I was anxious to check things out.

'I'm telling you, man, everything is organised. We'll be recording your whole commentary just in case the radiotelephone link to Australia is not working. And if we can't get through to Sydney we'll send it to the BBC and they can pass it on. Don't worry, we won't let you down.'

Jimmy made his way to the ring to the sound of 'Waltzing Matilda'. I was moved by the nostalgic melody and in more recent times I often wonder why it isn't Australia's national anthem. In 2005, Joy and I were in Sun City South Africa and their version of the Three Tenors came out on stage to entertain us. What did they sing when they knew we were there? 'Waltzing Matilda.'

Jimmy climbed through the ropes and sat in the number two corner, right above me. He looked down and winked. As is the custom, the champion would be the last to enter the ring. Bill McConnell was beside himself.

'I wish they'd hurry up, Jim.'

Carruthers said, 'Don't worry, let them take their time, it's a lovely night.'

Jimmy waited nine minutes before the champion arrived at ringside, but at last he was there. When the roars and applause died down, the ring announcer made the introductions. I was dishing out the colour, trying hard to paint the best word pictures I could for Australia.

Then the bell rang for the start of round one.

Toweel was slow out of his corner. Carruthers raced across the ring and threw a hailstorm of punches. Two minutes and nineteen seconds after the start of the fight, Toweel was counted out. Jimmy Carruthers was the first Australian in history to officially become a world champion. And I was the first Australian to describe a world title fight.

The crowd was going crazy.

I leapt into the ring. Jimmy was speaking into a microphone that sported the cut-out map of Australia my Dad had made for me. And now it was Bill McConnell's turn.

'I knew he could do it. And there's one thing I want to add. I know my wife'll be listening back in Balmain and I just want to say, "Millie darling, I loves ya".'

What a night, I thought. But I didn't know the half of it. Karl looked unhappy.

'Sorry, Reg, bit of bad news. We didn't get your broadcast through.' He hesitated. 'Well, actually, that's the good news.'

'What?'

'There seems to have been a bit of a misunderstanding about the recording. They missed part of it.'

'What do you mean? How could they miss part of it?'

'They didn't record the first minute of the fight.'

'But the bloody thing only lasted two minutes nineteen seconds! You mean I've come all the way to South Africa to call a minute nineteen seconds?'

I slowed down. Tried to calm myself.

'Okay. Can you set up for me to record the part you missed and have it edited into the live call? Can you organise that?'

Karl nodded.

But I had other problems. I had promised Qantas that there would be mentions throughout a fight which could have lasted over an hour— I needed some fill.

'I want to do some personality pieces with the celebs here. Now, you live here. You should be able to spot the personalities I should talk to. Find me some stars. Come on, let's get this done, then we'll go back to the studio and put it all together.'

Again Karl nodded. What else could he do?

'How much time before my call will get through to Australia?'

Karl looked glum. 'Studio says conditions are really bad. No chance of getting through for hours.'

But I moved fast anyway, recording celebrities then heading back to the SABC studios.

'We need some background noise.'

They found it. Crowd noise of people at an American baseball game.

I leaned into the microphone, closed my eyes and started talking. As Jimmy had thrown 147 punches in 139 seconds, it wasn't that hard to describe.

The recording was made on an EMI tape machine, as big as a washing machine and pale green. Beautiful. Miraculously, when edited to the real life call, the extra material sounded okay. Hopefully, no one would be able to pick it, as the recording would be debased by the swishing sounds which came and went in all transmissions back then.

It was well received, and no one questioned its authenticity.

Three happy Australians travelled back to Sydney, stopping overnight in Mauritius.

In the late afternoon, the new world champion, Jimmy Carruthers, his manager/trainer Bill McConnell and I, the triumphant fight caller, sat on the verandah of our hotel watching the golden light creep over the sugarcane fields.

Bill was ordering drinks and paying for them with the bank notes that almost spilled out of his jacket. As he patted his pocket, Silent Bill summed it up: 'Anyone can see I've never had any money'.

Back in Sydney I enjoyed my minor celebrity status for a short time. Then the balloon went up.

Bernie Stapleton, the man who had hired me, announced he was leaving the station. It was obvious this was a forced retirement so I immediately resigned, even though I had no idea why my boss had been sacked.

2SM was owned by the Catholic Church and although I was an Anglican, I had come to know more priests than do most Catholics and, on balance, found them to be great guys, generally crazy about sport. I took top sportsmen of the day to Catholic charity affairs and made a lot of friends. One of them, Monsignor Meany, took over the running of the station.

He called me into his office—the same office where Bernie Stapleton had hired me.

'Reg, there is absolutely no reason for you to leave. You're doing a great job. We want you to stay.'

But I steadfastly kept to the view that if they got rid of the man who hired me, then I had to go too. I was a very idealistic young man.

After I left 2SM, Jack Coyne took over the Rugby League call, covering both the reserve and the first grade games until a permanent announcer was hired. That man was Frank Hyde, who took over not just the League but the fights as well. This is what he said in 2005, just two years before he died.

I walked into 2SM and Tom Jacobs says, 'Just the bloke I wanted to see.'

Reg Grundy had just resigned and he'd been doing the boxing and the football and 2SM were in a bit of a hole. Tom says: 'We haven't got a broadcaster. How'd you like the job?'

Well, I wasn't too keen but he talked me into going to see Bryson Taylor who was the voice of the ABC at that time, and he gave me some voice lessons and I started off with the boxing.

FRANK HYDE

Frank became one of Sydney's best known sporting commentators with his non-stop descriptions of the League Match of the Day, and no one who ever heard him will forget his phrase: 'It's long enough, it's high enough, it's straight between the posts'.

My time at 2SM had been a rollercoaster ride.

I had wonderful memories, particularly of the fight game. But now it seemed there would be no more nights for me at the Tin Shed.

I was out of radio with nowhere to go.

A STROLL ACROSS THE PARK

I'd been out of work for three months. My mind was running riot: what if I never get another job in radio?

I'd left a good job on a station that wanted me to stay, simply because the man who gave me my break was leaving. Just when people were getting to know me too. Why did I do it? Why did I throw away my career?

I can't sit around like this any longer, I thought. I'll have to get a job of some sort. Maybe I'll wait another week.

I got the call with only a couple of days to go. It was all like a bad scene in a soap. Well, maybe a good scene.

Mr Callaghan had been the sales manager at 2SM. I didn't know his first name—I don't think anyone did—but he'd taken a job at 2CH and now he was on the phone.

'Reg, it's Callaghan here. 2CH want to offer you a job.'

I still didn't know his first name but I felt like kissing him anyway.

2SM had established me as a sports broadcaster, while 2CH played middle-of-the-road music and had no sports coverage. But what did I care? I was about to be back on air.

2SM was on the tenth floor of the Wynyard Building in Wynyard Street. Small in size, small in ratings.

2CH, just a stroll across the park, was spread over three floors of the AWA Building with its miniature Eiffel Tower dominating the Sydney skyline of the time. Big in size, but still small in ratings.

It was there, on the tenth floor, that I met John O'Grady—Jog—and began a lifelong friendship. On the eleventh floor was an auditorium where, in the future, I would make shows. General manager Reg Fox and his secretary were on the twelfth floor. Entry to this floor was by invitation or, more precisely, by command.

2CH had never been a station that programmed sport but it did now that I had arrived, and Jog was assigned to write four half-hour shows a week for me. I told him to stop complaining and be thankful: if it weren't for the fact that I was going to be back calling the fights on Monday nights, it would have been five shows a week.

Stripped sport on 2CH. It didn't make sense. But I was on air again and, miracle of miracles, back calling the fights. I walked into Sydney Stadium, down the ramp to the dressing rooms, and found Harry Miller.

'Didn't expect to see you back here, young Reg. Sorry we can't accommodate you at ringside,' Harry grinned. 'Come on, I'll show you your new position.'

Harry led me to a pole with a birdcage, which stood immediately behind the last row of ringside seats. I was looking across the ring to the privileged position I'd occupied just three months before. The pole was hardly a prime position but at least I was back, although it wasn't going to be easy being so far from the action.

In March the next year, Jimmy Carruthers fought Bobby Sinn. When Carruthers was declared the winner, the crowd booed and I declared it was one of the worst decisions I'd ever seen. I'd been fooled by my distance from the action and Sinn's bustling, walk-up style. The critics were unanimous that the crowd was wrong and that Carruthers had clearly won the fight.

Cinesound called the next morning for me to do the fight narration. Ken Hall who ran Cinesound and would later run Channel Nine Sydney looked at me, smiled and said, 'I listened to your call last night. It was one of the most exciting broadcasts I've ever heard. Pity it was wrong'.

I looked at the screen and saw the newsreel footage. I'd been wrong, all right.

'By the way, would you like your credit this week?' KG said to me. I had been asking to be credited for my narrations for some months.

No thanks, KG.

While I'd been at 2SM, the sales manager had given me some advertising agencies to service, which meant spending time each morning in a pub drinking beer with a rep. The result? I would leave the station by lunchtime and go home.

Soon I refused to attend pub meetings and found I still drummed up business. Maybe more.

But there was one time after I had moved to 2CH that I made the mistake of visiting a pub a few paces away. I had a Saturday morning sports show which featured celebrity sportsmen. Like the Bodyline fast bowler Harold Larwood, for instance, who was now living in Sydney and had a job driving a truck, delivering supplies of Coca Cola. He was a quiet, unassuming man, and the interview went well. The media had savaged him, but the poor guy had only been following orders.

And then there was Keith Miller, one of the great all-rounders of all time—a great lover of life both on and off the field. One Monday he came to 2CH to record an interview. I must have pleased him because he gave me a copy of his latest book and wrote in it: 'To the most difficult interviewer I've had the pleasure of meeting'.

When it was over he said, 'Come on, Reg, let's have a drink'.

How could I refuse? The drink became the drinks. At last I said, 'Look Keith, I've got a fight to call tonight. I don't know whether I'll make it'.

He spoke slowly and reassuringly. 'Sorry, Reg. Don't reckon you're much of a drinker. Why don't you call it a day and go sleep it off. You'll be right. But I tell you what. I'll listen tonight and if you're okay, just say "Jackson, everything's okay". Sort of want to make sure you're all right.'

I was. Everything was okay. He was a great man, and one I'll never forget.

The daily grind of coming up with a sports show every weeknight started to lose its appeal. The fights were okay; they were the meat and potatoes of my radio life. But how to fill the other nights?

After about a year, most of the shows we'd started out with had vanished but we were still making *Sporting Scrapbook*, a show for which Jog wrote a weekly script. It was a hastily thrown together mini-drama in which the essence of a sporting activity was expressed through the misadventures of a hapless fall guy.

The poor fool was played by Brian Henderson, then a 2CH announcer but soon to join TCN 9 and become Australia's longest running anchor for the prime time news. Needless to say, my friend Hendo doesn't put *Sporting Scrapbook* on his CV.

Many of those scripts survive and, despite loud objections from the author John O'Grady and the star Brian Henderson, I am prepared to release them if a suitable deal can be made.

On other nights, I attempted to describe sporting events from outside locations: ice hockey from the Showground and baseball from the Sydney Sports Ground, for instance. Although I had never seen either sport before, I was happy to give anything a try.

But I was starting to move away from sport.

Apart from my on-air duties, I was selling advertising time to supplement my income and this resulted in the creation of a new show, *Scoop the Pool*. It featured Dick Hyde, a used car salesman and auctioneer whose business was doing well, partly because of the radio show, which featured his remarkable ability to give accurate on-the-spot valuations of used cars based on listeners' enquiries.

As usual, I was the host.

Dick was much older than his wife, a very attractive blonde named Nola. I made sure that 'Nola', a popular piano piece from the 1920s, was used as the show's theme. I explained to Dick that the composer Felix Arndt had written it for his fiancée whose name was also Nola. I left no stone unturned when trying to make a sale.

Nola answered the calls as they came in to the 2CH switch, collected them and brought them to the studio. Dick read them on air. 'Mr Smith of Lakemba has a 1950 Holden in good condition. Mileage unknown. Green with beige upholstery. Well, Mr Smith, depending on the mileage, your Holden sedan should bring around 595 pounds.'

I like to believe that all the enquiries came from genuine callers. Whether they did or not, Dick certainly knew his stuff and the audience enjoyed his estimations.

Scoop the Pool was a grab bag for many different formats and some weeks we strayed from the valuations to present specials. At that time, promoter Lee Gordon was importing a stream of top performers including Frank Sinatra, Johnny Ray, Louis Armstrong, Bill Haley and many more. Our local guest for one night's *Scoop the Pool* interview special had dropped out at the last minute. I knew Nat King Cole was performing that night at the Stadium, so I called Harry Miller.

'Your timing's terrific. He's just arrived. Hang on.'

Within minutes, Harry was back on the line. 'You're in luck. I gave you a big build-up. Be here at 7.30.'

I had interviewed many sportsmen, but this was different.

I knocked on the door of the dressing room and heard that famous husky voice say, 'Come in'. I introduced myself. The great man held out his hand and said, 'Let's go'.

I was a great admirer of his piano playing style and relentlessly focused on his jazz background. He was good natured about it, even though it was obvious he'd rather talk about his singing. After all, that's what had made him a superstar and had brought in the big bucks. Eventually, though, even he got caught up in analysing his distinctive piano style. Amazingly, I still have a tape of that interview.

Lee Gordon was running a cash business and the bank notes handed over at the ticket counters were stuffed into hessian bags and placed in a room to be deposited in the bank the following morning.

Gordon knew the importance of the media, and invited all the press and radio people to visit the room after the show.

'Lee wants to show his appreciation of the publicity you're giving him,' said an underling to all of us. 'Just stick your hand in and grab a couple of handfuls of the moolah.'

A lot of guys moved over to the hessian bags. Some declined the offer. I was one of them.

I loved calling sporting events—being the eyes of the audience—and I was to take the concept to absurd lengths.

Sorbent, the toilet tissue manufacturer, entered the Sydney marketplace in 1952 and sponsored a panel show, which I created. It was recorded on the eleventh floor of the AWA building every Thursday at lunchtime, before a live audience. The auditorium had a stage and moveable seating for about a hundred people. Incredibly, all seats were occupied each Wednesday.

Visual clues were drawn on a giant pad. The artist was Kerwin Maegraith, a noted newspaper cartoonist. He was a colourful man who had known

Picasso in Paris, Einstein and Lawrence of Arabia in London, Hemingway in Hawaii, and had shared a flat with Errol Flynn in Sydney. We had both gone to the same school in Adelaide—St Peters College—although we'd never met.

The panel consisted of three celebrities, usually actors such as Pamela Page, Kevin Brennan, David Nettheim and Muriel Steinbeck—big names at the time. The panel had to try and come up with a word or phrase, or a name, from the clues they saw Kerwin drawing. The radio audience was supposed to try and solve the puzzle from the spoken clues.

Pretty sophisticated, eh?

But there were no angry letters or phone calls. The only person who seemed to be discomfited by it all was the much-put-upon young, quietly spoken, bespectacled man who was required to read the Sorbent commercials live from the apron of the stage.

I had to read toilet paper commercials in front of a live audience. Talk about embarrassed. I couldn't look them in the eye and read mostly to my shoes. One good thing though. It hardened me for those Clearasil commercials I used to do on Bandstand. *Clearasil was a breeze after that.*

BRIAN HENDERSON

The people who worked on the floor below unkindly called it the Sore Bum Show.

And what is the connection between a large papier-mâché giraffe and a roll of toilet paper? The Sorbent company can't remember, yet my assistant John O'Grady and I appeared with Millicent the Sorbent giraffe many times to advertise the brand, and occasionally at Taronga Park Zoo with the then president of the zoo's Trust, Sir Edward Hallstrom. Jog always came with me on those occasions but was rarely seen, since he was the front legs of the giraffe.

So what was the connection? Did Sorbent feature a giraffe in their advertising? Sorbent says no but I have a full-page Sorbent advertisement featuring the giraffe, myself and Hallstrom, and a photograph to boot.

It's a mystery that may never be solved.

* * *

On 21 May 1956, I called my one thousandth fight. A 2CH handout stated that I had spoken over six million words in describing some 10,000 rounds. This is six times as many words as there are in the English language. It sounded good, but whether it was accurate I had no idea. I hadn't been counting.

Now I was to be one of the commentators at the 1956 Olympic games in Melbourne, starting in November. The Federation of Commercial Broadcasting Stations had selected broadcasters from all over Australia.

Before the Games began half of the commentators were removed—I don't know why. But because I had been the first Australian to cover a world championship fight, I was chosen to call the final night of boxing— the gold medal events. As well, 2CH had allocated 7.00 to 7.15 each night, Monday to Friday, for my report from Melbourne. And I was to supply a daily one-minute report for NBC radio in America.

Apart from that, I was free.

Before the fights began, the founder and editor-in-chief of *The Ring* magazine walked over and put out his hand. 'My name's Nat Fleischer.' As if he needed to introduce himself. I wished I were somewhere else—I was still unsure of myself, and lacking in confidence.

At the end of the night Fleischer said, 'You're all right. Sound as if you know what you're doing'. He paused and grinned. 'Except for your accent. What is that?'

Weeks later, a 2CH accountant handed me a cheque from NBC made out to Red Grundy.

'You better sign it, Red,' he said.

It was for a small amount, but still welcome.

'After you've signed it, hand it back. You're an employee, so it's AWA's money.'

About forty years later, my company RG Capital acquired 24.4 per cent of AWA, including 2CH, and became the major shareholder. In the year 2000 we on-sold to Jupiter's. It was not one of our finest hours. We made a small profit of two million Australian dollars but lost about 2.6 million American dollars because of the exchange rate.

When everything was finally washed up, my dealings with 2CH/AWA resulted in a paper loss of US$60,000 plus, of course, that pesky amount of 50 American dollars, which should have finished up in the hands of Red—I mean Reg—Grundy. Perhaps I should have recovered that US$50 while I had the chance. With interest compounded over forty years, it would have been a useful amount.

Back in 1956, though, my sporting career was coming to an end. Frankly, my mind was on other things. I needed to move on.

And I had an idea!

GREASY JOE'S AND THE WHEEL OF FORTUNE

John O'Grady and I were having coffee in a York Street coffee shop less than a block away from 2CH. We called it Greasy Joe's. It wasn't really greasy, and it wasn't run by a man named Joe, and the coffee wasn't bad.

The coffee was unspeakable and came out of a jar labelled 'Coffee & Chicory'. I always had tea.

JOG

It was where we went to hang out to discuss our weekly schedule and sometimes our plans for the future.

We were on our second cup.

Jog looked sceptically at me. 'I see. So you've spent ten years in radio doing something you didn't want to do.'

I was impatient. 'That's typical of you. You know what I mean. Do you want to listen or don't you?'

Jog sighed in resignation. I think he felt he'd been here before.

'I never set out to be a sports broadcaster but once I got the hang of it I enjoyed it, loved it even. But that was when I was describing the action, not stuck in the studio reading your lousy scripts or pretending to be the Mr IQ of sport.'

'You haven't read one of my lousy scripts in twelve months.'

I ignored him.

'And you and I both know it's not working for me. I need to do something else, Jog.'

'So what am I supposed to do about it? I'm not even assigned to you any more.'

'But you could be again. So keep your shirt on and listen. Just imagine if we could do a show in the studio with people phoning in answering general knowledge questions and winning prizes. Maybe I spin a wheel or something. Think of it: I ask the questions, we hear the answers. We'd have all of Sydney listening and trying to get a go.'

'Like *Pick-a-Box*.'

'No, not like bloody *Pick-a-Box*. This would be on the phone. Every day. Afternoons maybe, two till four.'

Jog took his glasses off. A sure sign he was interested.

'So what's it called?'

I was wound up. 'I dunno. But if we have a sort of chocolate wheel, then I suppose we'd call it … err … Wheel something.'

'Yeah, that's catchy.'

Jog put his glasses back on.

It suddenly came to me. I stood up and pronounced: '*Wheel of Fortune!*'

I was on my feet waving my arms around.

'Radio's new hit is going to be the *Wheel of Fortune* … no … let's make it *Reg Grundy's Wheel of Fortune*. It'll be a new career move for both of us. You can write the questions, and sometimes I'll let you spin the wheel.'

I sat down, leaned across the table, shook hands with Jog and grinned. 'What do you think?'

'You're going to spin up prizes on a chocolate wheel no one can see?'

'It'll work.'

'Sure it will. Right after the pigs start levitating.'

Not everyone was as sceptical as my friend Jog, or perhaps I improved the pitch before I presented it to Reg Fox. He gave the okay overnight, and I was to have the Monday to Friday 2 pm to 4 pm slot. Exactly what I wanted.

I approached the Postmaster-General in Melbourne to arrange for the two-way communication system to be installed in the studio.

The official laughed. 'You're a bit ahead of your time, Reg. There's no way you can broadcast people calling into your studio. It's illegal.'

I was stunned. 'Why? Surely technically you can do it.'

'You'd be in breach of PMG regulations which prohibit "conversations between individuals by wireless". That's what the Act says.'

'There's got to be some way round that.'

'Hey, listen, we lined up that radio telephone link for the Carruthers fight for you. Reckon we looked after you on that one. But no can do this time. Look, Reg, I'm on your side. I know it's bloody silly, but rules are rules. You're just a bit ahead of yourself. It'll happen.' He laughed. 'Come back and see us in, say, ten years.'

It was an accurate forecast. In 1967, just ten years later, the PMG authorised the broadcasting of telephone calls and at midnight on 17 April 2UE went live to air with talkback calls; at 8.30 the next morning, Mike Walsh started his shift on 2SM with more of the same.

But that was 1967. This was 1957. It was a massive setback—but I'd had setbacks before.

My mind went into overdrive. I'll have to do a monologue every day, I reasoned. Be not only the quizmaster but the voice of the contestants as well. So what? I talked non-stop for an hour on my first fight broadcast, talked non-stop covering the Rugby League Match of the Day. This'll be a breeze.

I almost had myself convinced I could make it work.

So on Monday 16 June 1957, I opened my mouth and started talking. A quick intro and a general knowledge question, and the telephone lines lit up. Well, in a manner of speaking. We only had three lines and one telephonist.

Just the same, it seemed we were off to a good start.

From then on, those three lines were jammed every day for two hours with callers wanting to take part. The first to call in with the correct answer to a simple quiz question won the chance to spin the wheel.

The radio version of *Wheel* was to have many changes of format but was based on people at home answering questions to win prizes, which ranged from steam and dry irons to TV sets.

Jog wrote the questions and was my assistant in the studio. I'd spin that wheel which people could only hear and never see, and announce the number that came up to indicate what the prize would be. People believed me without question. There was no evidence of any levitating pigs and Jog seemed to be enjoying himself.

I repeated every contestant's um and ah, every sigh and laugh and every remark, no matter how trivial. I did this for ten hours every week. It makes me tired to think about it.

I even had my own letterhead, *Reg Grundy's Wheel of Fortune*, with my photograph on it. I don't remember asking permission—I just did it. I thought of myself as an entrepreneur even though I was on staff.

We'd been running for several months when Jog passed me a request.

'Do you think we could plug a book on the show?'

'What sort of book?'

'Well, the author's a chemist, never wrote a book before, but this is pretty good. Very funny.'

He handed me a copy.

That night I started reading. It was hilarious. I couldn't stop—read it all.

'Jog, it's terrific. Great title too. But who the hell is this Nino Culotta?'

'Oh, that's just a pen name.'

'So what's his real name?'

'O'Grady, same as me. He's my dad.'

We gave copies away on the show and I told my audience what a remarkably funny book it was. But *They're A Weird Mob* needed no help from me, and soon became a massive bestseller. I wonder if there are any of those giveaways still lurking in someone's bookcase. They were all first editions and would now fetch a few dollars more than the 16 shillings they sold for in October 1957.

The show was doing well but television had arrived a year earlier and many radio people were feeling restless. Jog was one of them, and he decided to move on. He announced succinctly and inaccurately, 'Radio's stuffed'.

He didn't go to television though. He got a job as advertising manager for a real estate company. He knew nothing about either, but ignorance didn't stop him any more than it had ever stopped me. Perhaps it was catching.

I was still enjoying myself, but by the time *Wheel* had been on air for two years I found myself growing increasingly frustrated by what I saw as the 'public service' attitude of the station management. I had started sending critical memos, impatient to move 2CH forward and to further my career.

Then Hamilton Huntley was appointed station manager. Decent man though he was, he seemed to lack any feeling for show business, and that included me.

So when Huntley called me to his office, I had a fair idea it was over.

Before he could open his mouth I announced, 'Hamilton, I'm moving on. Please accept my resignation as of now'.

My career in radio had really ended this time.

I was out of work again.

'WHAT DO YOU THINK IT'S WORTH?'

Once again, I had burned my bridges.

Despite my reputation as a salesman, I have always been reluctant to make phone calls. Day after day, week after week, I languished at home, undecided as to what my next move should be.

I had seen Brian Henderson broadcasting from Taronga Zoo on Mother's Day. Charm and confidence. He was on his way to becoming a television star.

I was now thirty-five, too old and too afraid to make the transition.

But I had to do something—I had a family to support. In the spring of 1954, I'd married Lola Powell at St Mark's Church, Darling Point. We'd met at 2SM. She was younger than me, but that didn't seem to matter to either of us. The observant reader might notice the beginning of a pattern here.

We had a quiet wedding breakfast at a friend's house and next day travelled by ship from Sydney to Adelaide. We found ourselves drinking coffee in a tiny shop in William Street, Adelaide, discussing whether we should stay on board until the ship reached Fremantle. I felt we couldn't afford it, and we flew back to Sydney where we moved into a flat on New South Head Road across the tramlines and just up from where I had lived with my parents.

We enjoyed our life together. Square dancing and charades were all the go and we spent many Saturday nights with our friends, enthusiastically going through our paces.

Eighteen months after we were married Lola presented me with a baby girl. Like so many men I was not prepared for being a father, but I fell in love with Kim Robin Grundy as soon as I saw her. I made daily visits to the hospital but after a few days could wait no longer.

'I hope I'm wrong, but I've never heard her speak. She's not mute, is she?'

Lola laughed and called me a fool. 'She'll speak, all right. You may be sorry then.'

Of course I wasn't. I was proud of her when she became head of the debating society at school.

Family men can't afford to lie around feeling sorry for themselves so, again after three months, I decided to take a chance or get out of show business altogether. I corrected myself: 'I'm damn well out of it now'.

Ken G. Hall, who had run Cinesound, was now chief executive at TCN 9. He certainly knew my work as a sports broadcaster, but had he ever heard of my *Wheel of Fortune* show? And would he take my call?

For days, I found reasons not to pick up the phone. When at last I did, I was put through to his office without delay.

'KG, I'm not sure you know what I've been doing since I last worked for you at Cinesound.'

Hell, that's a negative start, I thought.

KG replied, 'You've been doing that *Wheel of Fortune* show. Heard it a couple of times. Enjoyed it.'

It's now or never, I thought, plucking up my courage.

'KG, I believe I can turn *Wheel of Fortune* into a TV show.'

'Interesting.'

I nearly dropped the phone.

'Come and see me next Tuesday. Ten o'clock all right with you?'

It was better than all right. It was perfect.

But I was riddled with self-doubt. Today's Friday and I haven't a clue what I'll say to him on Tuesday. What if he actually gives me a chance? Then what will I do? Me on television? I reckon I'd die of fright. Radio was great once I got used to it. But TV? Might be okay for Hendo, but there's no way it would be right for me.

I had always prided myself on dressing well so it was natural for me to wear a suit and tie to the meeting.

It was Tuesday, 14 July 1959. The sun was shining in a clear blue sky as I drove into the parking area in front of the main entrance to TCN 9. But I wasn't interested in the weather.

The receptionist pointed to stairs leading to what I was to learn was the general office. 'Good morning, Mr Grundy, you're right on time. Let me take you through to Mr Hall's office'.

I'd never heard him described as 'Mr' at Cinesound. It was always KG.

We walked through a long rather narrow area dominated by a massive table. At the far end, a door was open and through it was a short, narrow corridor flanked on the left by his secretary's cubbyhole and on the right by the entrance to KG's office.

The door was open.

'Reg, come on in.'

I recognised the husky, slightly American-sounding voice.

He extended his hand and I shook it.

'Nice to see you. I'd like you to meet Alex Baz. He's the manager of the station. Take a seat and let's get started. Alex doesn't know your radio show, so perhaps you could fill him in.'

I did my best.

Alex listened attentively, then fired his first salvo. 'Wouldn't you say your main suit has been sport? Isn't a quiz show a bit of a stretch? And on television? How much experience have you had?'

I decided to play it straight.

'Alex, the next time I enter a studio will be the first time. Although I did watch that first night of TV. I thought the Johnny O'Connor show was terrific. Of course it was a bit cold standing in the street outside Arrow Motors in Double Bay staring through their showroom window at the TV they'd set up.'

Hall laughed. 'Okay, Alex, let's listen to what Reg has to say before we hang him.'

I plunged in. 'Here's a list of prizes I can get.'

I used the assumptive approach.

The two men studied the list.

Baz said, 'Do you really mean you can get this stuff? Radios, washing machines, cameras and TV sets? That's Bob Dyer's standard.'

They were a poor man's version of what Dyer was giving away on *Pick-a-Box* on Monday nights on Seven, but they were far bigger than any given away on TCN. Especially in the daytime.

Bob McGready's show with the dashing title of *Balance your Budget* had started a couple of months earlier. He was giving away packets of Crispies and other grocery items.

'I managed to have a pretty strong prize line-up on a radio station with not much of an audience. Why wouldn't I be able to do it on TCN?'

It was a rhetorical question and Alex Baz kept his head down.

I pressed on. 'Of course, I'd also write the questions, get the contestants and …' I hesitated. I wasn't all that sure what might be needed in television, so finished lamely with … 'pretty much do everything that needed to be done.'

It didn't occur to me to say I'd produce the show.

KG delivered the clincher.

'Okay, Reg, tell you what we'll do. Come back next Tuesday night at 6.30. We'll do a run-through, have a look at you on camera and take it from there.'

I floated out of the building. Me on TV. I didn't know whether to laugh or cry.

By Tuesday night I was a nervous wreck. I stood in the number two studio. Ken Hall and his assistant, Alec Kellaway, brother of Cecil Kellaway, the Hollywood actor, looked down at me from that narrow room I'd walked through to reach KG's office the week before. They could see me in the studio as well as on a monitor.

I did my piece, but had no idea whether it was awful or just plain bad.

Kellaway was the first to speak. 'Reg, if KG decides to give you a chance, I'll be able to advise you on a few things. Probably give you a couple of hostesses, good-looking girls in fishnet stockings maybe, dress the set with aspidistras, that sort of thing.'

I didn't know much about television, but I was certain he was dead wrong. Too old-fashioned. Not for me.

KG said, 'Obviously you're a bit green, a bit nervous. But you've got warmth—I reckon people might like you. So I'm going to take a chance. I'll give you a half hour on Tuesday afternoons for thirteen weeks and see how it goes. That's if we can do a deal.' He hesitated. 'What do you think you'd want?'

I answered with the line that was to haunt me for years to come.

'What do you think it's worth?'

I never asked that question again.

'WELCOME TO THE WHEEL OF FORTUNE'

I really didn't know how I was going to make this TV show of mine work. Still, I'd managed to persuade people that I knew something about boxing and Rugby League so perhaps, scared or not, I could fake it yet again. But I'd had a whole organisation behind me those other times. Now there was just me. And Lola.

We'd already decided that if this thing came off, Lola would be my production assistant and 'on camera' hostess. I guess I was trying to do the Bob and Dolly Dyer thing.

But I wasn't going to be on staff at TCN. I was a supplier—a packager—being paid a fee, modest though it was, to do everything: to get the contestants, secure those big prizes that had so impressed Alex and KG, write the questions, liaise with the station and, finally, host the program. I didn't think the two of us could handle all that on our own.

I'd kept in touch with John O'Grady and knew he wasn't particularly happy persuading people to buy land in Sydney's outer suburbs. Over coffee at the old Journalists Club in Phillip Street, I told him I was about to do what he'd been telling me since 1956 that I ought to do: I was taking the *Wheel* to television. Would he like to be part of the adventure?

Jog said he'd like that very much, thanks, but added a rider: 'I don't think you can afford me, Reg'.

He was right—I couldn't. But I wasn't going to let him know that, and a deal was done.

Jog headed back to his fancy Martin Place office to put in his resignation while I paid for the coffee and wondered if I should have told him that I only had a thirteen-week contract with TCN. If it didn't work, we'd both be out of a job.

And so Reg Grundy Enterprises was launched and began operating out of our Double Bay flat where work couldn't begin in the morning until my daughter had gone to kindergarten; Jog needed to use her room as an office. He remembers just two pieces of office equipment: a typewriter, and a card table on which to put it. His chair was my daughter's bed.

Tuesday 1 September 1959 was cool and cloudy in Sydney. The news reported that a Royal Commission was going on in South Australia, the ACTU was grumbling about lack of equal pay for women and, in India, Prime Minister Nehru was criticising China for an act of aggression. Grave and weighty matters. But I had more important things to worry about. I was live to air at two o'clock.

We arrived in plenty of time and someone told us how to find the make-up room. That was new. Hadn't needed make-up on radio. And then off to Studio One. Could this be the right place? It looked small and unglamorous. I noticed two cameras mounted on what I soon learned were pedestals, and a third on a wooden tripod. There were several crew standing around talking while another adjusted lights with a long pole. They all looked alarmingly young. Another, perhaps slightly older, greeted me cheerfully.

'G'day, Reg. I'm Ray Newell. I'm your director.'

I was only half listening—I was distracted by the set: two canvas flats painted an unattractive tan colour and decorated, if that's the word, with black cats and horseshoes.

It looked appalling.

In front of the flats—stretched canvas on wooden frames—was a lectern and on its right was the wheel with a ragged clacker. I never did get rid of that damn clacker. On a low platform, prizes were untidily displayed. I'd never seen such a mess in my life. Great prizes though. Who wouldn't be excited by a Luna Ray cooker, a Kriesler portable radio and a selection of Hestia foundation garments?

But today I had more to think about than the look of the set.

The moment had come. There had been no rehearsal. Nothing. A little red light was glowing on one of the cameras and floor manager Peter Honeyfield was pointing at me. I had a feeling of impending doom but I thought I'd better say something.

'Good afternoon and welcome to the *Wheel of Fortune*.'

For the first few minutes I was so fascinated by my image on the floor monitor that I talked to it rather than the camera. Then at last it was over. I walked out into the foyer wearing my Max Factor make-up.

'Mr Grundy, there's a call for you,' said Betty at the reception desk, smiling at me. 'It's Mr Gyngell.'

I wasn't quite sure who he was.

'Well done, boy. You were terrific.'

I soon discovered that Bruce was the programmer at TCN 9 and was already displaying some of the qualities that would soon make him a television legend.

And he liked me. Maybe I actually could make a go of this TV stuff. If I'd known that Louis Armstrong classic back then, I reckon I would have burst into song with 'It's a Wonderful World'.

I had hoped for nothing else than to survive the experience but perhaps I'd done a little better than that. Yet there was no feeling at all that I had just taken the first step towards an unimaginable future.

I soon settled down. I was no longer afraid of the cameras. It all seemed so easy and so natural.

And I was being noticed. Every week I was haunted by the manager of two boy singers. 'Reg, let them perform on your show. The audience will love 'em.'

My reply was always the same: '*Wheel*'s not a variety show, it's a quiz'.

Perhaps I shouldn't have been so rigid. One of the duo went on to international success. His name was Peter Allen.

After a few months I asked whether I could enter the control room. The director and the technical director laughed. Ray Newell said, 'We wondered how long it would be before the penny dropped.'

Soon I was asking for changes to the set, new ways to display prizes, even a new shooting pattern for the show. I was starting to realise the power I had over what went to air. There was no limit to what I could do. I was starting to think as a producer, not as 'talent'.

The word got back to Bruce Gyngell and one day, after the show, he called me to his office.

'Reg, there's some interesting stuff in bond. I'll arrange for you to have a look.'

I wasn't going to say I didn't know what bond was, but if Bruce thought it was a good idea then I was all for it. I found myself close to Darling Harbour in a warehouse which held hundreds of cans of film. Charlie Waite seemed to be in charge and introduced himself.

'See, when Channel Nine wants to look at a new show from the States but doesn't want to pay the duty, they have it delivered here where they can have a dekko without coughing up. 'Course, if they want to take it out they have to pay. It's a sorta no-man's-land. Bruce reckons you'd be interested in seeing one of them Yankee quiz shows so I threaded this one up. Called *Concentration*. See what ya think.'

At the end of the screening I couldn't get out of the building fast enough. I sought out Gyngell.

'It's terrific. I reckon an Australian version would knock their socks off.'

'Well, boy, if that's how you feel, let's go see the man.'

'KG, Reg thinks *Concentration* is a winner.'

'I see. Well, trouble is, Reg, you're already compering a show.'

'Oh, no, that's not what I meant.'

'What, you wouldn't want to host it?'

I loved the word 'host' Gyngell had just used.

'No, I'd get someone else to do that. Terry Dear, say. I'd just produce it.'

'Really? Well, if you and Bruce think it'll work and you can get Dear or someone of his standing, you can go ahead with a pilot.'

The enormity of the opportunity was hitting me. How to get Terry Dear, a former radio star and now a big-time television personality? That would be tough. And then I'd have to get the prizes. I was already giving away a lot of stuff on my own show and this would double or triple the merchandise I'd need. Well, I figured I'd damn well better pull it off.

Terry Dear proved easier than I thought. He loved the American kine—a filmed version of the TV show—and needed a new vehicle to boost his television career. He agreed to do two pilots.

The next bit was going to be harder.

I drove out to Diments of Hurstville who were advertising on the *Wheel* show. Emblazoned on the facade of the building was:

IRONMONGERY
PRODUCE & FUEL
GENERAL MERCHANT

I wasn't too excited about the first two but reckoned the last one would be the source for all the prizes I'd need.

I addressed the Diments management. 'Everyone knows and loves Diments of Hurstville. Exposure on my new show will bring shoppers from all over Sydney to your wonderful store. By donating the prizes to *Concentration*, people will see and get to know the superb range you carry and you're bound to increase customer traffic. That'd be good, wouldn't it?'

Old salesman's trick. Keep asking questions that demand a 'yes' answer. It worked. Diments were in.

The first recording session was soon upon me. The crude set was in the studio. The tiny audience was in place. Terry was doing the warm-up.

The day had come and I wished it hadn't.

Earlier that afternoon, Diments, my only source of prizes, had withdrawn its promise to supply merchandise. It would be impossible to replace them at such short notice. I was about to produce a game show with no prizes.

What was I going to do? I've got to go through with it, I decided. I'd just have to use the Diments stuff and worry about it the next day.

The *Concentration* board consisted of thirty three-sided blocks or wedges. The front sides of the blocks were numbered one to thirty. Players selected two numbers and if they each revealed the name of the same prize, the blocks were turned again to show two parts of a picture puzzle. First to solve the puzzle kept the prizes.

There'd been some trouble manually moving the three-sided blocks, but it was obvious that the studio audience had lapped it up.

The next day Gyngell and Ken Hall watched as the show was projected onto a screen in KG's office.

He was beaming. 'Good job, Reg. I like it. You're in business. We'll go into production right away.'

I didn't know whether to laugh or cry. What would I do about prizes? They had gone off at an alarming rate in the two pilots last night and I couldn't possibly afford to pay for them out of my own pocket. I had no option but to show the pilot to Diments executives.

They watched the show in silence.

'I thought we made it very clear that we were not contributing any prizes to this show,' said the general manager.

'I appreciate that,' I replied. 'But it was just too late to find replacement merchandise. Look, I'll pay for the prizes that were won, or you can decide to support *Concentration* and be part of a hit show.'

I think they'd been talking about it before I got there because the general manager changed his tack. 'Reg, we'll support you for four more episodes as long as you find other merchandise to reduce our risk. After that, we'll decide if we're going to stay or go.'

He held out his hand. 'I suppose if I'd been in your position I might have taken the same risk you did. We think it's a great show and we believe you're made of the right stuff.'

They actually applauded me. Wow—this is living, I thought.

Sadly, Diments of Hurstville, which had opened its doors for the first time in 1909, closed them forever in 1961, just one year after that discussion. I hoped I hadn't been responsible in some way.

The Broadcasting Control Board introduced the first content quota in 1960, regulating that 40 per cent of all programs be locally made, with four hours in prime time every month. There were no networks so all stations were independent and all in need of local product, preferably low-cost product.

I don't know whether that explained Bruce Gyngell's generosity towards me but it was certainly a good time to be an independent producer.

Wheel of Fortune was now turning strongly for an hour twice a week and as well there was *Concentration* and *Tic Tac Dough*, a live to air Saturday night quiz program that was another gift from Bruce.

There was a sudden increase in demand on the question writing department. That was Jog, who was secretly running around secondhand shops buying books of general knowledge questions. I turned a blind eye, so long as all question cards carried three supporting references.

One day a contestant gave an answer that was not on my card but sounded as though it might be correct. I announced: 'Let's see what our panel of judges have to say.'

The panel of judges was Jog, sitting in the control room armed with a copy of the single-volume Pears encyclopaedia.

We were live to air and all I could see was Jog shrugging his shoulders. I accepted the contestant's answer.

From then on the question review meetings held before each recording session became more stringent.

It was always difficult to get anything past Reg and those pre-show sessions when we went through the question box and I tried to convince him that the daily paper was a perfectly reliable authority still haunt my dreams.

JOG

Both *Concentration* and *Tic Tac Dough* were created by American game show producer Bob Noah. It was 1981 before I met Bob and offered him a job. He and I were to create a number of successful shows out of our Los Angeles office.

Tic Tac Dough was based on noughts and crosses and our version was hosted by Chuck Faulkner, a Woolloomooloo Yank whose American-sounding accent came partly from his birth in Belfast. The other part was phony. Chuck was a handful who gave me problems and sometimes made me laugh. Sometimes.

He made the whole station laugh when TCN booth announcer John Godson caught him with a 'Godson special'. Godson was a notorious practical joker and was quickly into action when Chuck bought himself a huge American convertible, roughly the size of Tasmania. Godson was straight on the phone, impersonating the car sales company. Very apologetically, Godson told Chuck they'd just heard from America that there was a product recall on that particular model because there was a problem 'in the big end'. It wasn't too serious and it could be quickly fixed if Chuck brought the car in next morning.

'Yes, of course, Mr Faulkner, you can drive it home this evening.' Then came the fatal postscript. 'But you *must not* drive it over ten miles an hour.'

Chuck was so excited about his new car that he did drive it home that night—to far away Seven Hills in Sydney's western suburbs. And there he was the next morning in peak hour traffic, other motorists cursing and horns angrily honking as he crossed the Harbour Bridge, still at a steady ten miles an hour. It took forever.

At one time I decided to use him for a studio demo of a show called *Seven Keys*. Chuck demonstrated how the champion would choose a key and insert it into each padlock on a series of seven showcases until one opened to reveal his prize. The camera watched every move as Chuck tried the key in padlock after padlock until only one was left.

'Unless I'm sadly mistaken it must be the refrigerator.'

It didn't open.

Later a stagehand used the same key and opened one of the showcases.

Why couldn't Chuck? No idea.

But that was not the last I'd hear from Chuck.

At the 1963 Logies Chuck Faulkner was voted New South Wales' most popular male for his role as Detective Sergeant Vickers in the Crawford cop show *Division 4*. It was to be his finest hour but before the night was over, he drunkenly threatened me for some perceived harm I'd done to him. Maybe it was that key.

Chuck Faulkner—part of the history of Australian television.

With three shows now in production, life was rosy, but the Diments experience reinforced my belief in two key points: that if my business were to continue growing, I had to stop being a one-man band; and that the prize area was far too important to take for granted.

We needed a prize coordinator—a good salesperson who wasn't afraid to knock on doors. Jog introduced me to Jess Williamson, a tough Scottish woman he'd worked with in real estate. He pointed out that anyone who could successfully sell blocks of land on the fringes of Sydney to people who didn't really want to buy them would have no trouble finding prizes for successful television shows.

So Jess joined us, and now we were four.

I was doing well, no doubt about it. And when videotape arrived in March 1961, I was to do even better. Once again it was thanks to Bruce Gyngell, although I didn't realise he had his own fish to fry. He had this to say when interviewed by Brendan Horgan in 1998 for the National Screen and Sound oral history archive, *Radio With Pictures*:

> When tape came I decided I wanted to do strip programming—five half hours a week, and now that we had tape we could record them all in one day. Suddenly I found I had a problem. I was paying Terry Dear 25 pounds to do one episode of Concentration, so now he wants 125 pounds to do five shows.
>
> Well, I'd have to put that past the boss to get authorisation and there was no way. It would have been a calamity if I'd put through 125 pounds a week when David McNichol was getting 75 pounds a week as editor-in-chief. Anyway, I wanted to do it and I negotiated him down to a hundred, but how was I going to get it to him? So I went up to Reg Grundy and I said, 'Reg, I'm going to put you into the packaging business', and he said, 'What's the packaging business?'
>
> 'Well, what happens is you produce the program for me and I'll pay you a lump sum and you pay the talent.'
>
> 'All right,' he said.
>
> 'You can do two half hours a day—ten half hours a week—and I'll pay you 650 pounds.'
>
> So that's how Reg Grundy got into the packaging business—for me to avoid being confronted by Frank Packer.
>
> BRUCE GYNGELL

Gee, and I thought it was because Bruce was impressed by my production genius.

Like the *Wheel*, *Concentration* offered a wide range of exotic prizes including the sought-after Fowler's Cook-a-Chook, a Fraser ironing board and the ever-popular Can-o-mat can opener. And of course there was our motto: 'Nobody goes away empty-handed'. Even the least successful contestants took home a sample bag containing, if nothing else, a Wettex.

Melbourne had its own version of *Concentration* hosted by Philip Brady but with all shows being stripped out of Sydney, poor Philip was doomed.

In 1961 I was on top of the world. I was twenty years old and hosting a local version of Concentration *at GTV 9 in Melbourne. Then things came seriously unstuck when I was told that from now on* Concen-tration *was to be networked out of Sydney, where it would be compered by Terry Dear and produced by someone called Reg Grundy.*

A few months later I met Reg in the canteen at Nine. He said he was sorry I'd lost the show but what with the coaxial cable now linking Sydney and Melbourne and with the advent of videotape, local shows were on the way out and soon all programs would be national.

'I give you my word,' he said. 'Eventually we'll work together.'

PHILIP BRADY

And so we did, eventually. Philip had to wait until 1968, but he was to host 3000 episodes of Grundy game shows.

There wasn't a lot of money around in those early days of television and certainly not a lot of it came my way. My contracts with TCN were simple letters of agreement.

Several have survived and show that I was being paid 60 pounds an episode for *Wheel of Fortune*, 65 pounds for *Concentration* and 50 pounds for *Tic Tac Dough*; a total of 650 pounds for eleven shows a week, out of which I paid all above-the-line costs. Broadly speaking, the TV station supplied studio and crew and other facilities. They were the items which were called 'below the line'. The producer paid for talent and production staff. They were 'above the line'.

As my prospects improved and more people joined me, I realised I must separate my family life from my business, and so rented the flat immediately above ours and turned it into an informal office. I didn't have far to go to work—it was an easy walk up the concrete steps that linked the two flats. I could be in my office in thirty seconds.

It didn't last long. I wanted Reg Grundy Enterprises to have a real business address so I took the plunge and rented premises at 83 Miller Street, North Sydney. I didn't have enough income to justify the move, but felt I had to show that I was here to stay.

Now I was on the same side of the harbour as TCN 9. TCN was my only customer, and it had been made clear to me that was how it should stay.

BOBBIE AND GEORGE

I was fortunate to have great parents.

From the earliest days, they'd been happy to see me making my own way. There was never a suggestion that I should get a 'real' job in, say, a bank or some other safe occupation.

Neither of them had any connection with entertainment although they'd certainly been influenced by the movies, the pictures as we called them then. Dad loved George Formby, the Lancashire comedian who had appeared in a 1940 hit, *Let George Do It*. Dad was always talking about him, so I started calling him 'George'. He seemed to like it.

Early in the thirties my parents had seen Fred Astaire and Ginger Rogers in *Roberta*. Dad started calling Mum 'Roberta'. As time passed the name shortened to Rob or Robbie, and by the time my father died everyone was calling her Bobbie. Somehow it seemed just right for her.

I'd named my daughter Kim Robin.

When I first met Kim Robin she was known as Kim but I thought she looked like a little robin and so, echoing Reg's mother's original nickname, that's what she became.

JOY CHAMBERS-GRUNDY

When I married for the second time, I began calling my wife Perce or sometimes Percy, rather than Joy.

It seemed I was to be the only one in this tiny family who continued to be called by my real given name. And I was named after an early movie star, Reginald Denny.

I was working at radio station 2CH when George died at age fifty-six. Too young. He was diagnosed with hardening of the arteries—athero-sclerosis. One of the causes of the condition is smoking, and he certainly was a smoker.

His health had been deteriorating for months and inevitably he found himself in hospital. My mother and I visited him every day. He had been there five or six weeks when we entered the ward one day to be told he'd been moved to a private room. We were shocked to find him propped up with stitches in his head. He had fallen out of bed. The guard rail which could have prevented the accident had not been in place. Gross negligence. But it was too late. It was obvious the room was set aside for patients who were on the edge of death.

He was unconscious yet breathing, and as we sat beside him his breathing stopped. I kissed him on the forehead. It was over.

As we walked out of the hospital I remembered how he had followed my career so closely: writing notes of my first fight broadcast, designing a cut-out of the map of Australia which I attached to the microphone I used to call the fight in South Africa. Dad died before I moved into television and I can only imagine how proud he would have been of the good fortune I was to have in the new medium.

The day after Dad's death I was scheduled to record an episode of the *Sorbent Show* with a live audience. I could have asked 2CH to substitute another host for that week's show, but I didn't. George would have wanted me to carry on so I recorded the show and went home to my grieving mother.

In the early days of my life in television Bobbie, my mother, came daily to our office in Miller Street, North Sydney and sorted the mail. It was a big job—as the number of shows increased, so did the bags of mail.

Ray Newell, who was our resident television director, on loan from TCN 9, bought her an electric letter opener—a small shiny object that cut a tiny sliver from the top of the envelope.

It was the first item of modern technology that we owned.

Email was light years away and my memos were written in a small book with numbered pages from which the master copy was torn out and passed on to the recipient; the carbon copy was left in the book.

I found this one from 28 April 1961:

Ray,

Could we secure some old ships' bells etc to be used for 10 sec time signals—wrong answers etc. You found it easy to spend my money on a letter opener, perhaps you could spend a few shillings on a sound effect.

RG

So here was this marvellous gadget, a device that everyone in the office wanted to try. My mother's pride and joy.

Each Grundy employee's approach was pretty much the same: 'Come on, Mrs G, you need a break. I'll open a few for you'.

Mum would have much preferred to open all the mail herself but graciously stepped aside for a moment or two.

ROB

Soon after the office moved to North Sydney, my marriage ended. Lola had become restless and finally left me for an even older man, a Melbourne barrister.

My small daughter, Kim Robin, stayed with me.

My mother came to live with us and it was she who really raised my daughter, showering her with the same love I had always been given. I called my mother Bobbie but Rob called her Mum. I suppose we were an odd threesome—my mother, my daughter and me. One thing I knew: there was much love between us.

But we were like gypsies as we moved from place to place. Kim and I loved swimming, so I tried to find locations that allowed us to have an early morning dip. At one time we were living over a greengrocer's shop near Manly baths. Later, I rented a house on the North Shore that had a swimming pool cut into the backyard lawn. Rob and I went swimming every morning. We swam all year round, sometimes in icy water. On Saturday mornings we went to the Double Bay Municipal Library and sat under an umbrella fondling the books we had just borrowed.

By the time I met Joy we had moved to Lindfield. And then I discovered a house in McIntosh Street, Gordon which had been built on a tennis court and had a swimming pool. No backyard. Just what I was looking for: a house pretending to be an apartment.

I was content with my lot in life. I ran the business while my mother ran the household and looked after Rob. When I fell in love with Joy, who again was so much younger, I thought it would be difficult for her to accept that her husband-to-be had a daughter.

It was not difficult at all. Rob was a lovely small child and for years we delighted in each other's company.

JOY CHAMBERS-GRUNDY

Joy had been coming to Sydney, staying with us, and she and Rob got along just fine. Maybe Rob saw in Joy the glamorous woman she herself could become. Maybe I'm wrong; maybe it wasn't so smooth after all. I only know that after we married, Rob switched off. The three of us lived at Bayview together but eventually Rob moved out and gradually we moved apart.

The loss of my daughter is the greatest heartbreak in my life.

I had lost a daughter and gained a wife who is the light of my life. If only the three of us could have lived happily ever after.

I hadn't heard from Rob for some time when she called me. 'Dad, you must do this. It's called EST.' That night, we had dinner together. Before we parted I promised her I would do it. EST stands for Erhard Seminars Training, named after the man who developed a system of self-awareness based on earlier versions of Zen. Participants were trained to get 'IT', although no one seemed quite able to say what 'IT' was. Perhaps it meant that we are what we are, and are responsible for everything we do. That's certainly the message I received from the experience.

Anyway, I did it, and after the first day I called her at around midnight Sydney time. I was in Vancouver. We talked about the effect EST had had on her and was already beginning to have on me. It brought Rob back into the fold, but it didn't last.

Years later, at her request, I flew from Canada to New York to see her. I arrived at her hotel but she was unavailable.

SAY WHEN

Ken Hall and Bruce Gyngell came to see me and suggested I take a drive with them. I thought that being taken for a ride could mean only one thing, and I was right. They were in no hurry to get to the point but after shuffling their feet a bit, they suggested I should stand down as host of *Wheel of Fortune*.

I wasn't surprised, really. I'd felt for some time that the pressures associated with running the business had made my performance as host less than brilliant. KG and Bruce may well have felt the same way, but they graciously told me I was of more value to TCN as a packager, running a business producing more shows for them. It was a view I accepted with suitable modesty, and handed over the *Wheel* to Walter Elliott.

I never hosted a show again.

I guess they might have meant what they said, because the next show wasn't long in coming.

It was Saturday afternoon and Bruce Gyngell was on the line. 'I've got a tape I want you to hear. I'll come round after dinner, okay?'

We sat in my study and listened to a stylish game show. *Say When* was a Mark Goodson production. It had the right pedigree. Goodson was the king of game shows at the time.

'What do you think, boy?' said Bruce, as he switched off the tape recorder.

'I love it.'

And I did. It was slick, smart and sophisticated and I couldn't wait to brief the troops on Monday morning.

There were eleven of us now, including art director Fred 'Cul' Cullen, brother of actor/artist Max Cullen. Fred designed a striking new company logo based on my signature, and his stylised version caught my eye. I changed my signature to match his logo and I'm still using it. Some people said I was eccentric, but it worked for me.

Don Davies joined the Grundy group. Don had worked as a producer for radio star Jack Davey, who was possibly the biggest radio star Australia ever knew, even though he was born in New Zealand. He had countless claims to fame, but one he could not have known about at the time: in 1955 one of Davey's contestants was sixteen-year-old John Howard, who was to become Prime Minister of Australia. When Jack died, a reported crowd of well over 100,000 people attended his funeral.

Pam Ferguson was the most recent person to join. Pam signed on as my secretary but I soon realised she was made for better things and switched her to production. She was to have—and is still having—a glittering career in the game show business in America.

'We've got a new show and eight weeks to get it up and running.'

Some of my crew didn't look too thrilled. They thought they were already flat out making eleven half hours every week. I pretended not to notice and outlined my plan to take *Say When* more up-market than our other shows by adding a few bells and whistles. I announced that I was going to hire the seriously good guitarist Don Andrews to provide live music over the prize descriptions and Valerie May as a hostess to model clothing and jewellery.

I was keen to have more fabulous prizes than any other game show around, so I sent our prize coordinator Jess Williamson on a shopping trip to Southeast Asia. Lacquerware from Japan, bronze incense burners from Korea and gold-plated chairs from Hong Kong were not as practical as the small kitchen appliances usually offered, but they were certainly more glamorous. Australia had never seen such prizes before.

I was determined that *Say When* would bring sparkle and glitz to daytime television, and it did.

But studio technology wasn't really up to the challenge. The turret cameras of the day had a definite drawback in that they had no zoom and a zoom was needed, essential even, to give visual punch when introducing the flashy line-up.

I remembered that TCN had a field zoom, which was used for sport, so I went to Bruce and asked if we could use it on *Say When*. The techies were against it but Bruce got Ken Hall's agreement, and that was that.

I was keen that *Say When* be hosted by Jimmy Hannan, who bubbled with charm and had the sort of looks that were made for television. Jog remembers that Jim turned up for his first meeting with us in a tiny bright red Isetta—a mini-machine for two, powered by a BMW one-cylinder bike engine. His new workmates watched as long, tall Jim unfolded himself like an emerging stick insect.

But common sense and, I suppose, network politics made general auditions necessary. I wanted to make sure Jimmy got the job so I added opening titles and music to his audition tape and did a voiceover introduction.

'And now, here's the star of the show … Jimmy Hannan!'

The salesman's assumptive close, once again. He got the job. And it wouldn't be the last time he worked for me.

In camera plotting the show, I was working from the studio floor and had Jimmy looking at a monitor while we established the spot where he should stand in relation to the set behind him.

Gyngell came down to the floor and instructed Peter Honeyfield, the floor manager, to tell Jimmy not to look at the monitor. I had a word with Bruce to let him know I was producing the show, not him.

'Bruce, just get out of the way. If, after you've seen the show, you don't like what I'm doing, then get rid of me. Until then, let me get on with it.'

Bruce backed off.

After the first show, Bruce, Ken Hall and the sponsor's representative were all over me. *Say When* had all the hallmarks of a hit.

A year later I handed over the production to Lyle McCabe, a former TCN 9 lighting man who had joined us and was showing tremendous potential as a producer.

One day I was standing behind him in the control room and had just tapped him on the shoulder for the second time. Lyle turned to me.

'Reg, only one of us can produce this show and you've said it's me.'

He was right. His words were echoes of what I had said to Bruce Gyngell. I turned and left the control room, and I never went back. For the rest of my life in television I stayed right away from the studio when a show was in production. I realised I could evaluate a program much better if I saw it as the viewer would see it.

It was while we were making *Say When* that I again crossed paths with Mr Callaghan from 2SM and 2CH. He was out of work and down on his luck. It was my turn to help him.

Say When was chewing up prizes. We needed someone to be a kind of watchman/custodian of the merchandise, which we kept in a building across the road from our offices in Miller Street, North Sydney.

I offered Cal the job and he jumped at it. I remember him in his grey dust jacket, smiling as he handed over prizes to winning contestants. Wish he was still around; I'd love to know who won that gold-plated bathroom chair.

With four shows in production, two of them running five days a week, TCN's studios were starting to be overcrowded. Bruce made it plain that one of the stripped shows would have to find other accommodation.

I got on the phone and made arrangements to use weekend downtime at QTQ in Brisbane and GTV in Melbourne. It was a pain, but there was an obvious upside. Both *Say When* and *Concentration* were running in those states and local production with local contestants seemed a good way of building audiences.

Say When was too complex to travel successfully, so it was *Concentration* that took to the road. Every other Friday the production team headed interstate to record five shows on Saturday and another five on Sunday before catching a late flight back to Sydney in time for work on Monday.

The set travelled by road and director Ray Newell always made it his first priority to check that it had arrived safely. Inevitably, there was a day when it didn't. No sign of it. It was Friday evening with a recording date at GTV in the morning. Ray got on the phone and found that the truck had overturned somewhere on the Hume Highway. He spent most of the night arranging for a second truck to collect and deliver the set. Somehow it arrived in time and the shows got made.

I didn't find out what had happened until the team was back at work on Monday. I was suitably impressed but when I eventually saw the episodes I called Ray into my office and pointed out that there was a mark on the flat behind the contestants. I accepted that the circumstances were difficult and realised it was a weekend, but surely a drop of paint could have been found somewhere! Obsessive and unreasonable? Ray probably thought so, and he's not the only one. I prefer the word painstaking myself.

Within a couple of years, ten shows a weekend looked like a lazy man's way to make television. In 1967 I told journalist Carmel Friedlander: 'We've made as many as fourteen half hours in a day and anything up to fifty-six in a week'.

Just the same, back in 1963, ten shows over the weekend was a feat considered not just groundbreaking but downright Herculean.

All our shows were doing well, but I believed Jimmy Hannan had more to offer than simply hosting *Say When*. He had a great singing voice. Why not use him as my entree into the record business?

Festival Records were open to the idea, and RG Records was born. Robert Iredale, Festival's top producer, agreed to put down the first tracks.

'Beach Ball' was chosen as our initial entry into the world of pop music and it was recorded in the Festival studios with vocal backing from three young singers who were to become famous as the Bee Gees. On the Grundy label they were not named, and simply referred to as 'Vocal accompaniment'.

How was I to know?

'Beach Ball' hit the Australian Top Forty in mid-December 1963, only held out of top place by the Beatles. It remained in the charts for fifteen weeks. What a great Christmas present!

I followed up with 'Hokey Pokey Stomp', giving the Second World War song new life with a 'Beach Ball' sound. It made the charts, then quickly faded away. I chased it with a forty-five, then made an LP of Jimmy singing standards financed by the Australian Wool Board.

Later, I persuaded Robert Iredale to leave Festival and join Reg Grundy Enterprises. His presence brought a flow of recording stars through the door, including rocker Johnny O'Keefe.

Joy was often in the office when Johnny turned up.

One day he made his move. 'Honey, let's go away for the weekend.'

'Johnny, you know I'm Reg's girl.'

'Yeah, yeah, I know, but just one weekend and I reckon I'd come up with a hit.'

Johnny didn't get the girl, Johnny didn't write the song and RG Records slowly went out of business.

It wasn't because of the O'Keefe incident.

GETTING THE CHOP

It was 1964: I got a call from KG.

'Like to see you today. Three o'clock okay?'

As soon as I entered his office I had a feeling it wasn't going to be good news.

'Reg, you've done a great job, but we're dropping your shows.'

Dropping my shows? What was he talking about?

'Not your fault. We're cutting back on transmission hours.'

Not all my shows. He can't mean all of them.

But he did.

It didn't matter that they were all way ahead in the ratings, winning their slots by a country mile. Soon they'd be gone. My career in television would be over. I'd be out of work … again.

I left KG's office and walked along the overhead passage. I paused for a moment in the area that served as the boardroom and separated the CEO from the general office. There below me was the number two studio where I had first faced a television camera and where I had made so many episodes of *Concentration* and *Say When*, *Wheel of Fortune* and *Tic Tac Dough*.

It was hard to believe that after all the struggle, all the effort to establish myself, my loyal group and I would be without a show. Reg Grundy Enterprises would soon cease to exist.

My eyes moistened. I felt ashamed that I couldn't accept the verdict. But I couldn't. It had come out of the blue. One moment I was the pioneer who had 'invented' independent packaging, yet soon I would have nothing.

When I'd started, I often thought, 'What if TCN drops my show? I'm hanging by a thread. What the hell will I do if the *Wheel* stops turning?'

I'd had an irresistible desire to succeed, to grow my business, and I'd pushed ahead until I felt secure with four shows. When strip programming was introduced I was like a kid in a candy store. The sky was the limit.

I was bursting with ideas, pushing for more daytime productions.

Safety in numbers, I'd thought. Nothing could happen to me now. But it did.

I straightened up and left the boardroom, and made for the wooden stairs that led down to the reception area, beyond which lay the two studios and the property storage bays. I didn't look to the right as I moved through the general office area. Maybe some of those people sitting there already knew that my shows were to be axed. I kept looking straight ahead.

At the front desk I forced a smile and said, 'Betty, mind if I call my office?'

'Of course not, Mr Grundy.'

Narelle Powers, my secretary, took the call.

'Get your car and meet me at the corner of Willoughby Road and Chandos Street.'

I got there just as she pulled up.

'They've dumped me. I'm losing all my shows.'

'All of them. Oh dear.'

I couldn't show my emotions in front of her, but I was close to letting go.

'I don't want to go back to the office. Tell anyone who asks that I've had to move on to another meeting and I'll be in in the morning.'

'What are you going to do?'

'Oh, I'll go home, climb into my shell and have a think.'

The following morning was tough. Apart from my secretary, there were twelve people to tell. Don Davies went white. Later, I saw him in a corner whispering to Pam Ferguson. The sardonic Fred Cullen acted as if he didn't care. Ray Newell was supportive, but would have known that he could go back to TCN 9 if nothing else turned up for us. My secretary, Narelle, shed a tear.

It was not my finest hour.

'I don't want you guys to despair. I regard you all as family. You'll all stay on full salary and I'll do everything I can to get us out of this hole.'

I don't think any of them were convinced.

The next day *TV Times* reported:

Television viewers will see the last of Terry Dear's Concentration *from TCN 9, on February 28.*

Mr K.G. Hall, Chief Executive of TCN, said: 'A Melbourne-produced program called Key Notes *starring Alastair McHarg will replace it'.*

Not exactly what KG had said to me.

I think what really happened was a simple case of arm-twisting. Station affiliations had changed and TCN 9 had just hooked up with GTV 9 in Melbourne to form what was called the National Television Network; GTV was insisting that it should provide part of the daily program line-up. My shows all emanated from TCN in Sydney, so had to go to make room for Melbourne productions.

Whatever the reason, *Concentration* was finished and my other shows would soon follow. The future looked bleak.

It was later that night when the idea hit me: when facilities in Sydney were stretched, hadn't we made *Concentration* in Queensland? Maybe I could talk Jim McKay at QTQ into making it a permanent arrangement.

What a ludicrous idea. QTQ was running *Concentration*, but had been paying TCN only a small portion of the actual cost. Was I seriously going to ask Jim to carry the whole load himself?

It was a long shot, but I couldn't think of a better move. I called QTQ and set up a meeting for the following afternoon. I didn't sleep well that night, and as I flew towards Brisbane I gazed out the window at the clouds below us. I was looking for a silver lining.

QTQ 9, together with BTQ 7 and the ABC, sited its studio on top of Mount Coot-tha, from where the whole of Brisbane could be seen. They would eventually be joined, in the middle of 1965, by TVQ 0.

It was a beautiful day as the cab drove up the winding road lined with gum trees.

Jim McKay, a quiet man, stood up from behind his desk.

'Sorry to hear about your problem with TCN. I've got a feeling your visit might have something to do with it.'

He'd given me the opening and I jumped right in.

'Jim, we're six weeks ahead with *Concentration*. Your crew know the ropes. If we switch full production up here, the show can continue without a break.'

I paused and thought: if he says no, I'm finished.

He didn't say no. He didn't say anything.

'Of course, I wouldn't expect more than the licence fee you're already paying.'

What was I saying? Who did I think was going to fund the rest?

I hurried on. 'Maybe we could do a deal where we sell the show to some of the country stations and split the income.'

Not a bad idea actually. I wondered why I hadn't thought of it before.

Jim finally spoke. 'The show is doing well for us.'

I went for the closer.

'And if the rest of the network picks it up again, as I'm sure they will, you'll have a national show coming out of your studios. We can knock out a whole week's episodes in a single shift and I reckon we might be able to do more if we really try. What do you say?'

Jim smiled. 'Let's see if we can find a way.'

I could have leapt over his desk and hugged him.

I was still in business.

Jim did find a way and soon we were managing to record fifteen episodes on a weekend allowing Terry Dear, the host, to visit Brisbane once every three weeks.

I enjoyed working at QTQ. I loved the bush setting. The crews were friendly, the atmosphere tranquil. But by the year's end all my other shows would be gone and the income from Brisbane wouldn't go near to covering my staff's wages. I had to get more work, make more programs, just to cover overheads.

Still, the move to Brisbane kept me in the game. What I didn't know was that it would also change my life.

MONEY FROM OLD STAMPS

I took a break. It had been a tough few days.

The following Monday I walked up the stairs to our office at 83 Miller Street. Jog was sitting in his office looking smug.

He got in first. 'Seems we don't always need the great white master to keep us in business.'

'And what the hell does that mean?'

'Well.' He paused to keep me hanging. I waited. Two can play that game. He cracked first.

'Compton Advertising has approached us to make a kids' game show.'

'Who for?'

'Ampol.'

'And what did you say?'

'I said we were far too busy.'

I was impressed. It was the first time we'd been approached by an ad agency.

'All we need is a format.'

'I'm your man.'

Jog grinned. 'Thought you might be.'

I once told Matt White, the entertainment reporter for the *Daily Mirror*, that I was 'cursed with enthusiasm'. Now seemed the time to prove it.

The show was called *Ampol Stamp Quiz*. The idea was that postage stamps would be distributed at all Ampol stations. The kids want the stamps, Dad fills up with Ampol. Major prize: a trip to Disneyland.

It was a fairly straightforward format with state finals and a grand final. We decided we'd like pop stars Dig Richards and Little Pattie to be host and hostess.

Pattie quickly agreed.

I called Dig's agent, Bill Watson.

'What's the money?'

'Well, it's a daytime low-budget show, so …'

Bill jumped in.

'Okay, Reg, you don't need a sob story. I remember when I worked for Lee Gordon at Sydney Stadium. I was there when you were taken to the room with all those hessian bags full of banknotes. They told you to take a couple of handfuls and you declined. Not many did. So I reckon you'll do the right thing by young Dig. Let's make it easy. Whatever you offer, we'll accept.'

And what was the series' most memorable moment?

Reginald Goldsworthy was the agency account executive who travelled with the show. When asked how he was, he inevitably replied, 'Like a lion'. He was one of the most charming and colourful of men, and often one of the least sober.

We were staying at an Adelaide motel when the fire alarm went off in the middle of the night. Guests lined the balconies and watched the fire brigade drag a smouldering mattress into the courtyard. Reg Goldsworthy, rumpled in a bathrobe, watched forlornly. He had fallen asleep with a lit cigarette in his hand, setting fire to his bed.

Next morning he was as cheerful as ever and tucking into his breakfast. When asked how he felt after the night's traumatic incident, he waved a slice of toast: 'Like a lion'. Yes, Reg Goldsworthy always felt 'like a lion'— even when he'd almost burned himself to death.

The *Ampol Stamp Quiz* was John O'Grady's final credit with Reg Grundy Enterprises. Jog spent the Christmas break contemplating his navel and decided that he wanted to be writing something other than quiz questions, prize copy and game show run-downs. He left at the beginning of 1965.

It would be forty years before we got together again.

NEW YORK, NEW YORK

I'd had my new passport for over a year. I'd applied for it in a moment of optimism after *Concentration* returned to TCN 9 in 1965 with what we were calling the Gold Coast version.

The Gold Coast look was reflected in the prizes. Pam Ferguson had the job of contestant coach, and told them to look happy no matter what prize they won. The eighty-five-year-old woman who won the surfboard did her best.

The old show was again a hit around Australia and I was happy that my prediction to Jim McKay had come true: QTQ was the first station outside Sydney and Melbourne to produce a national daily program.

With *I've Got A Secret* booming as well, I felt that we might have turned the corner and that the time had come for me to get up close and personal with some American game shows by actually seeing them going to air.

It was August 1966 and the first of many, many trips I was to make across the Pacific. Someone with too much time on their hands has estimated that I have now made that crossing hundreds of times.

I can remember asking Reg to take me with him and he replied, 'Not this time, but I will take you in the future, I promise'. He certainly did—I reckon I've made that crossing hundreds of times too ...'

JOY CHAMBERS-GRUNDY

The flight was long, stopping at Honolulu and Los Angeles before finally arriving in New York.

Wearily, I struggled out of the airport and into a cab.

'Where to?' demanded the driver.

'The Hilton Hotel. Avenue of the Americas, I think.'

'You got it,' growled the little man behind the wheel, a week's stubble on his face and the stub of a cigar clenched between his teeth.

He was just like the taxi drivers I had seen in American movies. Amazing.

The yellow cab was filthy and even the windscreen needed a wash. It might have helped the driver see where he was going but that wasn't necessary—the cab and the cabbie had done this route hundreds, maybe thousands, of times. But for me it was the first time, the time one never forgets.

I slumped in the back, falling into a reverie as the cab battled its way towards Manhattan. I was tired, dog tired.

How had I managed to make it to Gotham? From pig and cattle results to this. How had the whole adventure in entertainment come about? What was I doing in show business anyway?

The years rolled back, and I tried to piece it all together. An eight-year-old on stage in top hat and tails, singing and dancing in front of a chorus line of little girls. A twelve-year-old lying in bed listening to the *Hollywood Reporter* on the wireless. A fifteen-year-old at school doing impressions of the comedy acts of the time with his best friend, Max Short, who was to lose his life in the war less than five years later.

And to think of the life that had been given to me. A nineteen-year-old working in the District Finance Office as Pay Sergeant, at the Showground on Wednesdays putting on a show and singing. Two young men in a small recording studio in George Street, Sydney, me singing 'Pennies From Heaven' to Valdemar Smith's accompaniment. Leaving with the precious, fragile acetate.

And to think that soon I would be in Manhattan where Carnegie Hall was located—where Artie Shaw would have performed. I remembered being at the Trocadero in George Street, the best dance hall in Sydney. Being there with American soldiers and uniformed Australians listening to Artie Shaw playing clarinet in front of his big band. Standing on the ballroom floor as the magical music filled the air, the Yanks looking marvellous in their tailored uniforms with ties and shiny shoes; the few of us Aussies in rough serge and heavy boots, making the most of the moment.

'Mister.' It was the cab driver.

'You been to the Big Apple before?'

'No.'

'Where you from?'

'Australia.'

'Yeah? You got any cities out dere or is it all, you know, whadya call it, outback?'

'No, we've got cities.'

'Amazing.'

'I'm pretty tired. I think I'll just close my eyes for a bit.'

He grunted.

I returned to my reverie. Sunday nights at a little studio dance hall on the first floor of a building in Pitt Street, where members of the 2KY Bing and Swing club danced and performed. Like a karaoke bar without the alcohol. Dreaming of being Australia's answer to Bing Crosby, stepping up on the stage, singing my heart out. Longing to do it, but lacking the courage to make the move.

Working at night, operating a spotlight at the Grace Auditorium, a ballroom at Grace Brothers, Broadway. My father, the manager, giving me the job of spotlighting the singers and generally controlling the stage lighting. The old carbon arc filling the small bio box with almost unbearable heat, the arc fiercely burning as I turned the knob to bring the two carbons together.

Bob Hudspeth, who owned a chemist shop just down Bayswater Road from Kings Cross, conducting the resident band at the Auditorium, giving me the chance to sing a couple of songs during intermission at the local movie theatre. There I was standing on stage with a fourteen-piece band roaring behind me. Giving myself a stage name, 'Bob White', taken from an old Bing Crosby track called 'Bob White, What You Gonna Swing Tonight?' Appearing a couple of times with the band and then my singing career ending. Bob White swinging no more. Why did I sing under an assumed name? No valid reason that I could remember, as nobody knew me under my real name anyway.

I'd answered my own question. It was clear I was destined to be in show business.

'Hey, mister, we're here.'

The towers of New York were above me. Peering up at the canyon walls, I caught my breath. I was right in the middle of it all, at West 53rd Street and the Avenue of the Americas (6th Avenue), and I was about to watch game shows. Just as soon as I got into my room.

I waited impatiently in line behind the red velvet rope that funnelled new arrivals to the check-in counter. At last I was in the elevator—even I knew better than to call it a lift. I walked eagerly along the corridor towards my room. The door was open. The maids were inside.

'We won't be but ten minutes.'

It was 10.45. I knew the block of morning game shows was going to air right now.

At last I was inside. I turned on the TV. Colour. It was still a decade away in Australia. I lay on the bed, willing myself to keep my eyes open. Smart sets, smooth MCs, big prizes and bright contestants—the glamorous world of the American game show.

At noon the credits for the final show rolled down the screen. I closed my eyes and drifted off into game show heaven.

I need not have gone to New York. I could have watched the same shows on the three network affiliates in Honolulu or Los Angeles. But I didn't know that. I was single minded, enthusiastic … and naive.

On the return trip I stopped over in Los Angeles and booked into the Hollywood Roosevelt. It reeked of nostalgia. So many stars had stayed here. So many liaisons had been made.

I went for a walk to clear my jetlag. Right across Hollywood Boulevard was Grauman's Chinese Theatre. I turned left and soon passed Schwab's Drug Store on Sunset. That's where Lana Turner the movie star was discovered, I thought, gazing in wonderment.

After a couple of hours the landscape changed. I was passing an elegant hotel named the Beverly Wilshire. How could I realise that some fifteen years later, Joy and I would be living in an apartment in this very hotel?

I crossed the road into Rodeo Drive. My eyes were dazzled by the glamorous shops. I was in Beverly Hills.

Later that afternoon I lay beside the Roosevelt pool with my feet up, exhausted. I'd walked over 16 kilometres.

The tears were rolling down my cheeks. I was not unhappy. It was just the acrid smog assaulting my eyes.

What did I care? I was in Hollywood, the home of show biz.

AMERICA IS PINCHING
MY SHOWS

If you've been around long enough and managed to have some success, rumours will abound.

I suppose the most prevalent one about me is that I knocked off American game show formats and illegally produced them in Australia.

Dame Edna Everage put it more kindly at my eighty-fifth un-birthday show:

Reg, you had all those wonderful ideas for quiz shows. It's extraordinary that they came to you while in America watching television.

Norman Gunston, the satirical character played by Australian actor Garry McDonald, said on his return from a visit to the US:

I feel sorry for Mr Grundy; the Americans are pinching all his shows.

Yes, when I was in America I sat in hotel rooms and made audio recordings of game shows, and took black and white snaps of the television screen as well. Then I'd fly back to Australia and pitch the shows to whomever I thought might buy them.

But nothing I did was ever illegal.

At that time America had not signed the International Copyright Agreement so none of the US producers involved were entitled to protection. I was in the clear.

Here's the rub. While I certainly didn't have the money to pay for rights at that time, I didn't know I was in the clear. So the rumours were wrong, but I thought they were right!

Kerry Wright, our erudite legal counsel of some thirty years, who has been with us through thick and thin, thinks I should put it in a more flattering light by saying: 'I used the shows and the ideas for the shows when I was entitled to. When I wasn't entitled, I didn't.

There was only one copyright holder who ever tried to take us on. Although I made many changes to the format, it would be hard to deny that *Temptation* and *Great Temptation* were actually inspired by the original American production of *Sale of the Century*.

Al Howard owned the rights and hired Australian lawyers who tried to assert that we were breaking the copyright, but they had no case and were forced to back down.

By the time the Nine network decided that it wanted us to produce *Sale of the Century* with the original title, the USA had signed the Berne Agreement and Howard's rights were protected. I negotiated with him and bought Australian rights.

The first few shows I made for television—those from the early 1960s—had a slightly different story.

For instance, my first production, *Reg Grundy's Wheel of Fortune*, was created by me so there was no copyright issue. My *Wheel of Fortune* was totally different to the American show, which eventually I was to make in 1981 after buying the rights.

And those old favourites—*Concentration*, *Say When* and *Tic Tac Dough*—were all handed to me by TCN 9, so copyright was a matter for them, not for me.

These days, shows are seen and bought worldwide, but I was the only one doing it back then. Australian networks knew that I was the man on the spot when it came to American game shows, and I made sure I was first to get those shows on air back home.

And they were certainly well received. As Dame Edna once said:

If Reg Grundy hadn't made all those TV shows, Australian families, in the evening, would have had to talk to one another.

A FINE ROMANCE: WE'VE GOT A SECRET

I was in the boardroom at QTQ 9 Brisbane with Jim McKay, the man who called the shots.

'*Concentration*'s going well, Reg. Ratings are up.'

'Maybe we ought to capitalise on it,' I said.

'Like how?'

I'd been working on an idea. Now seemed a good time to spring it on him.

'Maybe a local show like *Tell the Truth* with local stars.'

'How does it go again?'

'Simple enough. Three people pretend to be the same person. The panel has to pick who is the real one. We could do a pilot.'

'Just one?'

'Yes, we'd only need a crew for less than a shift.'

Jim thought for a moment. 'Doesn't seem to be much downside. Okay, you're on. Let's drink to it.'

The next morning I ran into John Frank, the QTQ 9 program manager—we always got along well. Jim had told him the idea and John was keen.

'I like the sound of this show you're doing, Reg.'

I was jubilant and I was worried. It was a great concept, but it wouldn't be as easy to pull off as I'd led Jim to believe.

If the show worked and was stripped each weekday, we'd need to record five shows in a day. That would mean coaching ten groups of two people trying to pretend to be the real person, plus ten real people, adding up to thirty people each week.

I'd pitched the wrong show.

We should be making *I've Got A Secret*, I realised. Four panellists attempt to discover the 'secret' of each guest. No rehearsal needed—just a supply of guests with good secrets. That shouldn't be too difficult.

I didn't want to go back and tell Jim of my concern. He might cancel the whole thing. There was only one thing to do: make the wrong show. Make *I've Got A Secret* instead of *Tell the Truth*.

I did.

Panel games are notoriously difficult to make well. They are essentially feather-light concoctions of warmth and humour with very little to keep them upright other than the charm and quick wit of the panellists. Get the casting wrong, and the most promising format will fall over with an embarrassing thud.

I needed to get the casting right.

I chose a local publican, Joe Borsellino; a lecturer from the University of Queensland, Fred Indorf; and Babette Stephens, the grand dame of Queensland theatre—a strong combination of wit, charm and brains. I already had the host, Don Seccombe, QTQ 9's nightly newsreader.

I needed one more. How about a gorgeous young woman with personality? Never hurts to add a bit of glamour.

Three hundred young women turned up for the audition to find my 'Golden Girl'. Don Davies, my assistant, eyed them as they milled in the station foyer.

'Okay, Don, bring them in in threes. Let's see if any of them can look good, ad lib and make us laugh all at the same time.'

I faced the first three girls and started the audition, asking them questions like: 'If you looked over a fence and saw somebody sunbathing in the nude, what would you do?' Or, 'You have one minute to talk about the wind.'

It was a long night. At 10.30 I was back in the foyer.

'Well, ladies, thanks for coming. We've seen you all. We'll get back to the finalists later this week.'

As I started to turn away a slender arm was raised at the back of the crowd.

'You haven't seen me.'

I turned to Don. 'She's two and a half hours late. Get rid of her.'

'Aw, come on, Reg, let's take a couple of the other girls back in and see what she's like.'

I grudgingly agreed.

I started with the 'wind' question. Most of the girls had failed to give any sort of response; the others had just delivered a few cliché-ridden sentences.

But she said, 'I'm not going to try to describe the wind. Shelley said it all in "Ode to the West Wind" and I can't top that'. She laughed.

'Do you remember any of it?' I asked.

'Certainly. Here are the last two lines:

"The trumpet of a prophecy! O Wind,

If Winter comes can Spring be far behind?" '

I moved on. The exchange was not what I'd expected or wanted. I wasn't looking for a bookworm—I wanted a fun girl who could get a few laughs. Yet there she was grinning at me. Fabulous figure, real good-looker.

For the first time that night I felt I was losing ground.

'What show business experience do you have?' I asked.

'Well, I used to recite poems on the Ipswich bus when I was little. Lately a friend and I have been singing together and calling ourselves The Shades. And I've been in lots of plays.'

'Is that it?'

She nodded and her golden hair shone in the arc light. 'That's it.'

She was smart, funny and too damn sure of herself. Anyway, the videotapes would tell the tale.

At ten the next morning I was in the tape room.

'Arthur, you've dubbed off the six finalists and added in that last girl?'

Tape editor Arthur Gough nodded.

'Let's play the first six.'

Arthur pressed the button.

After I'd seen them I knew there was only one who had a chance—an attractive woman with an intriguing Swedish accent.

'Okay, let's look at the seventh.'

I watched in silence, then asked him to replay the segment.

'Well, I guess that's it,' I said. 'We've got our golden girl.'

'Which one do you reckon, Reg?'

'The last one.'

Arthur was talking to himself: 'Yeah, hadda be, hadda be her!'

So the latecomer got the job. And she got me.

But that was a way off yet.

Jim McKay never asked me why I made the wrong show. Why would he? *IGAS*, as it became known, ran for almost ten years.

The girl was terrific. I was pleased that Don Davies had persuaded me to give her a chance. Isn't it funny how one decision can change your whole life?

Over the weeks of run-throughs I saw another side to Joy Chambers, a side I liked a lot. Now I had a problem. I had a made it a rule never to date a woman working on one of my shows.

When Lola walked out on me, I decided to throw myself into my work and from then on women played a very small part in my life. The few who did were not in television and so had nothing to do with my shows.

Yet I wanted to get to know this fabulous, glamorous vision. The age difference was huge. At a stretch, I could have been her father. But I couldn't help myself—I badly wanted to see her away from the studio. Just the two of us. To hell with the rule.

On the day of the pilot show everything went swimmingly.

'Well done, panel, you were great. I reckon we might have a hit.' I tried to sound nonchalant. 'Joy, there's just one thing I want to go over with you.'

I guided her behind one of the backing flats. It was now or never.

'Would you consider having dinner with me?'

The vision smiled. 'I'd love to.'

Joy was living with her parents in Ipswich. I was living in Sydney with my mother and daughter. I'd planned to return to Sydney but now decided to stay over if Joy would have dinner with me the following night.

'I'm staying in Brisbane with my aunty.' She gave me the address.

'I'll pick you up at 7.15.'

She was simply dressed but there was radiance about her. At least to me there was.

We walked down the broad stone steps to Chez Tessa on Wickham Terrace, Brisbane's only first-class restaurant then. I had never felt so uncomfortable with a girl since I took Beverly Watson from DJs' model department out to dinner that distant Friday night before the war.

I ordered a bottle of Hamilton's Moselle. I was to learn a little more about wine over the years.

As she studied the menu I said, 'You know, you knocked me out at the audition when you mentioned Shelley's "Ode to the West Wind". You must love poetry'.

'I got it from my Dad. He's a lot older and more learned than my girlfriends' fathers. I suppose he could almost be my grandfather from an age point of view. A bit like ...'

She didn't finish the sentence but I knew what she was thinking.

The only poem I knew was the first line of 'The Man From Snowy River'. But I'd been doing my homework and had memorised a few classics.

"Shall I compare thee to a summer's day? Thou art more lovely and more temperate."

She laughed and looked away.

'Should I stop?'

She smiled and said very softly, 'Oh, no. I like Shakespeare'.

"You take the breath of men away, Who gaze upon you unaware." I shrugged. 'I guess I'm just an old romantic.'

An old fraud is what I was.

Joy was visibly impressed. 'Fancy your being interested in poetry.'

We were both settling down, feeling comfortable with one another. The brash young woman from the audition was disappearing. She was telling me about her parents and her brother and sister.

I was more reticent. Too soon to talk about my broken marriage and my young daughter, I thought. Not that this was going anywhere. Enjoy the moment, I told myself.

I took her back to the house where she was staying.

'Aunt Millie will be up. She always waits until I get home. Come in and meet her. We'll all have a cup of tea.'

Aunt Millie was tiny, thin as a rake, with a lined face and a broad north of England accent.

We instantly liked one another. Millie had married a man much older than herself, a man who had died in her arms not long before I met her. Perhaps she saw in Joy and myself a mirror of that part of her life.

The next day I returned to Sydney. I had a lot to think about and it wasn't all about television.

After that Chez Tessa night, Joy and I saw each other whenever I came to Brisbane. Saw each other outside the studio, that is!

When I first met Reg I was happily going out with a handsome young soccer player. But as time passed by and I saw the qualities of the man who was Reg Grundy I realised I wanted to spend my life at his side.

JOY CHAMBERS-GRUNDY

Later I would hire Bill Mason. He had been producing the George Wallace variety show on rival station BTQ 7. Bill took over from me on *IGAS*. He would eventually head up all my game shows throughout the United Kingdom and Europe.

But for now, I was still the line producer and handled the briefings of the panel. That meant I spent a lot of my time on recording days with Joy. I didn't mind a bit.

I stayed at the Tower Mill Motel on Wickham Terrace, Brisbane and on Friday nights we would have dinner in the circular restaurant on the top floor of the building. Magical.

There were changes to the panel after the pilot. Indorf, believing I would want to keep the same line-up of panellists used in the pilot, demanded a higher fee. I dropped him. I didn't want four panellists all deciding they were worth more money. I simply didn't have the budget. Well, I really didn't have a budget.

I replaced him with John Morris. He was a sunny, funny man with an encyclopaedic knowledge who left the panel after a year or so and, in 1980, appeared as a contestant on *Sale of the Century*.

That's when Ron Cadee joined the panel. Slightly overweight, big voice, laughing his way through the show. Poor questioner, but who cared? He got the laughs and the audience loved him. A big, huggable teddy bear.

Finally Reg decided on the permanent panel members: Babette Stephens, Ron Cadee, myself and the voice of ABC breakfast radio, the charming

Russ Tyson. At first Reg was a little concerned that Babette and I had to share QTQ's only tiny private dressing room. Babette was a very mature woman of the world and I was a teenager. He need not have worried— we immediately liked each other and that friendship lasted until Babette left the world. She certainly was one special gal.

JOY CHAMBERS-GRUNDY

The rapport between Joy and Ron was immediate. Ron sometimes disregarded the questioning and started talking to her.

'Joy, you're not wearing it.'

'What do you mean by that?'

'What do I mean? I mean the ring I gave you last night. Why aren't you wearing it?'

Joy had no idea what he was talking about but played along.

'Oh,' she said, 'I wouldn't wear it on TV. That's private, Ronnie.'

Joy and Ron were firmly entrenched as Brisbane's favourite TV twosome. One was rarely seen without the other. They went together like fish and chips and many believed that if they were not romantically involved then they should be.

I knew better, but wasn't going to interfere. The ratings went sky high.

Ron and I were simpatico. Our TV roles took us out and about together. We laughed at the same things and shared similar attitudes. Probably drank too much at times, but we never stopped laughing. He was my dear friend and I miss him.

JOY CHAMBERS-GRUNDY

Sometimes the secrets weren't that great but the panel made the most of every one of them. For a number of years *I've Got A Secret* won the Queensland Logie and for a few years running, Joy and Ron won individual Logies.

Don Seccombe used to enjoy himself so much he sometimes forgot to clarify for the panel what a guest had said.

We took those secrets pretty seriously. I remember how the panel used to get annoyed when Don would laugh and mislead us instead of clarifying a point made by a guest with a secret. But hey! In retrospect it was all fun and helped to get the show big ratings.

JOY CHAMBERS-GRUNDY

Now and then we came up with some people who had truly memorable secrets.

The woman who spent three years in Spain as a professional bullfighter.

A nurse who cared for Ringo Starr during his bout of tonsillitis in London.

The pilot of a Lancaster bomber who wore no parachute. The aircraft disintegrated around him after being hit by German flak in the Second World War. He was falling through the air expecting to die, when he hit something and grabbed it. It turned out to be his rear gunner's legs. The miracle was they descended together on the rear gunner's parachute.

The lovely elderly lady who had been a survivor of the *Titanic* sinking in 1912. She had been a child at the time.

And the outlandish tale of a woman who lost her teeth in the surf. Six years later they were washed up on a beach 80 kilometres up the coast, close to where she lived. She produced the teeth to support her story.

Many famous people from all walks of life came on *IGAS*: Chips Rafferty, the Bee Gees, Jimmy Edwards, Mickey Rooney, Edmund Hillary, Michael Powell, Dick Bentley, a host of local stars like Johnny Farnham, Bert Newton, Don Lane, Dawn Lake, Bobby Limb, Barry Crocker … and of course a sprinkling of sports figures, mayors and politicians.

Apart from *IGAS*, Joy was appearing on the Friday *Tonight* show. She was the sidekick to the star, Irish comedian Jerry Gibson. So on many a Friday night after dinner, I found myself driving Joy up to the studio, then waiting in the parking lot until she finished.

Neither of us wanted it known that we were—I hesitate to use the word—dating. Joy was the exception to my rule, and we wanted to keep the secret between ourselves for as long as we could.

Joy had confided in her mother, who had accepted the fact that we were seeing each other. May expressed no concerns regarding the age difference, relying on her daughter's good sense. When I phoned Joy at home, May, whom I came to care deeply about, would call out, 'Darling, it's the man with the beautiful voice'.

When the show settled down I went to London and was staying at the Westbury on Bond Street. The sky was grey. Had been for days. I was lonely, missing Joy, but Joy's father, Alan, older sister Coral and her brother Jack happened to be in London. Her father was sceptical about us, and he was right to be. A much older man who was a television producer?

This was the moment to introduce myself.

I invited them to have dinner with me. We assembled in my room and I suggested that we should record our getting-to-know-you chat. I was Mr Showbiz with a flashy tape recorder.

RG gave a Gold Logie performance and any queries we might have harboured about his suitability for our Joy were happily resolved in a night of good fellowship. He even made a tape recording of messages for my mother (already a fan) in Ipswich. And as the years passed, Reg and I, without being brothers, became brothers.

JOHN (JACK) H. CHAMBERS

The ice had been broken.

We still have that audiotape and from time to time Joy and I play it. It's very nostalgic for us.

And what was the score?

Well, Jack and I hit it off straight away. Coral seemed to like me. And Joy's father was smiling. Alan Chambers soon got the measure of me and would talk to anyone who would listen about the Grundy Network. When he was terminally ill I used to fly up every Wednesday to Chermside Chest Hospital in Brisbane and visit him. He was a good man, a thinker, very philosophical.

IGAS was soon joined by other Grundy panel shows until we were on every night, Monday to Friday. I tended to use Joy and Ron in them all as their patter and rapport worked so well, but QTQ's line-up of stars including Muriel Watson, Del Ward and Hugh Cornish all appeared in *Play Your Hunch* and *Funny You Should Ask*.

How good could it get?

Just before I met Joy she had become Queensland's Miss Surf Girl and, as part of her prize, was to go on an Australian tour of all the capital cities. Her aircraft stopped in Sydney. I was at the airport. We looked into each other's eyes. I embraced her. We talked non-stop. Then it was time for her to fly away from me.

'I don't want to leave you,' she said.

'I love you,' I replied.

Joy hardly ate on the flight.

'I was too much in love to eat,' she says now.

I found myself humming a tune, then realised it was 'Everything's Coming up Roses'. I laughed out loud.

I've Got A Secret ran from 1965 to late 1974 and Joy never missed an episode.

All those secrets over all those years. And the best one of all, for part of that time—that Joy and I were the perfect match. Somehow the age difference wasn't causing a problem.

We'd been going out together all those years but I wasn't expecting Joy to be first to make a move.

'Reg, you say you love me and I know I love you. So why don't we get married?'

I hesitated, thinking of all the things that could go wrong. My age, the fact that I had a daughter. I had a laundry list of negative thoughts.

'Maybe we should wait a little longer,' I said.

I must have been insane. I'd just said no to this gorgeous creature.

'Okay,' she said and looked away.

It was two years before I formally proposed. She said no because I'd said no. Six months later we had a summit meeting and both agreed we should get married.

We planned to fly to Hong Kong, then Rome, then London.

It was 6.30 the night before we were to leave. I finished my last phone call. Joy was waiting outside my office. I wondered how she could put up with my preoccupation with the business. I remembered the day in Brisbane when she called me just after nine one morning. I'd returned the call at—I looked at my watch—yes, at around this time. Six thirty.

'Sorry, Honey, I got a bit caught up.' Those things never bothered her—she is very patient.

I brought Joy into my office. She looked at me, shook her head and smiled.

'Joy, I've got great news.'

'Sold another show?'

'Better than that. We're getting married tomorrow morning.'

'No, we're flying to London tomorrow morning.'

'Before we go to the airport.'

'You're mad,' she said.

'Everything's organised. Reverend Roger Bush will do the honours and your Mum and Coral are arriving from Brisbane first thing in the morning. I want us to leave Australia as Mr and Mrs Grundy.'

She moved in on me.

'You're incorrigible.'

We hugged one another.

She had the last word.

'I've got nothing to wear.'

I had expected to buy a wedding dress in London and had no idea how I could find something in Sydney before tomorrow. Early the next morning I rang Farmers in Gordon—they used to open quite early back then— 8.30 I think. But I rang before that and told the story to a very nice man who said I should come round straight away and they'd let me in even if they weren't open. So Reg's daughter Rob and I both went emergency shopping. I wanted to wear white and there was only one white dress in my size in the entire store. It had flowers round the neckline and hem and I hated it. But I bought it anyway.

Then, oh my goodness, the wedding ring! We found a small jeweller's shop in a side street. It wasn't open either but there was a man inside and

REG GRUNDY
116

we knocked on the window until he tentatively opened the door.

When he heard the story he was quick to respond and within minutes I had a ring. It hadn't been a difficult choice. Like the gown, there was only one ring in my size—a plain gold band.

JOY CHAMBERS-GRUNDY

Which goes to show. Everyone loves a love story.

We were a small group inside Roger Bush's church. Joy's mother May and her sister Coral—the matron of honour—my mother Lillian, Kim Robin, my secretary Di Ayres, Geoff Harnett, our accountant, and my best man, Charles Kenna.

Our personal driver handed Joy a yellow rose. He had run round to a florist and bought it for her. She carried it for the ceremony and pressed it later. She tells me she still has it.

At precisely 9.30 am on 20 October 1971 we became man and wife. The media had been tipped off and photographers with flashlights popping captured the moment when we arrived at Kingsford Smith Airport.

As we taxied for take-off, I gave my wife a gold charm bracelet. Jess Williamson, who was still in charge of prize acquisition, had found it—a plain gold bracelet with a single charm; a gold heart. We were off to a good start.

But the honeymoon was markedly lacking in honey. Now that we were man and wife we were noticing the differences. We realised that we would both need to make compromises. Hong Kong saw us rubbing one another the wrong way.

But by Rome we were settling down.

And by London we knew that our love was the constant and our irritations were minor.

We were as happy as Larry, but for Joy there was something missing.

'I know we're married,' said my new wife in London, 'but I want a proper wedding in my own church when we get back home.'

So the search for a 'proper' wedding gown started.

Reg was out with Bruce Gyngell one morning and told him that there would be a second wedding back in Brisbane for all our friends and relatives. 'She'll need a special dress for that,' said Bruce, 'and I know just the place.'

JOY CHAMBERS-GRUNDY

Bruce and I headed off to Harrods. We found a dress we both liked a lot.

In their defence I should say that they didn't actually buy it, but when I met them for lunch they told me about it.

Bruce was a very persuasive man and he was keen for me to see it so I accompanied them back to the shop expecting to hate their choice, but it was an absolute delight—a beautiful, teal blue velvet and white lace dress, long and flowing. I was thrilled with it and have it still. In fact at the gala night which Reg refers to on the very first page of this narrative I wore a duplicate of it.

JOY CHAMBERS-GRUNDY

Our last stop was Hawaii where we stayed right on Waikiki Beach at the Halekulani Hotel.

Then the honeymoon was over.

We landed in Sydney. The Mercedes was waiting at the airport. We drove from Mascot across the Harbour Bridge. Joy was not all that familiar with northern Sydney; all she knew was around Gordon where I lived.

We turned down Mona Vale Road heading for Church Point and stopped on a circular drive outside a big white house with green gables and many trees. This was 'Rathmore', 1788 Pittwater Road.

I turned to Joy and kissed her on the cheek.

'I think you'd better get out.'

Joy hesitated and looked at me questioningly.

'We're here.'

'Where?'

'Darling, this is our new home.'

This was just Reg's way. I was quite young and it seemed perfectly natural at that time that Reg, being older and with so much more experience, would make decisions like buying our first house on our behalf and surprise me.

JOY CHAMBERS-GRUNDY

I took her by the arm. We walked down three stone steps, opened the latched gate and moved towards the front door. The grand old house was on a terraced double block that led down to a long, narrow jetty on Pittwater.

Facing north, we could see right up to West Head and Lion Island. We walked down the flowered terraces and along to the end of the jetty.

'That's our mooring out there.' I pointed to the round marker bobbing in the water.

We both started to speak at the same time.

'Maybe we could get a boat one day ...'

We laughed and hugged one another again.

Joy said, 'Oh, Reg. It's all ... wonderful!'

We were to live there happily when we were in Australia until we left for Bermuda in 1982.

I'd bought the house for $135,000, a lot of money for me to spend at that time. It was worth it.

We have spent almost every waking moment together from that time on. All our offices and studies are side by side. Even now, every day, we find plenty of things to say to one another. Not bad after thirty-nine years.

A FINE ROMANCE, PART TWO: JOY REMEMBERS

It was a hot Monday in February and I had been modelling in Brisbane all day. Around 6 pm, I met my father who was head of security for ACI (Australian Consolidated Industries) and we drove for over an hour to where we lived in Ipswich, 23 miles [37 kilometres] to the southwest, driving into the sun, which sat on top of every hill.

On arrival at Idolwood, our house, Mummy handed me a letter. It was from Hugh Cornish—the then publicity manager for QTQ Channel Nine in Brisbane. I had been writing to Hugh for a couple of years, in the hopes of getting work on TV, and he was a semi-friend. I was a teenager, pushy and sure, as they tend to be, and I believed the TV world needed Joy Chambers. I had always been a performer: at four and five I recited to the captive audience on the North Ipswich bus, standing up behind the driver while my beautiful mother looked away out the window. I began acting in Little Theatre at eight and had learned Art of Speech later and sang and danced.

The letter from Hugh informed me of an audition—taking place at Channel Nine that very same night and beginning at 6 pm.

I looked at my father. 'Oh, no, I'm tired and the audition started ages ago. I'm too late, I won't go.'

But my wonderful father took me by the shoulders. 'You're being foolish. This is what you've been wanting for years, get back in the car, we're going.'

I slipped into a long lemon dress, which recently I had worn as a bridesmaid, and, with our dinner uneaten on the table, we drove back to Brisbane as the short Queensland twilight fell.

We had never been to Mount Coot-tha, where the TV stations stood on the summit, and we became truly lost. I was being negative and saying we should turn back, but my father was the opposite and finally, in the darkness, around 9.30 to 10 pm, we found the building and the tall transmitter beside it.

Hundreds of girls milled about in the dimly lit grounds. In those days QTQ 9's foyer was on the opposite side of the building to where it now lies and I left my father and made my way through the crowd. I met a girl whom I had modelled with that day; she gave me a haughty look. 'You're too late—it's over.' She flashed her long false fingernails at me.

This exchange annoyed me and I was now imbued with some of my father's enthusiasm. The foyer was full of young women and their mothers and I stood at the back wondering what to do next. Suddenly, two men entered from the far side. I could see one had a moustache and wore a 'Prince of Wales' checked suit and appeared to me to be a nice-looking 'old' man. (I have never since considered his age.) The loud buzz of chatter died as he spoke in a clear resonant voice. 'Thank you very much for waiting. But after seeing you all, we have decided on our six finalists.'

It was now or never. I raised my hand at the back and called out, 'But you haven't seen me!'

He paused and I saw him frown and turn to his companion. They went into a huddle and I squeezed through the assembled women towards them.

I could feel my heart accelerating as the man with the moustache, obviously the leader, spun back and met my eyes and delivered the words which forever altered my world: 'All right, follow us and come along into the studio.'

The studio was dark except for an area of light where two cameras and their operators faced a long desk and some chairs.

The second man from the foyer—younger, with a kind, clean-shaven face—sat me with three of the six finalists, and the other man, standing in the dark, began to ask us a series of questions, which we answered in turn.

I can see him now, just visible in the gloom beyond the pool of light, to the side of the camera; slender, almost too slender, his face sun-browned, oozing energy and concentrating intently, absorbed in all that was said. He is still like that today—focused and single-minded, giving complete attention to his current situation. I liked his voice, though I do not believe I was attracted to him that night. I already had a boyfriend. The attraction came later as I learned to know the essence of the man.

I recall three of his questions: 'Tell me what you think of the wind,' 'What's the best thing that ever happened to you?' and 'If you looked out your window and saw the man next door sunbathing in the nude, what would you do?' I gave my answers; I was loquacious and not nervous and was young enough to feel confident—vulnerability comes with age. I remember I quoted the final lines of Shelley's 'Ode to the West Wind'. At times this man with the moustache disappeared and the other took over; I now know he had gone upstairs into the control room to briefly watch proceedings on the monitors up there.

When it was over, outside standing waiting for me, as he did so many times in my life, was my exceptional father with his high forehead, calming smile and intelligent pale blue eyes.

On looking back now I realise how tired he must have been. It was late, he had not eaten since lunch, he was over sixty; this was his second long road trip that day and he was to rise again early the following morning. It was he alone who had urged me along to this audition—I had been the reluctant one.

If not for Daddy, I would not have gone to that audition; I would not have met Reg Grundy; I would not have fallen in love with him and he, with me.

Thank you, Alan Chambers.

The following Friday evening, the phone rang. It was the man with the moustache whom I now knew was Reg Grundy. He told me I had succeeded in getting the job. I remember the elation as I replaced the receiver and ran through to my mother in the kitchen cooking dinner. 'I got it, Mummy. I got the television job. Won't Daddy be pleased? Can you believe it? Out of all those hundreds of girls he chose me!'

JOY CHAMBERS-GRUNDY

TWO CANS OF FILM: SALE OF THE CENTURY

I had learned the game show business by studying *Pick-a-Box*, not for Bob Dyer's performance but for the structure of the quiz elements. But it was the American game shows and their polished production techniques that really hooked me.

Reg Grundy's Wheel of Fortune had commanded up to 70 per cent of the audience in daytime—impressive even in a two-station commercial market.

But why bother to create shows if I could have the pick of the best American ones?

I hired Charles Michelson, an American distributor, to send me kinescopes of new game shows as they came along. In September 1969, two cans of film arrived—DVDs didn't exist back then. I threaded up the 16 millimetre projector in the living room of my home in Gordon on Sydney's upper north shore.

I knew that hit shows were few and far between in any genre so my hopes weren't high. But one show I was about to view was to be my passport into the exciting world of American network television.

The first reel was the Ralph Andrews show, *It Takes Two*. Earlier in the year I'd stood in line to be in the audience for the pilot at NBC studios in 'the Valley', as the San Fernando Valley is called locally in California. I wasn't impressed then, and I wasn't impressed now.

I threaded up the second film and watched as the opening title appeared on the wall: *SALE OF THE CENTURY*. I liked the title and loved the show.

The host was actor Jack Kelly who had been co-star in the Maverick series. Better in the western than in this, I thought. The network must have agreed, because he was soon replaced by Joe Garagiola. By the end of the episode I knew I had to make an Australian version. I knew it would work.

Bruce Gyngell had left Nine after a dispute with Sir Frank Packer and had moved to the Seven network. He was stirring things up with the Seven Revolution and the slogan 'Seven Is Revolting'.

I called him.

'Bruce, I've just seen an American game show I want to make for you and the Seven network. I want you to see it before I pick up the phone and call somebody else.'

Bruce laughed. 'Where's your smooth, laidback selling style?'

'Bruce, I want you to see it now. Can you come to my place on your way home tonight?'

As Gyngell lived in Bellevue Hill in the Eastern suburbs and I was on the other side of the Bridge, it was a bit of a stretch.

'You serious about this, boy?'

'I am.'

'Okay. I'll see you around six.'

Bruce watched the show in silence.

'Not mad about Jack Kelly but the format's good, bit different to most. Put a hold on it for me.'

He looked me in the eye. 'Do you have the rights?'

'Don't need them, and anyway I'm going to make big changes including the title. When I'm finished, it'll be twice as good as it is now.'

'What will you call it?'

How many times had I heard that?

'Well, its appeal is the fact that contestants can use their winnings to buy merchandise—even a car—at a fraction of its real value. Every woman will go crazy about that. And as we're tempting players to spend some of their money to win prizes, which will, at the same time, reduce their lead, how about *Temptation*?'

I was too excited to stop.

'Don't you see, Bruce? It's terrific.'

Bruce spoke slowly and quietly.

'Reg, let me give you a piece of advice. Don't try to sell something that you've already sold.'

That was good enough for me.

I sent a message to Charlie Michelson in the USA: 'I believe *Sale of the Century* has terrific potential. I showed it to Bruce Gyngell last night and I think he's going to buy it for Seven. I'm going to make big format changes so we don't need any rights'.

First we needed a host, and Lyle McCabe remembers how that happened.

Bruce had some ideas about the compere. One of them was to use that jaunty bloke going down the street whistling on the Winfield commercial. It had become very popular but I don't think we were all that impressed with Tony Barber at first. But he was a fast learner and was pretty good and with his own style by the time we made the pilot.

LYLE MCCABE

Bruce also wanted it sponsored by Coles so he, Lyle and Tony Barber flew down to Melbourne to present the show to the Coles Board. I was overseas.

Their boardroom was quite spartan and above their big store in, I think, Collins Street and there they all were, all of them it seemed to me in their seventies and eighties and including three of the Coles family. So we do the presentation and they seem interested, especially when one of them says, 'We want you to have lunch with us'. I thought we were on the right track then. Off we go downstairs to what I presumed would be the executive dining room but which turned out to be the public cafeteria where we lined up with all the shoppers.

The old lady behind the counter says, 'Same again today, Mr Cole?' to the man in front of me, and he says yes and then I get asked the same question. I say, 'Oh, I'll have what he's having', and that's what I got—pie with mashed potato and gravy. And then this old Coles family member says proudly, 'We can go back up now. They deliver it right to the boardroom you know'.

You couldn't help but be reminded of Are You Being Served *and young Mr Grace.*

LYLE MCCABE

Lyle produced the pilot. It took a whole shift to get it done. Normally, we would make five half hour shows in that time. It wasn't the slickest thing I'd ever seen, but it was enough to show the Board at Coles.

I had recently acquired an open reel 2 inch [5 centimetre] quadruplex machine, which was propped up on a chair in our kitchen at Lindfield. Just imagine—now I could watch in my own home what had been going on in the studio.

Astonishing how far technology had advanced in a short time. It was just a few years earlier that I was using a Pyrox wire recorder at 2SM. It weighed a tonne and actually recorded on wire. If the wire broke, as it often did, the only way to do an edit was to unravel the wire with a pair of pliers and join the ends together in a knot.

Coles New World *Temptation* went to air as a daytime strip on 1 June 1970 and was to run through into 1974.

I received $670 an episode to start, and had to pay the host and hostess. The contract was to run for six months but in October Bruce Gyngell extended the deal to the end of the year. Tony Barber knew he was on a winner and his agent Harry Miller was pushing for more money. By 1973 we were getting $2800 an episode, which added up to $14,000 a week.

We had a hit.

In Queensland, BTQ 7 was after us to come up with a strip to follow the news. Hayden Sargent hosted a radio talkback show. Everyone listened to him. How about a television version? We'll take the best items from the news, put Hayden on camera with a couple of experts, and we'll have talkback television. We called it *Hotline*.

I reckon we may have been the first to do it anywhere in the world.

Of course the danger was that one of the phone-ins would use an unacceptable word or two. BTQ's chief engineer came up with the answer: 'Let's pass the tape from one machine to another, giving us 8 seconds to prevent foul language going to air. As well, we'll have a guy in the booth with a bleep button, just in case'.

The show was so successful that ATN 7 in Sydney ran its own version. And then it happened. The words went to air: 'The Prime Minister is a bastard'.

The newspapers had their headline: 'BTQ CALLS PM A BASTARD'.

The Broadcasting Control Board threatened to take away BTQ's licence. It was touch and go. The station promised to have two guys with two bleep buttons in the booth in future.

Me? Well, I was standing on the sidelines because I had *I've Got A Secret* on Nine and *Hotline* on Seven, both going to air at the same time.

When things settled down I suggested Hayden Sargent could do another TV phone-in show in daytime. 'Let's call it *Heartline* and give the people of Brisbane the chance to open up their hearts and talk about their problems.'

Hayden jumped at the chance.

When discussing *Heartline* Bill Mason, who was running the Queensland office, often used to say, 'This is not merely a television program, it's a social obligation'.

What a year it had been.

GREAT TEMPTATION

A brash and colourful twenty-eight-year-old hillbilly singer arrived in Australia in 1937. Bob Dyer, wearing yellow boots and playing a banjo, performed songs like 'The Death of Willie' and 'The Martins and the McCoys'. He dubbed himself 'The Last of the Hillbillies' and topped the bill at the Tivoli, the vaudeville house in Sydney's Haymarket.

In 1948, Bob moved into radio with a quiz show called *Pick-a-Box*. It attracted big audiences and when television started in 1956, the show transferred to the new medium and really took off.

Dyer, like myself, hosted and got the prizes.

Twenty-five years later, *Pick-a-Box* was still getting good ratings but by the start of the 1970s Bob was becoming careless.

'Oh, Doll,' he called to his unseen assistant and wife, 'I've left the questions for the next round in the dressing room.' Off camera, Dolly was heard to say, 'I'll get them, Bob'.

He made small talk with the challenger until Dolly walked into the shot with the question cards. The show was being recorded on videotape. It would have been so easy to stop tape until the missing questions were in his hands.

In 1971, Bob announced that the show would end in July. He'd had enough.

At that point I picked up the phone and called Bruce Gyngell who was now managing ATN 7 and was visiting London.

'Bruce, you've had a loyal game show audience on Monday nights with Bob, and you'll lose them if you don't put a new game show into the slot.'

'Got something in mind, Reg?'

'Well, *Temptation* is doing great. Let's do a night-time version.'

'Interesting. What would you call it?'

That was the second time Bruce had asked me to name the same format.

'It'll have bigger and better prizes, so how about *Great Temptation*?'

'Can you get it ready in time?'

'Sure can.'

'I'll be back in the office next Tuesday and we'll put the deal in writing. Come in at ten.'

Simple as that. Bruce was a great programmer. He didn't need audience study tests or focus groups. He went with his instinct—his gut feeling.

Great Temptation began transmission in the old *Pick-a-Box* slot in July 1971. In 1974, the Seven network cancelled the show. Who knows why?

And there's one might-have-been.

Glen Kinging was programming the Seven network and called me.

'Can I come down to your place after work tonight?'

Glen turned up and we sat in my office. It was a large theatre-like area, complete with projection booth, that we had tacked onto the original house. I called it the Bijou—the 'little jewel'.

As we looked out onto Pittwater, Glen told me the reason for his visit.

'Reg, we've got a problem at six o'clock. I want to put a game show in.'

I knew exactly which one it should be.

'Glen, you should never have cancelled *Temptation*. Put it back at six. I'll add a few bells and whistles and you'll kill 'em.'

'No, I want something new. I reckon *Temptation* and *Great Temptation* are yesterday's news.'

I tried to talk him into it, but he wasn't having any. The show we finished up with, *Celebrity Tattletales*, had Dave Gray as host and lasted twenty-six weeks. Glen will still tell anyone who'll listen that it was the worst programming decision he ever made.

In June 1980, Joy and I were staying at L'Ermitage on Burton Way in LA when I heard that *Temptation* was coming back as *Sale of the Century* on the Nine network in Australia. It was going to air in a couple of weeks. By then, my friend Ian Holmes, who had begun his career at GTV 9 in Melbourne and moved to Sydney to run Channel 10, had joined me and was CEO of my Australian operation.

I was pretty concerned. 'We can't call it *Sale of the Century*; we don't own the rights,' I said.

My lawyer, Kerry Wright, was equally concerned. The USA had by then signed the Berne Convention and the earlier defence against any action by Al Howard wouldn't stand.

Years later I discovered that at that time in 1980, while I was in America, Ian Holmes had written to Lynton Taylor, then program director at Nine: '*Sale of the Century* is a working title but we are considering several others'.

Bob Crystal, my LA representative, who also became my great friend and is still with me after thirty-eight years, arrived to see me right at that moment. I filled him in.

'Bob, do you know Al Howard, the guy who owns *Sale of the Century*?'

'No Boss, but I will as soon as he answers the phone.'

'Well, get hold of him and tell him that we intend to remake *Temptation* and call it *Sale of the Century*. Tell him he'll get a good royalty.'

Bob made the call and revealed himself to be in Olympic class as a double-talker. I barely understood a word he was saying and I doubt that Howard did either. But Howard picked up that we were offering money all right, and agreed to accept a licence fee.

We were in the clear.

Great Temptation returned as *Sale of the Century* on 14 July 1980 on the Nine network. And Al Howard started receiving regular cheques.

The series ran for years, and was taken off only to come back yet again in 2005 under its original Australian title of *Temptation*—the title I came up with back in the 1970s.

It ran, on and off, until January 2009.

By then, the show that I'd projected on my wall at Gordon so many years before had become the longest running game show in the history of Australian television.

MONEYMAKERS

Bill Mason was running the Queensland operation from a small office in Charlotte Street, Brisbane. I flew in every Friday to review the week's production schedule.

One week in 1971 we drove along Coronation Drive through Toowong, then followed the road as it wound upwards to the peak of Mount Coot-tha. Our target was Ron Archer, general manager of TVQ 0, the most recent of the TV stations to begin operating in Brisbane.

Ron had been a Test cricketer, but never mentioned the game to me. He was an all-rounder who, in the third Test of 1956, sent Colin Cowdrey, Alan Oakman and Peter Richardson back to the pavilion. All before lunch. He would have succeeded Ian Johnson as Australian captain for the 1957–58 South African tour had he not been injured in Pakistan, ending his cricketing career at the age of twenty-three.

And now we were seated across the desk from him.

He was a big, quietly spoken, decent man and we had a pleasant conversation about some of the things we might be able to do for the station.

'You know, Ron, it's about time a good old-fashioned quiz show was made here to give locals a chance to win some money.'

He was interested. 'What do you have in mind?'

'Well, I've been working on an idea that could be a real knockout.'

'What will you call it?'

Same old question.

'I'm calling it *Moneymakers* and that's exactly what it is. A good enough contestant could win $20,000.'

I gave him a general idea of the format.

'I reckon it'd go well stripped at seven o'clock.'

'I'm interested,' Ron replied. 'Let's make a pilot.'

As we drove away Bill said, 'Where did that come from?'

'I'm not sure. But we got a pilot.'

The pilot was hosted by Philip Brady who did his usual capable job for me. It went well and we got an order for thirteen weeks.

Twenty thousand was substantial money for a local quiz show but I didn't think we'd be giving it away too often. A contestant had to beat twenty-five others to take home the big bucks.

The show started in May and by July it was agreed that our production fee would be increased to $400 an episode. An extra $2000 a week plus 80 per cent of sales to Sydney, Melbourne and Adelaide.

Ian Holmes was running Channel Ten in Sydney at that point and I very quickly asked him to give it a try.

'Sorry, Reg. Don't think a Brisbane show is right for my schedule.'

After twenty-six weeks my $2000 per week moved up to $3850. Almost a 100 per cent increase. Plus I could add the returns from sales to country TV stations. I was getting $16 an episode from NEN 9 Tamworth with a relay to Taree thrown in. And Ian Holmes did eventually pick up *Moneymakers*, and stripped it at seven o'clock on Ten in Sydney.

After production and transport costs, I was doing all right. I wasn't going to get rich but at least I was going broke more slowly. Not much of the income came from syndication but the idea of on-selling a show and picking up a few dollars more without having to do any more work appealed to me.

I had been on a roll with the Ten network for some time and had five shows a week there including the *Marriage Game* and *Blind Date*. It was almost embarrassing when the press started to refer to Ten as Network G. That's when I met distributor Max Dutch.

I remember going to see Reg at his office in North Sydney and we did a deal. His arrangement with Ten was Reg supplied just about everything and Ten supplied facilities. Then they went fifty-fifty on distribution. I got 15 per cent, of which Reg paid half and Ten paid half.

I think the first show of Reg's that Ten did was Marriage Game *but there were lots more—*Blind Date *was a real favourite. I took them first to Adelaide where they were very keen to get Reg's shows—and the same* with Perth. Not too sure how much I got for them; maybe as much as $250 to $500 dollars an episode in the bigger markets and perhaps as little as $15 an ep in the regionals. Probably doesn't sound like a lot of money, but they ran five days a week and went on for years.

MAX DUTCH

I was happy to make a similar deal with Ron Archer for *Moneymakers*. Ron and I always got along fine and I made a lot of programs for him over the years.

In 2005, Ron and his lovely wife attended the opening of my show at the Queensland Art Gallery featuring images from my book *The Wildlife of Reg Grundy*. It was really good to see him again after such a long time.

A year later I heard that he was terminally ill and called him at his home in Brisbane. He answered the phone and we had a brief conversation. What do you say?

Ron's last words to me were, 'Thanks for the call, Reg. But I reckon this one's going to clean bowl me'.

He was right. He died on 27 May 2007. Ron Archer was one of the good guys of television; a great Australian and a hell of a cricketer.

WHO'S MINDING THE STORE?

My American adventure started in 1972 when I began making regular trips across the Pacific.

By that time we were producing more television shows than anyone else in Australia. In March of 1972 we turned out 156 half hours and twenty-three one hours, with thirteen shows running on forty-one of the forty-eight stations in the country. At least that's what *TV Week* reported in its 17 June issue.

I reckoned it was time to break into the American market but had no idea how to go about it. I needed someone in LA to give me a hand. Someone who knew the ground rules and who could perhaps introduce me to the people I needed to know.

Russell Watkins, who represented the Australian Nine network in America, recommended Bob Crystal.

Bob had worked for Doris Day running her music business and, more importantly, had been involved in television in Australia where he'd produced both the Tommy Leonetti and the Stuart Wagstaff shows for the Seven network in the late 1960s—so he knew about me.

Joy and I met 'Bobby', as we tend to call him, in 1972 at the Beverly Hilton Hotel in Beverly Hills where we had a suite with an outdoor terrace. The terrace was actually the roof of a garage building, but it had been turfed over and I could work out there in the sun. I used to enjoy the sun. Joy says I've had sunstroke more often than anyone she has ever known.

I told Bob what I had in mind.

Basically Reg said, 'I'm looking for someone to knock on doors and introduce me around. I want to make this market my next step'. We shook hands and I've been with him ever since.

BOB CRYSTAL

I was in and out of America several times a year and soon needed office space. It wasn't long before we sublet a floor on West Pico from Israeli producers Menahem Golan and his cousin Yoram Globus.

In Los Angeles we stayed at the Beverly Hilton whenever we were in town until we decided to move to L'Ermitage, an elegant boutique hotel on Burton Way where one of our neighbours was Anthony Quinn. He was a nice man who had many children who used to play in the corridors and kick up a fuss.

Then Joy announced that she was sick of packing and unpacking, and why didn't we look for some permanent accommodation? We found a very nice place on Beverly Crescent, in the hills above Sunset Boulevard—the house where Richard Burton always used to stay when he was in town.

It came with Mercedes, a Mexican woman who didn't speak English, but was one of the best housekeepers we've ever had. Bob Crystal insists that she made the best cookies in town.

She spoke no English and my Spanish began and ended with 'ensalada sólo, ningún postre' (salad only, no dessert). But we liked her a lot.

I now have a Spanish-speaking sister-in-law. I sure could have done with Maria then.

JOY CHAMBERS-GRUNDY

We were there for about a year when the Beverly Wilshire opened a new wing of apartments. We went to inspect one and were mildly astonished to find a motorbike on one of the little half circle balconies off the living room. It was Steve McQueen's old apartment. Steve had turned the dressing room into a sauna and, perhaps surprisingly, had a library with an eclectic collection of books. Bob Crystal says dismissively, 'He bought them by the yard. They all do'.

We returned the sauna to its original purpose as a dressing room but left the handwritten message we found on one of the timber walls:

'When the going gets tough, the tough get going.'

STEVE McQUEEN, JR

It was written in lead pencil, thickly, as if he had gone over and over it. It was obviously important to the boy who had marked it there, and painting over it would have been a shame.

We loved the place. So did Bob Crystal. It meant that when we were away he had a parking spot at the Wilshire Hotel right in the middle of Beverly Hills.

And someone else liked it: the wife of the President of the United States. Nancy Reagan preferred to stay at the Wilshire hotel whenever she was in town. Once, when we were in residence, the manager called and asked if we'd mind moving out for two nights. You can't say no to the President's wife. So we moved to a suite the Wilshire gave us right across the hall. The corridor was full of secret service agents. Joy says it's the safest she's ever felt in a hotel.

The secret servicemen came up and down in the private lift with me. They always stood at the back of the lift facing out: ready for anything I suppose.

JOY CHAMBERS-GRUNDY

We're not at the Wilshire any more. When we were coming to the end of the lease we decided we needed a larger apartment and bought our current LA address where we've been ever since.

Throughout the 1970s Joy and I were spending more and more time in America and although I kept in close touch and made many trips across the Pacific, I was not in Australia often enough to manage the daily running of the business.

So who was minding the store?

In 1972 I appointed Bill Mason and Lyle McCabe joint general managers. Ian Holmes, one of the best programmers I'd met, had become a close friend.

'Bad idea, Reg, to have two managers. Better to have only one person at the top of the tree.'

And so it worked out.

Bill decided to leave us and follow his own star. Happily, he came back after a couple of years and then, together with his wonderful wife Anne, left to look after our interests overseas. Lyle was left in charge but eventually resigned because of ill health although, miraculously, shortly afterwards he joined John Collins to form a television production company.

I had no choice but to start running the Australian operation again. I was back at the concrete desk in the main office. Well, I think it was concrete. It might have been stone but it was a huge immovable slab that came with the building.

One day Ian and I were having lunch at our favourite haunt in Castlereagh Street when Ian said, 'I'm leaving Channel Ten. Going to set up my own production company'.

'Why don't you come and join me?'

He smiled. 'Good idea.'

We shook hands.

But it wasn't that easy.

Ian insisted that I follow him to London where the miracle would happen and I would appoint him Chief Executive of the company. Yet another international flight was the last thing I wanted, but I went along with it. I'm still unsure what it was about, and I think Ian is too, but perhaps it was something to do with the fact that, as general manager and programmer at Ten, he had only a week before ordered the first series of *Chopper Squad* from us.

We flew to Paris for a day or two; pleasant days, and Ian bought me a belt with 'RG' on it.

I stopped over in Singapore on the way home and got a call from Channel Ten's chairman in the middle of the night.

'What the hell do you think you're doing hiring Holmes? And what are you doing with *Chopper Squad*?'

I played a straight bat to him. And hung up.

I went to see him when I got back and he was all sweetness and light. The Singapore call was forgotten. Very odd.

Subsequently, I was invited to a dinner at his Rose Bay home where a group of people were putting their hands in their pockets to support a politician. I passed.

Ian Holmes took over the company and it became the Grundy Organisation. Joy and I kept trotting around the world, and that's how it went until I sold the company.

It was during the time between Lyle McCabe running my Australian company and Ian Holmes taking over that it had become obvious we needed more office space. Reg Watson turned up one day in the office we had in Arthur Street, North Sydney carrying a model of an office building. He showed it to me. 'I think this is just what we're looking for.'

It was a forced sale but there were a number of caveats on the building and Kerry Wright and our company secretary, Frances O'Brien, whom I would never think of addressing as anything other than 'Miss O'Brien', went to a barrister for an opinion. They were told that legally things seemed okay but it was a moot point, because no mortgagee would loan on the building anyway.

In her usual quiet way, Miss O'Brien said to him, 'We'll be paying cash.'

'What? All of it? Nobody has that much cash.'

She smiled. 'We do.'

At that time we were still using the Bank of NSW at Double Bay and the bank wasn't too keen on us taking out so much cash. There was a recession and things were tough, even for banks. In fact, the Double Bay branch asked us to please not take any more money out of our account, because they needed to keep all the cash they could and our account was so important.

Then I was advised that one of the caveats on the building might be troublesome. BorgWarner had never been paid for installing the lift and, not unreasonably I suppose, wanted to see their money.

I thought about it for a while and then called Kerry.

Reg instructed me to tell BorgWarner that they could remove the lift but if in doing so they damaged the structure of the building in any way, we would take action against them. It was a decision worthy of Solomon.

KERRY WRIGHT

We didn't hear any more about it and when we moved in the building on the Pacific Highway at Artarmon in Sydney was renamed Grundy House.

It was from that Artarmon office one weekday morning that I was picked up in a taxi to go into Sydney's CBD. The taxi driver pointed to the sign 'Grundy House' and remarked to me, 'Of course, Reg Grundy has been dead for years. That's just a name they use!'

I replied, 'Well, he was pretty much alive when he got out of bed beside me this morning.'

JOY CHAMBERS-GRUNDY

'UNADULTERATED SALACIOUS CRAP': CLASS OF '74

We were in London on our honeymoon and staying in a pleasant ground floor apartment in Queen Street, Mayfair.

Bruce Gyngell dropped in and as the housekeeper was out, I asked Joy to make us a sandwich.

I remember getting the bread and butter and the cold meat out and cutting up a tomato. I was working away when Reg appeared at the kitchen door. 'Darling? What's wrong?'

I looked up. 'Nothing. Why?'

'Where's the sandwich? It's been half an hour ...'

I stood there, knife in hand. Suddenly we both started to laugh. I'd lived at home until I married Reg and I recall my wonderful mother doing everything for me. I suppose I just wasn't the fastest in the kitchen! I can assure you I make a sandwich more swiftly now.

JOY CHAMBERS-GRUNDY

That same week Bruce Gyngell introduced me to Bob Monkhouse, the English movie star, TV host and comedian. Bob invited us round to his home in St John's Wood for dinner where we met Jackie, the lovely lady he was soon to marry. Bob was a movie buff and had a major collection of old films with which he entertained his guests, projecting onto the white wall of his living room.

The same way I first saw *Sale of the Century* on the wall in our house in Gordon.

We had a wonderful night and he invited Joy and me to come to ATV Birmingham to see his hit show, *The Golden Shot*, go live to air. We went by train and while we were there Bob arranged dinner at the Albany Hotel with a couple of Australians who were working for ATV. One of them, Mike Lloyd, was to direct *The Golden Shot* next day. The other was Reg

Watson, producer of *Crossroads*, a successful daytime serial watched by millions of people throughout the United Kingdom.

It was obvious Mike wanted me to be his ticket back home while Reg Watson was clearly content with his current work and had no intention of returning to Australia.

Reg Watson and I immediately hit it off and I left Joy to talk to Mike while I tried to get a fast education from Reg on how to make serial drama. The night went fast and I learned a lot.

From then on we travelled to Birmingham to see Reg Watson whenever we were in England. A strong friendship developed and has continued to this day. Reg is a special man with a very inventive mind and we've shared some amazing moments along the way.

Australian television content regulations had been working in my favour up till now, but an aggressive 'TV—Make It Australian' campaign and the new Senate Standing Committee enquiry into Australian content on TV were against low-cost programs in favour of much more expensive drama. The writing was on the wall.

Ian Holmes, still at Ten Sydney, called me to say that he was looking for a prime time serial. I submitted an idea. Ian liked the concept but warned that he was more interested in another producer's project.

The other project turned out to be *Number 96*, which was a winner for Ten.

In 1973 things got worse. The new federal government announced that it was introducing regulations that would influence not just the quantity but also the types of Australian-made shows television stations would transmit. This was the 'points system' by which Australian programs would earn one point for each hour that went to air against a minimum quota.

But game shows were to be rated at half a point an hour which meant that television stations would be penalised for scheduling them; the government was going to reward the more expensive and more labour intensive drama productions.

It seemed to me that the government had decided to dictate to Australians what they should watch rather than what they might want to watch.

At the time, the press was saying that I was the biggest producer of

Australian television outside the ABC and that I was making twenty-four hours of television every week. But while I made some light entertainment my shows were mainly game shows and I saw myself yet again facing the loss of all my productions.

There were only two major independent production companies back then, and both of us were facing imminent doom. Hector Crawford's cop shows had been cancelled. He needed a new show to save him from closing down. And somehow I had to get into drama.

Once again I was about to jump in at the deep end and start swimming. But this time I might as well have had a gas stove tied to my foot.

I spent a weekend trying to come up with something and by Monday morning I had an idea. I called Reg Watson who was still in Birmingham.

'Reg, I've got an idea for a teenage serial. It's about a group of teenagers in their last year of school before moving out into the world … It has two major themes—the students' interest in the opposite sex and the behind-the-scenes lives of their teachers.'

I even had a title in mind: *Class of '74.*

I told Reg Watson: 'I'm out of my depth. Do you reckon you could help us create a sort of bible?'

In this context, 'bible' refers to a summary of the characters, plot and so on in TV drama.

'I've got a few characters already: there's Julie who's this attractive teenage student who's confined to a wheelchair. Then maybe a beautiful young teacher who meets a priest, but at their first meeting, she doesn't know he's a priest … and, well … other students and teachers.'

I'd run out of gas.

I took a deep breath.

'If I send some material over to Birmingham, could you have a look at it and help me get the thing off the ground? That's if I can sell the damn thing. I'd better, or I'll be out of a job.'

Reg Watson agreed to help and eventually we had created a presentation. I'd pitched the idea to John Doherty at Seven and he liked it. But what about 'Rags' Henderson?

Rupert 'Rags' Henderson, managing director of Fairfax who controlled Seven, had bought Crawford Productions in 1972 and sold it back to Hector Crawford the following year.

Strange.

Since then Rags seemed to be casting a jaundiced eye at independent production companies and particularly at Grundy.

Would he agree to go ahead with *Class of '74*?

John Doherty remembers.

We were always looking for higher ratings and I was particularly concerned that our audience was skewed towards the wrinklies. Number 96 on Ten was giving us hell and something had to be done.

We decided we wanted to do Class of '74 *but, of course, Rags Henderson had to OK the deal.*

Reg Grundy had a script and some storylines and I sent them off to Rags. His eyesight was failing and I'll swear black and blue that he never read a script. I'm sure that Betty Buckland, his secretary, did the reading.

The meeting was set for New Year's Eve 1973. It didn't matter to Henderson what day it was so off I went with Norman Cottier, our finance manager, for our late morning appointment. Norm came with me because we had to put up a business plan and guarantee network support.

As usual, Henderson kept us waiting but we got in at last.

Now I'm quite sure that Rags Henderson had just two suits and both of them the same colour and made from the same material. Impossible to tell which of the two he was wearing that day but he was behind his big desk in shirtsleeves and braces and, as usual, he had slipped right down in the chair so his waistband rode up to just below his breasts. His technique was to say nothing but to wait until you spoke. There was silence for a bit and I finally said, 'So, what did you think of the script, Mr Henderson?'

'Mr Doherty,' he said, 'it's just unutterable, unadulterated salacious crap and I don't like it.'

Well, that was a bit of a shock and there was silence for a while and I wasn't sure what to say. Then I thought, 'Oh, bugger it, I'm going to speak up. If I don't, I'll forever regret it'.

So I said, 'Well, it's not designed for your age group, Mr Henderson.'

He stared at us for a while then said: 'Ah, get out—do it'.

So I wished him a Happy New Year and got out.

JOHN DOHERTY

My daughter and I were staying at the Palace, St Moritz, Switzerland and Joy was in London with her mother and brother Jack when Lyle McCabe called me to say that the Seven network had given us the green light to go into production.

Kim Robin and I left the snow and via London returned to Sydney.

A production group made up of Grundy people and a few new faces who had some experience in the production of television drama was pulled together.

Soon we were in trouble, failing to produce the five half hours per week that would be required to launch *Class of '74*. I was sending scenes from the production across to Reg Watson in Birmingham who later said how very difficult they were to follow.

No doubt.

If only I could persuade Reg Watson to come to Sydney and sort us out! We badly needed him.

Joy and I flew back to London and booked into a flat at 20 Hereford Street, behind and parallel to Curzon Street in Mayfair, not far from where we had stayed in Queen Street on our honeymoon.

I called Bruce Gyngell, who by now was in London as deputy chairman of the ATV network, working with chairman Lew Grade.

'Bruce, I've got a problem. Any chance of dinner one night this week?'

'What are you going to try to sell me this time?'

'Nothing. But I sure need your help.'

Bruce and I sat at our table at the Mirabelle Restaurant, 56 Curzon Street. White starched tablecloths, great service, superb food and wine. Very fancy.

▲ My first car. The green Rolls Royce
I got later on was better!

▶ My only contact with show business as
a child was when I appeared on stage at
the Port Adelaide Town Hall in a variety
concert at the tender age of eight.

◀ Dad and I on the beach, showing off our balancing act. No wonder I suffer from vertigo!

▶ I'm in the army, 1942; just call me 'Signalman Grundy'.

▼ Mum and Dad farewell me at Sydney airport, 1952. I am leaving Australia for the first time, flying to Johannesburg for the world championship fight between Jimmy Carruthers and Vic Toweel.

◄ We featured the Sorbent giraffe in a panel show at 2CH in 1954. John O'Grady is at the front end.
© *Ern McQuillan*

▶ Sports broadcaster to game show producer. I had no idea this was to be a watershed moment in my career.

▼ 2CH's *Wheel of Fortune*: I am delivering a TV set to the first phone-in winner, a major prize in 1957.
© *Ern McQuillan*

2CH
AUSTRALIA'S **GREATEST, RICHEST** RADIO QUIZ EVER!

TOMORROW 2–4 P.M.

REG GRUNDY'S ✶ FABULOUS...

WHEEL OF FORTUNE

A SINGLE PHONE CALL COULD WIN YOU

A COMPLETE RANGE OF FAMOUS A.W.A. PRODUCTS—including . . . .
"DEEP IMAGE" TV Sets ; Hi-Fi Radiograms ; Washing Machines ; Refrigerators ; Pressurate Car Radios ; Mantel, Clock and Portable Radios and Electric Clothes Dryers.

Return air trips by ANSETT AIRWAYS. MOFFIT-VIRTUE Frymatics and Diver-matics ; HAWKINS Pressure Cookers ; SLEEPMAKER Mattresses ; A.W.A. FRASER Kitchen Furniture and Ironing Boards ; WALTZING MATILDA Portable Barbecues ; MAXWELL BOWERMAN Permanent Waves ; COMPLETE RANGE OF KING GEE Products ; Home Child Studies by PHOTOGRAPHIC ILLUSTRATORS ; L.P. Records ; Books ; Theatre Passes ; Month's supply of Petrol by ATLANTIC ; HANIMEX Cameras ; ARGUS Previewers ; ARGUS 300 Projectors and many many more.

A FORTUNE IN PRIZES
TOMORROW
AND EVERY DAY
MONDAY TO FRIDAY
2 — 4 P.M.

anyone can compete from HOME

2CH

▲ In 1964 I have my own record label, RG Records. Here's my only artist, Jimmy Hannan, getting ready to record his first album.

▲ *Everybody's Talking* on TCN9, 1967. Panellists Ron Cadee, Joy Chambers and Terry Dear with the producer. That's me.

▲ Ian Holmes and I watch an episode of *Prisoner* at Grundy House, 1978.

▲ Joy and I celebrate our second wedding anniversary in Brisbane with the cast of *I've Got a Secret*.

▲ Bert Newton awards me a Logie in the mid 1970s.

After dinner we walked along Curzon Street towards Park Lane.

'How about a nightcap?' I said.

We moved through Shepherds Market past Tiddy Dolls restaurant and on by Shepherds Pub where Douglas 'Tin Legs' Bader and other Second World War pilots had hung out when on leave.

We entered Hereford Street. At number twenty, we walked up the stone steps to our temporary London home. Bruce and I talked for hours. Joy left us around midnight and went to bed.

'We need Reg Watson to sort us out or we're sunk.'

Bruce looked me in the eye.

'Reg Watson is a very loyal guy. But his contract ran out light years ago and Lew hasn't ever got around to renewing it.'

I jumped in. 'And I reckon he'd be interested in spending some time back in Oz.'

'And joining you?'

'Well, I don't know if he'd agree to that. Maybe just come back for a while until we get things sorted out. He's got *Crossroads* running like a Swiss clock. He reckons you could almost put it on auto pilot.'

We were sipping champagne.

'Well, boy, I have to be loyal to Lew and ATV but if Reg says he's got to go back to Australia for a while—' He interrupted himself. 'I know he's got leave owing. And if he reckons *Crossroads* will be okay then I wouldn't stand in his way.'

Bruce added, 'Maybe he's got a close relative who's critically ill ... or something.'

We talked and drank the night away. Unfamiliar behaviour for both of us. I called Bruce the following morning. He had arrived home at 7.30 am, had a hangover and was in bed reading scripts. I wasn't feeling all that great myself. Obviously neither of us would make it as serious drinkers.

I had to stitch this up. 'Bruce, in terms of what we said in our half-drunken state last night, if I were to get Reg Watson to say to you that he wants to go to Australia, leave without pay, sick leave or whatever, for some weeks or perhaps as long as to the end of April, what would your reaction be?'

I paused, then continued.

'Look, I know this isn't easy. If Reg goes to Australia the disadvantages to you could be great. On the other hand, you would find out, once and for all, whether *Crossroads* can get along without Reg Watson, which is something you don't know at the moment.'

Bruce sounded sick. He breathed loudly into the phone.

'Tell him to ring or cable Francis Essex [production controller of ATV] and say something like "Have serious family problem. Would appreciate a month's leave" … or "Would like to stay in Australia to the end of February" or something … Anything he likes, really. If he says he wants to stay in Australia for another month after that for family reasons, I'm sure they will be able to find some way of getting round it.'

At last Reg Watson arrived in Sydney with his brother, to look over the Grundy operation.

Reg Grundy put us up at Noah's Motel in North Sydney.

I was used to working for ATV, who were extremely cautious with money as far as the employees were concerned. If you wanted a cup of tea, you had to pay for it. And when I worked in sales, they'd give you sixpence to go to J. Walter Thompson and people like that to sell a million dollars worth of advertising. You went in the bus, tuppence each way, and the tuppence in change you had to give back. And you had to produce the ticket as well.

Even Bruce Gyngell had some problems with them. Once he took me to lunch and said, 'How do you get on with these bloody expense accounts? There's this woman in London demanding receipts! Excuse me a second'. And he went over to where somebody had dropped a receipt and put it in his pocket. 'I'm determined to fix the bitch.'

When I got to Noah's, there was this kitchen and I said to my brother, Barry, 'We have to be careful about money so you go out and get some chops or something and I'll cook'. So there we were paying for meals while next door, the guys working on the show were ordering complete meals including oysters.

I thought it was going to be a holiday but I was handed all these scripts.

'Would you mind reading these?'

Reg Grundy kept on at me about working for him and would say, 'Why don't you come back? We'll get you great accommodation right near me'.

I wasn't too sure that was a good idea but nevertheless Barry and I went to look at a place called Possum Hill near where Reg and Joy lived. Even the taps in the bathroom were gold and Barry was saying, 'Take it, take it', and I was saying 'Shut up. I don't want the job.'

REG WATSON

One day not long after that Reg Watson and I were in my study at Bayview. It was a beautiful day with sunlight filtering into the room. There through the window was *Carolyn J*, our sturdy 13-metre Grand Banks, sitting off the end of our jetty with the glinting blue water lapping her hull.

I was asking Reg yet again to join me as head of drama.

'Why don't we find you a home here at Bayview. Maybe one with a few kangaroos and kookaburras. And let's all live happily ever after.'

Reg looked out along the gleaming water to Lion Island sitting off Palm Beach and thought of the grey days, so many of them, in Birmingham.

'*Crossroads* is now the number one show in England. I've done it—there's not much left for me to do there.'

I could sense that he was weakening.

'Reg, let's do it.'

I held out my hand and he took it.

We smiled, then we laughed.

I said with conviction, 'We'll never look back'.

And we never did.

But the start of our adventure together wasn't smooth. Reg W. gave three months notice and, during those three months, he actively worked with me on *Class of '74* from Birmingham. Not so easy in those days without modern communications—it was mostly done on the telephone.

I gave ATV three months notice and went back to work it out. Reg kept sending me these clunky half-inch Umatic tapes of monochrome rushes.

I was supposed to send back notes.

I finally got to Sydney in April of '74.

REG WATSON

Full-scale production had begun on 21 February and we were in desperate trouble.

When I came back to Australia it was really chaotic. The show was way behind schedule.

My first question: 'How far ahead are you?'

'One week.'

'Strewth,' I said.

'We need people with four-camera experience. Let's use some of your game show directors,' I told them.

REG WATSON

Bill Mason approached Mike Murphy, who was running our Melbourne office, and asked him if he would come to Sydney to direct some episodes. Mike was hot to trot. He was joined by ex-game show director Hal Croxon.

But the crew were saying to me, 'We don't do things like that here'. So I had to be bloody-minded and say, 'From now on, you do things my way'.

We had an Italian film director who sat on the floor and never went into the control room and I had the job of saying to him, 'This isn't working', and as he didn't speak English very well he said, 'No, you are so right', and I said, 'You'll have to go', and he said, 'Yes, I must go back to work', and I said, 'No, you have to leave', and he said, 'Yes, I will leave now', and I said, 'Yes, good', and he said 'I'll go back to work', and I said, 'No', and so it went on.

In the end I said, 'Look, you are fired, you are finished, you are out, kaput!' He burst into tears and said, 'You can't do this to me', and I said, 'Yes, I can'.

I phoned Reg Grundy and said, 'The only way we will get this done is if I go into the control room and direct', and Reg said, 'Are you sure you are doing the right thing?'

I said, 'Yes.'

The floor manager was so disgruntled that he sat on the pedestal of one of those old cameras and let the director direct on the floor. So I got him and said, 'This is your one opportunity to take control of your studio. You do it through me from the control room and control that floor, and if you can't do it then you shouldn't be here'.

The next day he came in and he took control of his floor and gradually it all came together.

REG WATSON

Reg Watson had saved the show and had moved into Possum Hill at Narrabeen, overlooking the lake.

But we were not out of the woods yet.

Hector Crawford also survived his drama crisis and came through with a serial set in a television station. It was called *The Box* and featured plenty of sex and semi-nudity, but seemed to be immune from interference from the Broadcasting Control Board.

We went to air with *Class of '74* a month later and some scenes had to be edited because they were not approved by the Control Board.

The Box was produced in Melbourne while *Class of '74* was made in Sydney. Interestingly, the Control Board's head office was in Melbourne.

The press decided that *Class of '74* was about everything that was unacceptable at 7.30. The first script is credited to writer Peter Hepple and was directed by Peter Maxwell. It featured, though not necessarily in this order, an affair between a teacher and a student, a hint of devil worship, some pornography and the deflowering of the school virgin.

Advance news of the content didn't hurt the show's audience. On the first night *Class of '74* dominated its slot with a thirty-seven rating, the highest ever for a seven o'clock show. But network executives were worried. The Broadcasting Control Board had issued a caution that the show might have to be moved to a later time slot.

Myles Wright, the Board of Control chairman, pontificated:

At these times (4 pm to 7.30 pm) parents should be able to feel secure in allowing children to watch television without supervision. The Board considers the general tone of Class of '74 *to be totally opposed to this rule.*

MELBOURNE AGE, 20 MARCH 1974

While there were plenty of protesting phone calls from viewers, the ratings confirmed that the majority of the audience loved the show just the way it was. We didn't think *Class of '74* needed to be cleaned up but the Sevens did and, in particular, HSV 7 in Melbourne.

Ron Casey, the general manager of HSV 7, had his own problems. The Mother Superior of the school his daughter was attending had called him.

'Mr Casey, *Class of '74* is a disgrace and you should take it off the air.'

Alarm bells were ringing.

Lyle McCabe and I flew to Melbourne and spent the night in the station's tape room, editing the first week's episodes.

I'm saying, 'Stop tape. Replay that bit. The priest is looking at her ... was that longingly? Better drop the look.'

It was getting to the ridiculous stage.

On Wednesday of the first week the show was moved to 8 pm in Sydney and 7.30 pm in Melbourne. Just for three nights. The next Monday it returned uneasily to the 7 pm slot, with continuing Control Board scrutiny.

In March 1975 the writing was on the wall when Channel Seven in Melbourne moved the series out of its prime time slot, replacing it with repeats of the US sitcom *Bewitched*. A spokesman for Channel Seven Melbourne said the move was prompted by 'falling ratings towards the end of 1974 and early this year'.

The show was unceremoniously consigned to 8 am Saturday mornings in Melbourne—a strange timeslot if the intent was to keep the show away from the eyes of children.

On the plus side *Class of '74* had started with a bang—plenty of media attention and high ratings. At least we had shown that we could make drama that people wanted to watch.

No doubt the show had been too racy for the times, but it has the distinction of being the first teenage television serial produced anywhere in the world.

It had been the start of Reg Watson's extraordinary career as my head of drama—the most important appointment I ever made. His record in creating and developing serialised drama is nothing less than astonishing.

1974 *Class of '74/'75*

1975 *Until Tomorrow*

1976 *Young Doctors*

1977 *The Restless Years*

1979 *Prisoner*

1981 *Punishment*

1981 *Dangerous Women* (USA)

1982 *Sons and Daughters*

1983 *Waterloo Station*

1985 *Neighbours*

1988 *Richmond Hill*

Watson developed them all and, with the exception of *Class of '74*, which started before he arrived in Australia, set their style by writing at least the opening episode for each production.

RON McLEAN AND A BOTTLE OF SCOTCH

If we were to stay in the drama business we needed to follow *Class of '74* as quickly as possible.

My friend Lynton Taylor, the program director at Channel Nine Sydney whom I'd known well since he worked in Adelaide at ADS 7, was sitting in the beautiful green leather wingback chair in my study in our house in Bayview. It was the same room where I'd clinched the deal with Reg Watson.

'There's no doubt you've got a find in Reg Watson but we're looking for series, not serials. Why don't you get hold of Ron McLean? Tons of experience, worked with Roger Mirams on *Spyforce*.'

So Ron joined us.

Reg Watson, head of drama, has this to say:

Ron's idea of how to write a script was to have a bottle of scotch in the filing cabinet. After the first week, he said to the floor manager, 'Get some money from Reg Watson for a bottle of scotch'. So the young guy came in and said, 'Ron wants a bottle of scotch', and I said, ' What for?' and he said, 'To drink'.

REG WATSON

With or without whiskey, Ron soon came up with a concept for a prime time adult drama called *Two-Way Mirror*.

Kerry Packer approved a movie-length pilot.

The plot ran like this: the head of Mirage Cosmetics dies with many secrets. It is revealed that he was a voyeur. A painting on the wall of his office slides away to reveal a two-way mirror through which he watches Jimmy, the house photographer, posing nude models and sometimes making love to them.

We didn't expect any problems from the Broadcasting Control Board as the show was planned for 8.30 pm or even later.

Reg Watson remembers:

I was to produce the pilot.

Everybody in the office had a point of view about it, including Lyle McCabe and Bill Mason.

I thought, well, I'm a stranger here so I'd better listen.

I was told I needed a nude model and Jimmy should show her from every angle.

My God, I thought, what sort of country have I come back to?

In the end I decided that the photographer would wrap the girl in Gladwrap.

In the end, I had to do the wrapping and I felt sorry for the poor girl.

We shot it in an old film studio and just about everything went wrong.

REG WATSON

We sent the pilot to Kerry Packer but there was no enthusiasm for the show. Not even for the nude.

I viewed the pilot recently and, while some of the performances were poor, the concept was intriguing.

Two-Way Mirror would have had a chance if it had gone ahead.

And here's a bit of soapy trivia I bet you didn't know. The theme music for *Two-Way Mirror* was written by Nine's musical director, Geoff Harvey. When the show didn't go ahead, Geoff, never one to waste good work, recycled it as the theme for *The Sullivans*. So what became a Hector Crawford theme tune had been written for his only rival, Reg Grundy.

After the demise of *Two-Way Mirror*, Channel Nine ordered a pilot of a second Ron McLean concept called *Case for the Defence*. John Case, played by actor John Hamblin, was a Queen's Counsel—hence the title. The pilot was made in August 1975 and a series of nine movie-length episodes were commissioned in 1976. They were well made, but for whatever reason Nine didn't bother to transmit them.

In May 1978 Channel Ten, at the time struggling to meet its Australian drama quota, picked them up and put them to air and they did well.

Ron McLean's next concept for Channel Nine hit the spot. It was a copy show called *King's Men*. Gordon Glenwright, who had been the school janitor and amateur counsellor in *Class of '74*, was cast as Inspector Harry King, the head of the Kings Cross Police Station. The pilot was average or worse, and the cast worked hard with pedestrian dialogue.

Again we sent the pilot into Consolidated Press in Castlereagh Street where Kerry Packer had his office. Kerry was soon on the phone to me.

'It's not bad, son. Not great, but not bad. I reckon you're nearly there. We'll have a good think about it and get back to you.'

After their think, Nine decided to go with *King's Men* and ordered thirteen one-hour episodes. Production started 15 March 1976.

Many changes were made to *King's Men* after the pilot and before series production started. Inspired by the American series *Mod Squad*, we introduced young undercover cops. Even the opening title sequence was about to be changed.

We had started with *King of the Cross*, which became *All the King's Men* and, finally, *King's Men*. We liked the final short name much better. My executives and I were seated in our small viewing room at Grundy House. An advertising agency man was talking at us.

'I can make this show a hit. Start with a cat walking along a wall, and you can't miss.'

Dramatically he proclaimed, 'Watch this!'

Projected onto the screen at the end of the room was footage of a cat walking along a wall accompanied by moody music and finishing up with the show title: *KING'S MEN*.

A cat walking along a wall? I wasn't convinced it would make the show a hit. Yet somehow the new opening title with the cat was accepted.

I had an idea. I called Reg Watson.

'If we're going to use a cat in the title then we should get a trained cat which can lodge itself in King's in-tray. Sort of ties it all together.'

Reg Watson's credit read executive producer, but he says that the only part of the show he can remember is 'looking after the bloody cat'.

Reg Grundy had this idea. Gordon Glenwright was playing Inspector King and RG felt he should have a cat like the one in the opening sequence, which would sit in his in-tray. All right, so we need a trained cat. This woman comes in and says, yes, she has a trained cat but it turns out it isn't really trained and keeps jumping out of the tray. I was the only one the cat would listen to, so I had to go and get it. On and on and on it went—this cat jumping out of the tray and not doing anything you wanted it to. It drove me mad.

Then one day the woman comes in and says, 'The cat is dead'. I thought, 'Jesus, I've got to tell Reg Grundy. He loves that cat.'

So I go to Reg and say, 'Reg, I've got some bad news for you'.

'What is it?'

'The cat's dead.'

REG WATSON

We stood there silently in my office for a moment before we both started to laugh. Watson was looking at me pleadingly.

'Do you want me to find a replacement?' he asked.

I felt sorry for him … and for the poor cat.

'No, just write in a scene about King being upset by the loss of his cat.'

Reg Watson asked again. 'No replacement?'

'No replacement.'

'Good.'

And he was off, whistling.

ABBA

In 1976 the Swedish pop group ABBA arrived in Australia.

Brian Henderson's *Bandstand* had ended but we had brought back the show as a Reg Grundy Production, hosted by Daryl Somers. We devoted a special episode to ABBA, and it went through the roof. It has been reported that more people saw it than watched the first moon landing, and it started an ABBA fever in Australia that had only been equalled by The Beatles' visit in 1964.

When we met, I hit it off with ABBA's manager, Stikkan Anderson—known as 'Stig'—and I became ABBA's unofficial representative in Australia.

Alex Hamill, then an account executive at George Patterson Advertising Agency (later its chairman), marched into the Grundy offices one day with $50,000 in a brown paper bag. He announced that he was prepared to pay serious money for an exclusive on the Swedish pop group to endorse one of the George Patterson client's products.

George Patterson finished up paying $105,000 for the rights, beating the Bank of NSW (later Westpac), which offered $100,000.

Hamill wanted ABBA to promote National, an electronics company that had a solid reputation for its TV sets but needed to publicise its many other appliances. Alex Hamill believed that ABBA were modern, international and had cross-generational appeal. The campaign was so successful that National cut back on its advertising allocation because of the overwhelming demand for their products.

Joy and I took Stig out in our Grand Banks 42 one weekend. We hung off a mooring in Refuge Bay in the Hawkesbury River on the Saturday night, eating and drinking the Swedish national drink, aquavit. Stig kept telling Joy she was not Australian but Swedish, because of her blonde look.

'Joy my darling, you are blonde and beautiful, there is no doubt you are

Swedish.' He would raise his glass high and swallow another mouthful of aquavit.

I was not used to drinking much alcohol, as the earlier all-night session with Bruce Gyngell revealed, and the Swedish aquavit was a killer. Amstel light beer has 3.5 per cent alcohol by volume. Most wines are around 14 per cent. Aquavit is a whopping 40 per cent. No wonder Joy and I woke with throbbing headaches on the Sunday morning.

Yet I reckon it was worth it. The night before I had thrashed out a deal with Stig for us to make a road movie starring ABBA.

Stig seemed unaffected by the aquavit, and we spent the morning chatting on deck in the sun while he told us of his early life and how he had met the four stars in the ABBA pop group.

Some months later Joy and I were in Europe and we travelled to Stockholm to visit Stig and his wife. Both were former schoolteachers who had made it big when they hooked into ABBA. We had dinner in their modest apartment, fairly sparsely furnished, and yet the walls were covered with modern art; actually, famous masterpieces.

The next day we visited the ABBA office in a small building in the city, up one flight of stairs. There was a lift but it was out of order. Why? Because it was stacked full of paintings. Stig never quite explained why they were stored in the lift; perhaps lack of space.

Joy had broken a capped tooth and Stig made a phone call and got her in to see a dentist that same morning. In Stockholm, waiting time was up to six months. That confirmed Stig's influence in Sweden.

When we returned to Australia I was feeling uneasy. The road movie which Grundy was making with the four ABBA stars had completed shooting and was being edited back in Stockholm. What if they were making a mess of it?

I called Bruce Beresford, who was in London at the time, and asked him to fly over to Sweden to make sure everything was okay. His report was reassuring and he gave me comforting news: 'Don't worry, Reg, it's going well; they know what they're doing'.

On 24 November 1977 *ABBA: The Movie* opened at the Regent Theatre in George Street, Sydney.

Stig and I agreed we should arrive at the theatre together.

For the first time in my life I decided to wear a white suit. Joy and I arrived at the Sebel Townhouse, Kings Cross and I knocked on Stig's door. It was opened by a smiling man wearing a white suit! So off we all went to the opening and there Stig and I sat in the front row of the circle for the premiere, looking almost like twins in our snappy white suits.

Afterwards, we hosted a splendid six-course dinner for Stig at the Hilton Hotel in Pitt Street.

The movie did well but was not the sensation that we had hoped for. It was not the fault of the movie—it was a matter of timing. Although the kids yelled and spilled out onto the pavements outside the Regent in George Street, the peak of ABBA excitement had passed.

ABBA: The Movie is a perennial on cable TV. Try to catch it—I'm sure you'll enjoy it. Australian Robert Caswell, who wrote the script, went on to great success in America, being nominated for a Golden Globes award. *ABBA: The Movie* was released on DVD in 2005.

MESSING ABOUT IN BOATS

My association with water, apart from its use for drinking, having showers, and other matters of hygiene, got a start when I was in radio at 2CH and Jog and I would go fishing in a rented dinghy on Sunday mornings on Botany Bay and the Georges River. The highlight of those outings was the day I caught a very large flathead. The local fishermen were full of praise.

'It's a beauty, best fish that'll be caught on the river today.'

All I had done was drag it into the boat. No protest by the fish, which seemed disinterested in the whole affair.

This trivial event is only mentioned in this personal account of my life as an early sign of my interest in boats, although I've rarely done more than sit in them. Back then, I let Jog do the nautical business of adjusting the fuel flow, pulling the strap to start the Chapman Pup motor and manning the tiller. I just pointed the direction in which I wanted us to go.

Something I've continued to do, I suppose.

Many men seem to enjoy things like changing a light bulb, fixing a vacuum cleaner that suddenly won't work, or tuning up the lawnmower. Practical things bore me, maybe because I haven't the slightest idea how to deal with them.

Sometimes my lack of competence has made things difficult for me. I remember as a young man renting a small dinghy with an outboard from Halverson's Marina at Bobbin Head. The girl with me seemed happy enough for us to putter across to the far side of the river—the uninhabited side. I dragged the dinghy up onto the shore and we decided to eat our sandwiches and drink our Cokes near to where we had landed. An hour later, when we returned, our small boat was perched precariously on a large rock. The tide had gone out. We were stranded.

I suppose the cynical reader is thinking it was deliberate—a nautical version of the car running out of gas. It was not. I was not a pushy young man—completely the opposite. So we hung around the boat until the tide came in and we could float away and return to Halverson's on the other side of the river.

In spite of this experience, I loved being on the water and continued to go fishing. I was okay, as there was always another man present who could do all those things that the average practical male seemed to enjoy.

After Joy and I married, it was natural that we should buy a boat. There it was, early in the 1970s, attached to the pontoon at the end of our jetty, which jutted out into Pittwater north of Sydney—a Savage Lancer, 8 metres long. A plastic wonder, and our delight.

Two of our close friends were Sophie and Ed Williams—Ed had been a mentor of mine in my early radio days, and Sophie and Joy had hit it off. They became our first boating guests. It was a grey day, but the weather was not my concern; I was trying to work out how to move away from the pontoon at the end of the jetty.

Later I was to realise that it's inadvisable to turn the wheel hard away from the pontoon and accelerate. But that was exactly what I did, slamming the stern into the pontoon. I pretended to be unconcerned and kept up the banter. Our good friends appeared not to notice the lack of seamanship, which was remarkable, considering the noise of the impact.

In spite of my lack of nautical know-how, we had a marvellous time with our small boat. We would motor up to Coasters Retreat halfway to West Head, then slowly return to our long jetty. No thoughts of tying up somewhere or beaching the boat or dropping the small anchor. To get into the boat, edge up Pittwater and turn back was enough of an adventure for us.

But as time went by, I gained confidence and started thinking about buying a real boat. In September 1974 our new Grand Banks cruiser was delivered. She was built in Singapore and Peter Skelton remembers her as being 'of enormous size'. Actually, she was 13 metres, a semi-displacement hull wooden boat which was to give us great pleasure and introduce us to the art of entertaining on the water.

Joy had been christened Carolyn Joy, so it seemed appropriate to name the new boat *Carolyn J. Joy C* didn't sound right.

Although we were to own floating palaces, my favourite will always be

Carolyn J. I don't think Joy feels that way, but I do, and we could take it out on our own. We spent many weekends on the Hawkesbury River and the bays of Cowan Creek. The forward cabin stored a Umatic machine, which played VHS tapes of shows I thought I needed to see.

Catamarans zipping across Pittwater made sailing on Saturdays a dangerous exercise for the inexperienced. So late on Fridays we would embark, travelling around West Head to return on Monday mornings. Sometimes the water was mirror smooth and we would cut the engines and look down from the fly bridge at the fairy penguins as we floated by. There were times when a strong swell would be rolling in from the Tasman Sea, and rounding West Head on the return journey on Monday morning could be an adventure.

Carolyn J turned out to be the boat on which we entertained the most people. There was a comfortable feel about her, although we also had more embarrassing moments on her than any of our other boats.

Many of those moments involved people who were famous or extremely wealthy or both.

One of them was John Kluge, the owner of Metromedia, the largest independent television business in the USA, which he later sold to Rupert Murdoch for a reported four billion dollars.

Metromedia's Australian representative was Max Dutch, who had been distributing my shows around Australia. Max was in the money distributing Metromedia hit shows like *Charlie's Angels*, *Starsky & Hutch* and *S.W.A.T.*—shows which had elevated Max onto a very different level than he'd been accustomed to when working for me. Max had not met John Kluge and was surprised when he called.

'I'm making a quick visit to Sydney and there are two people I want to meet—Kerry Packer and Reg Grundy.'

Max called me and suggested that I take John for a day cruise on *Carolyn J*. I was happy to supply the boat but explained I would be out of Australia when Kluge was in Sydney. So Ian Holmes, who was running the Australian operation, John Fowler and my secretary Di Ayres took Kluge for a cruise up to the Berowra Waters Inn, one of Sydney's top restaurants and accessible only from the water. Of course, Max Dutch and his wife were on board, as was the woman who was to become Kluge's next wife, and a Chevrolet dealer from New York who was one of Kluge's best friends.

While Kluge and his Chevy dealer mate played cards, the rest drank champagne and somehow managed to get lost. Hard to understand how you can get lost getting up the Hawkesbury to Berowra Waters, just as it's hard to imagine how it's possible to run aground on a clearly marked sandbank—but they managed that as well.

They were two hours late for lunch.

John Kluge had a dinner appointment in town but it was nearly dark by the time they got back to Bayview and it would have been about 9.30 before he got to his dinner appointment, still wearing his casual clothes.

Kluge didn't mention that abortive day when we met a few months later in New York. And I certainly didn't remind him.

Glen Kinging, who programmed the Seven network for years, remembers another cruise.

Reg and Joy entertained quite a lot, often on their Grand Banks cruiser. I remember he had an industry day outing on the harbour and quite a lot of us were on board. As usual, Reg and Joy were terrific hosts and of course there was lunch with decent glassware and china—none of your paper cups and plates—and what I think was real silver cutlery. I'm not sure quite what happened but I think my neighbour bumped me and I dropped the fork I was using. I watched in horror as it bounced on the deck and then neatly flipped over the side. I couldn't believe it. What was I going to do? I thought that the cutlery would certainly be counted at the end of the day and the fork would be missed. But what if a whole place setting was missing? Mightn't they just think there'd been some sort of typographical error on the list?

So I went and found the matching spoon and knife and tossed them over the side to join the fork.

No one ever came knocking on my door, so I assume I got away with it. I hope there's a Statute of Limitations on that sort of thing.

GLEN KINGING

Glen, we knew you'd done it, but your secret was safe with us. Except, of course, for the many guests we had on board after that day. We would always cut the engine and glide past the spot, and I would say, 'That's where Glen Kinging threw the cutlery overboard'.

Peter Skelton, who lived on Pittwater at the time, had his own boat. It wasn't a cruiser of any sort, let alone a Grand Banks. As a matter of fact, it was a 4.5 metre aluminium runabout with outboard that he used for occasional fishing, so he was happy to accept an invitation to go to sea on something bigger.

Peter had a great day on board with other Channel Ten execs, enjoying our usual hospitality. As he got off I said, 'I hear you've got a boat?'

'Err, yes.'

'I'd love to go out in it sometime.'

After the day he'd just had, Peter was mortified at the thought of entertaining Joy and me in his tinny. It was a while before he realised that the reference was to the boat Channel Ten had just bought to entertain clients and which was almost as big as ours.

But not quite.

Peter liked to tell people that even the engine room of *Carolyn J* was covered in white shag carpet.

Again, not quite!

In 1975, stars of the *Laugh-In* cast from the USA sailed up the Hawkesbury River with us, and so did a number of American television notables. Among them was Ron Howard, who became a Hollywood film director. But when he came aboard he was with Henry Winkler who played the Fonz; Ron was Richie Cunningham in *Happy Days*, the American hit show of the 1970s.

Ron had married his high school sweetheart, Cheryl, on 7 June 1975. They had come to Australia on their honeymoon. He turned up at Bayview wearing a check shirt, just as he might have when he played Opie in the *Andy Griffith Show* in the late 1960s. The newlyweds and the other guests appeared to have a wonderful time.

Ron made it very clear that he saw his future not in front of the camera, but behind it. He wanted to be a movie director. We had a long chat that afternoon. He was still talking about directing when the cruise was over and we stood beside our front gate. It was time to say goodbye when he made his pitch.

'How about I make a movie for you for $150,000. I've got a good script. Matter of fact, it was written by Rance Howard, my dad.'

I didn't know what to say. One hundred and fifty thousand dollars was a lot for me to consider at that time. Ron sent me the script, 'Tis the Season, but I passed.

Two years later Ron Howard directed a low-budget movie, *Grand Theft Auto*, for filmmaker Roger Corman. The script was by Ron Howard and Rance Howard and both were in the cast. Ron never looked back after that.

In retrospect, it wouldn't have been a terrible mistake to have been the producer who discovered Ron Howard as a director. But heck, I've got nothing to complain about.

There was another Australian (actually a New Zealander) who appeared in two Grundy shows, *Young Doctors* and *Neighbours*, who did get together with Ron Howard on *A Brilliant Mind* and *Cinderella Man*. Russell Crowe.

Stirling Silliphant, who had won an Academy Award for his screen adaptation of *In the Heat of the Night*, came to Australia to follow up on meetings we had in Los Angeles. I had commissioned him to write the script for a movie based on the serial killer Eddie Leonski, an American soldier stationed in Australia during the Second World War, who murdered a number of young women and who was subsequently hanged in Pentridge Gaol, Victoria on 9 November 1942. The working title was *The Brown Out Murders*.

I flew Stirling and his Vietnamese wife to Sydney for more discussions and to do a little pre-promotion of the project. We found ourselves on board *Carolyn J* one Sunday. Stirling looked across the calm waters of Refuge Bay as he told us how he felt.

'You know, if I hadn't got into the business, I reckon I might have been a sailor. There's nothing better for me than to be out on the water. Strangely, my wife and I love to go out in tough conditions and test ourselves in bad weather.'

We didn't volunteer to oblige him.

I caught a radio interview he gave when he was in Sydney. 'I'll be back in ninety days with the script and if everything goes well it should be in the theatres by the fall of 1980.'

As the months passed by I had my hands full with other matters. *The Brown Out Murders* just slipped off the table and never did get made. Director Philippe Mora's version of the Eddie Leonski case was called *Death of a Soldier*.

One Sunday we entertained three famous British actors: Roy Dotrice and his daughter Michele Dotrice, and the man she was to marry, Edward Woodward. We all hit it off, and swam around the boat and ate a wonderful lunch Joy had supplied. At the end of the day we relaxed in our Pittwater home and played charades.

One charades team consisted of Roy, Michele and Edward. Edward Woodward had appeared in many acting roles and had received the British Academy Television Award for Best Actor. As well, he recorded twelve albums of romantic songs. Edward gave me copies of all twelve, and I still have them.

Roy Dotrice was a Shakespearean actor who had served with the RAF during the Second World War and had been a German prisoner of war. Now Roy was in Sydney performing in a one-man show at the Sydney Opera House. Roy, who was the same age as me, took a real shine to Joy and called her almost daily to have lunch with him.

He never got his wish.

Michele Dotrice was best known for her portrayal of Betty, the long-suffering wife in *Some Mothers Do 'Ave 'Em*.

Our charades team was Joy, Coral—Joy's older sister, who was staying with us—and me. Some might think the odds were stacked against us. There was much laughter and it was late when the game was over. But, after that long hard game, amazingly—our team won!

One of the most offbeat *Carolyn J* stories belongs to Noele Gordon, the star of *Crossroads*, the immensely popular English serial which Reg Watson had produced for ATV in Birmingham.

Reg persuaded Noele to come to Australia and stay with him, and we took her for a cruise. The next day she was leaving to return to the UK. Noele came to Reg Watson and said, 'Reg, you better have these'.

She opened a suitcase. Toilet rolls spilled out onto the floor.

'I was told in Birmingham that you didn't use toilet paper in Australia. So I brought my own.'

Although I now had plenty of experience with the Grand Banks I was never going to win an award for my boat handling. It was yet another beautiful sunny Sunday and the top executives of TCN Channel Nine were about to arrive for a day's cruise. I had *Carolyn J* alongside at the end of our jetty. The tide was going out, so I needed to cast off and move the boat to our mooring 200 metres out in the bay. I started to steer her through the maze of bobbing buoys.

And then it happened.

The tiny vortex created by the movement of the twin propellers had sucked up a buoy and wound the line around the port shaft. Before I could turn off the engines, I had a huge concrete block hanging from the propeller just below the surface of the water. There was only one thing to do. Cut the line free.

I grabbed a Stanley knife from the boat's toolbox and dived off the swim platform. It was a slow and dangerous procedure. Take a deep breath, dive in, and saw on the rope. Lungs nearly bursting, take another deep breath and continue.

I felt like Harold Lloyd, the actor who performed daredevil risky scenes in his silent movies. Harold didn't talk much and neither did I, as I dived in and out of the water.

In the middle of this, our guests arrived at the house and were ferried out to the boat and scrambled on board.

Dripping wet I said, 'Welcome. Sorry, won't be long. Got a bit of a problem. Be with you in a minute'.

These were my customers and here was I, acting out a scene from a Harold Lloyd silent movie. Lloyd made over fifteen million dollars for performing his stunts. Me? My act was a freebie.

It must have been twenty minutes before we were able to move away.

The sun had been beating down on me. I was exhausted with the constant diving and hacking. I was smiling and making small talk, wondering if *Carolyn J* had been seriously damaged—we were limping along with only one propeller turning. I was the captain and would be on duty for the next eight hours or so.

Eventually, the day was over.

Of course, I was wrong—it was not over yet. We had invited our guests to stay for a barbecue in the terraced grounds of our home. Everyone was having a great time. That is, everyone but me. It was after midnight when they left. I fell into bed.

And what happened to our beautiful *Carolyn J*? She was taken to Halverson's at Bobbin Head where the bent shaft was straightened out.

And the really strange part? Strange to me anyway. The CEO of the Nine network who had been on board was anything but my friend at that time, and yet he was the last to leave. He had his reasons for disliking me, and I can guess at what they were. But I'm not going to speculate in these pages. The point is, he stayed at that barbecue right till the end.

Many years later Joy and I sat in the Concorde lounge at London Heathrow airport, waiting to be called onboard. I looked to my right through the glass at the beautiful machine waiting on the tarmac.

I turned back, and there he was—the man who'd been last to leave the barbecue that night so many years before. We'd had a lot of water go under the bridge … some of which is still to come in this yarn I'm telling.

I knew he had seen me, so I turned to Joy. 'I'm going over to speak to him.'

And I stood up, strolled across to his table and said, 'We never did like one another, did we?'

He looked up and replied, 'No, we never did'.

Sam Chisholm and I laughed and shook hands. It didn't mean that from then on we became firm friends, but let's say the past remained in the past.

Although *Carolyn J*, the Grand Banks, had served us well, by 1980 we decided to move up to a bigger boat. We were in America at the time and naval architect John Carlton was commissioned to find her. He recommended a Bertram 58.

Joy and I travelled to Florida and went for a trial run through the canal, passing wrecked boats which had probably been used for drug running before US customs had put them out of action. Then on out into the bay, looking back at Florida with its hotels stretching down the sandy foreshore as far as the eye could see. It reminded us of a greatly expanded Surfers Paradise in Queensland where Mayor Bruce Small had taken the idea of canals, after seeing Florida.

'It's a wonderful boat,' said the Bertram rep, 'but of course if you want to do any serious fishing, you could have a 10 foot [3 metre] cockpit added and you'd have a magnificent 68 footer [21 metre].'

'What's the cost of the extension?' I asked.

'Only 90,000 US,' smiled the salesman.

And then he mouthed the immortal words of a salesman's 'close'.

'You'll never regret it.'

I was hooked, just like the fish I hoped to catch.

So we added the extra 3 metres of cockpit and made her a 68 footer.

And the all up cost? Near enough to a million US.

Joy and I were still swallowing hard at that dollar price tag when we were faced with another financial hurdle: the cost of freighting her as deck cargo to Sydney was enormous.

So what would be wrong with sailing her out on her own bottom? The answer should have been 'A lot!' but that didn't enter my mind. It meant a voyage through the Panama Canal and then across the Pacific to the east coast of Australia.

A crew was assembled to take her on this epic journey halfway around the world. Architect John Carlton agreed to be the captain and he hired a first mate, a crewman and an engineer.

But there were more problems to be solved before the new *Carolyn J* could set forth. The Bertram had a capacity of 1900 US gallons [7200 litres] but to cross the Pacific she'd need to carry 3800 gallons [14,400 litres] between refills. The problem was solved by installing a temporary tank under the stern extension, and sixteen 50 gallon [190 litre] tanks in the cockpit. Just as well we *had* a cockpit.

By the time she got to Sydney the fuel bill had reached $25,000 dollars—

about a dollar a kilometre. But there was worse to come.

The voyage had hardly started when John realised his three crew members were not up to the job. There were endless delays due to mechanical breakdowns and it had been a hair-raising passage through the Panama Canal and up the west coast of America to Newport, where the three-member crew was paid off.

Carolyn J was stuck in Newport for some forty-two days before new crew came aboard. It took a while, because this time we did the recruiting in Australia. It paid off.

We replaced the three original crew with just two new guys.

New Zealander Keith Thiele was the new mate. He was a top navigator who had served as a wartime bomber pilot. Snowy Hitchcock from Sydney became the engineer. He operated a diesel and marine electrics business and what he didn't know about GM marine engines wasn't worth knowing.

Now the real journey started. The promised deadline was November 1980 but with those early delays it was May 1981 before we took delivery in Australia.

At last we got the word that the boat and crew had arrived on the Australian east coast and my driver and I flew north and got aboard in Coffs Harbour for the last leg to Sydney.

As soon as we got into open water the Bertram started to move. It had a stiff action, as I was discovering. John Carlton had skippered the boat on its long crossing but it was Snow Hitchcock, a pretty tough cookie and the engineer, who grinned at me and said, 'G'day, Reg. We've got a nice baked dinner for you with gravy, and a great red wine to wash it down'.

My ability not to be seasick was being tested.

The wind was picking up and reaching Beaufort 6 or 7 as the spray flattened out across the sea. The boat's movement was becoming more drastic as the minutes went by. Standing upright on deck was trying. If you let go, you found yourself propelled to the other side of the boat in a moment. My driver was asleep on the round bed in the main cabin. There was just a mattress. During the night I crept down into the cabin and shared it with him.

And for this we'd paid almost a million dollars?

By morning the wind was still blowing hard and it stayed that way all down the coast. I was very relieved when we passed through the heads and moved down Sydney Harbour.

Joy was waiting on the dock as we tied up. With a last look back at a dirty battered boat, we left *Carolyn J* Mark II behind, and travelled home to Bayview. We were not there when the Customs officers arrived, but I'm told Snow greeted them with the following words: 'She's fucked'.

John Carlton has never forgotten the epic journey and is said to boast that he once drove a 68 Bertram from Miami to Australia. He thinks he may be the first person to have crossed the Pacific in what he unkindly calls a production plastic motor boat.

While we had happy times on board she was not the same as the Grand Banks which, with its displacement hull, gave us a smooth, stable ride. She was quiet—the Bertram was not.

We had a mooring near Dangar Island in the Hawkesbury River, and we would take the Bertram from our back door in Pittwater around West Head and up to Dangar Island. We could not anchor—that was too difficult because a 21-metre boat is a lot for two people to handle. But we could just manage to take her from mooring to mooring.

Reg drove and I was the entire deck crew. There were many times I nearly fell overboard trying to pick up that damned elusive Dangar mooring with the boat hook.

Reg misses those small boats … but I don't.

JOY CHAMBERS-GRUNDY

But actually, owning a boat was becoming a distraction.

So it was ten years later before we bought *Reverie Rose*, a 33.5 metre Benetti, and renamed her *Idolwood* after the house in Ipswich, Queensland where Joy was living with her parents when I first met her.

We celebrated our twentieth wedding anniversary aboard the *Idolwood* in Golfe Juan, a small port on the Riviera, with our senior executives and close friends who flew in for the weekend event.

As always, I sang to Joy an old song written by Irving Berlin called 'Always'. It's our theme song, I suppose. When I first met Joy it was 'I Wish You Love', but as the years have passed it's become 'Always'. I get a bit teary and my voice wobbles and she takes my hand and holds it … same every time. I'm an old romantic at heart, I guess.

At our twentieth anniversary the small group of musicians on the aft deck were all Italians who did not know the 'Always' tune. I stumbled through it, kissed Joy, made a speech and sat down. But Joy was holding my hand and smiling so that made it a success for me.

In 1991, some fourteen months later, we sold *Idolwood*. We were again looking at yachts for sale. I found one in a boating magazine—shot from a helicopter, beamy and beautiful at 45.5 metres long and 9 metres wide. *Katamarino* had been built in Japan of aluminium supplied by Kaiser, the aluminium king. Because of that, the aluminium was very thick and she was as sturdy and solid as if she were made of steel.

But it was the width of the beam that really attracted us. We inspected her. Joy proclaimed that the drapes and carpets would need to be replaced— the smell of cigarettes was everywhere. In spite of that, we were hooked.

That yacht really smelt terrible. The previous owners had obviously been serious smokers; so I did a cleaning and redecorating job and she ended up looking and smelling brand new.

JOY CHAMBERS-GRUNDY

Halfway through 1992, we bought her and called her *Idolwood II*.

Soon we were in Canada cruising the St Lawrence River right up to the Great Lakes and back to the Saguenay River and through the Gulf of St Lawrence on to Prince Edward Island.

On Prince Edward Island we went ashore with Reg Watson and Peter Connah, Di and John Ayres and the rest of our friends. It was an important night—Reg Watson was paying! At the end of the meal, Reg opened his wallet only to be told by the manager that the mayor had paid for us. He had left a message saying how honoured he was to have us anchored in Charlotte Harbour, and he hoped we would enjoy the rest of our stay.

We were amazed and thought it very generous of him. The next day we tried to contact the mayor, who ran the local garage. We were told that he was away. We never did find him but it didn't matter to Reg Watson, who hadn't been forced to cough up. He was smiling.

The following night the alarms went off in the early hours of the morning. Everybody tumbled out of their cabins and the crew ran all over the place. Attached to the stern was a dinghy. On the deck stood a man saluting the flag. He was escorted off and we all went back to bed. The next night he returned a little the worse for wear. Same thing: alarms ringing and our 'friend' saluting the flag. This time we contacted the police.

The sergeant said, 'Don't worry, he won't get aboard again. He's the local drunk. Completely harmless, but all the same we'll lock him up until you leave. He's used to his favourite cell, I assure you.'

Aboard *Idolwood II* Jerry Pike, an Australian, was our chief engineer and also a PADI (Professional Association of Diving Instructors) diving instructor. So I decided to take up diving. But I needed a buddy to learn with me. Captain 'Ginger' Steve volunteered. He had been skippering the yacht prior to our purchase of her and had remained as captain.

The night before the first dive I imagined all the things that could go wrong. I was a bit hesitant the next morning but events took over and I was soon out on deck with Jerry and Ginger Steve. I had been told that my first task, after proper instruction, would be to touch the anchor. Most owners never get to do that, said Jerry.

We were only in about 12 metres of water so the task didn't seem unreasonable. Pike was tough.

'Now, you need to get into your suit and do everything yourself. In an extreme situation your buddy can help you. But only then.'

So we back-flipped into the water and down we went. It was a strange feeling, made stranger by Jerry putting his hand out palm first, signalling for me to stay on the bottom while he took Ginger back up to the surface. I moved over and touched the anchor. At least that was one thing achieved and out of the way. Eventually Jerry and Ginger Steve dropped down beside me and the lesson continued.

At last we had gone through the underwater stuff, and now only the written exam had to be attended to.

'Jerry, it'll have to wait until next time. We've got to get off in a couple of hours.'

Jerry replied, a serious tone in his voice, 'You've got to do the written test before you get off today, Mr Grundy'.

'What's the hurry, Jerry?'

'You've just got to get it done. You're the oldest and wealthiest student I've ever had. I'm not letting you get away without doing it.'

I did it … and passed.

We had a new chef on *Idolwood II* and the standard of the meals zoomed way up. He was meticulous, presenting daily handwritten menus to Joy for breakfast, lunch and dinner.

In spite of that, our breakfasts didn't vary much. Cereal and fruit was just about it. Lunch also varied little—often just a sandwich but extremely tasty, first class. Dinner we largely left to the chef's selection. He had been briefed on what we would and would not eat. Crustaceans and pork were out, as were cucumbers, raw onions, melons and offal of any kind. I wasn't too keen on citrus fruit or berries either. No problem. He didn't as much as blink at the list.

His food was superb and I was amazed at how he cooked twelve perfect soufflés in that relatively small galley oven. I remember he gave a number of our guests cooking lessons. He was generous with his time like that.

JOY CHAMBERS-GRUNDY

One night after the evening meal we invited the chef to have a drink with us and after a glass or two of wine he said, 'I love working for you two but I'm going to leave you one day. My dream is to open a restaurant in London'.

We certainly knew how good his food was and how beautifully he presented each meal. I bet he'll be successful, I thought—maybe we should back him.

But I knew nothing about the restaurant business and, in any case, he might never make the move. We left it at that but we said that if ever he felt he needed help to come back to us. He never needed it! He opened many restaurants and is possibly the best known chef in the world.

His name? Gordon Ramsay.

Gordon has based his fame not only on his skill as a chef, but also on his use of expletives. Yet aboard *Idolwood II* we never heard him say 'damn' or even 'dash'.

There's a little more to the story of Gordon's *Idolwood II* days though.

It was his first transatlantic crossing and a couple of days out from Antigua in the Caribbean, Captain Ginger Steve gathered crew members for drinks on the upper deck to celebrate the crossing. The captain, who could not hold his liquor and would become tipsy even after one or two drinks, was drinking excessively and became aggressive. The women crew members were frightened, and Gordon stepped forward to constrain him. Ginger threw a couple of punches and Gordon replied with a right to the jaw.

Gordon and the chief engineer scooped the captain up and carried him to his cabin. They decided to leave him there to sleep it off. The next day Captain Ginger was still in a fighting mood and they had to lock him up again until the yacht arrived in Nelson's Dockyard in Antigua.

We were not on board and got the news later, secondhand.

It was obvious that he should be relieved of his command so two of our senior executives flew to Fort Lauderdale and removed him from *Idolwood II*. Within days Ginger Steve had skidded his Harley Davidson into a truck on a freeway in Florida and ended his life.

We liked Ginger Steve but he had lived in a world created by his imagination. An unreal world. Just before *Idolwood II* was to leave Europe to cross the Atlantic he had requested leave to visit his girlfriend in France who was having a major operation. Later we were to learn that no such girlfriend existed. He seemed to have lost touch with reality.

The first officer became the temporary captain with unfortunate consequences. He too was a nice guy but not up to the job. In St Thomas in the US Virgin Isles he anchored in the fairway, right in the path of cruise ships. Jerry Pike, who was still chief engineer at the time, had gone ashore and watched aghast, waving to *Idolwood II* to move which, at last, she did.

And there was yet another incident when our temporary captain backed over one of the tenders. The crew stood frozen in place. The woman in charge of the interior, a lovely girl who was the wife of the temporary captain, stood crying.

The tender was fast sinking when the chef left the rest of the crew standing and took action—Gordon dived overboard, bailed the tender out and brought her alongside.

In 1996 we sold *Idolwood II* to Stephen Cannell, a Hollywood writer and novelist who produced many television hits including *Magnum*.

Early in 2009 we were dining at the Peninsula Hotel in Beverly Hills. I was munching on my Cobb salad when we saw Stephen Cannell at another table. Joy thought for a moment and then decided. She marched over and introduced herself. He was pleased to meet her and came over and shook my hand, saying to us, 'We love the boat. Glad we bought it from you'.

YOUNG DOCTORS

It was still the late 1970s. At last we had finished *King's Men* and delivered all thirteen episodes. Now we waited for the verdict.

To renew or not renew.

The phone rang in my office. It was Bruce Gyngell.

'Hi, Reg. I've got Jim McKay with me.'

This was not the Jim McKay who ran QTQ 9 in Brisbane, but another Jim McKay altogether, and the Nine network programmer.

'We've decided not to renew *King's Men*.'

Once again I'm out of drama. Déjà vu! But Bruce was still talking. What did he just say?

'Sorry, I didn't catch that.'

'Jim and I have an idea for another show we want you to make.'

Now I was listening.

'I'm in the program meeting and Kerry and all of us are excited about this concept. We're calling it *Young Doctors*. I'll call you in a few days to go over it.'

Bruce had left Nine to join Seven a few years before. Now he'd moved on again and was acting as a consultant to Kerry Packer while at the same time, and presumably with Kerry's knowledge, also working for me as an adviser.

Bruce had saved my bacon. He'd given me another chance. I'd better get it right this time.

But *Young Doctors*? I couldn't imagine a more banal title. Later I was to realise that it was a perfect title because *Young Doctors* was about, well, young doctors.

And now I come to think about it, *Neighbours* is about neighbours.

Perhaps a couple of our other shows might have worked if their titles had been more explanatory. *Taurus Rising*, for instance, and *Waterloo Station*.

I talked to Reg Watson about *Young Doctors* and he started to develop the concept. I needed to speak to Bruce but he was in Los Angeles. Or somewhere. Nobody seemed to know. At last he phoned and we discussed the heart of the show, the direction it would take. It was to be not too serious. Mostly about the lives and loves of the doctors and the nurses. No heavy medical stuff. Or, as Reg Watson puts it, 'It was slap and tickle and nurses chasing doctors and vice versa'.

Young Doctors was shot at the Eric Porter Studios in North Sydney, not far from our old offices in Miller Street. The studio was dated, and new flooring had to be put down to accommodate the pedestal cameras. When there was heavy rain, the roof leaked and the crew had to run around with buckets and mops. Like most film sound stages, it wasn't fitted out for television. There was no control room. So an OB van ('outside broadcast' unit or mobile control room) arrived and was hooked up every morning.

When I looked at the first episode, I felt it was too soft for an opening show. I called Reg Watson.

'I don't think it's strong enough.'

'You mean you want me to make an entirely new opening ep?'

' 'Fraid so. Punch it up a bit.'

'You're kidding.'

'No, I'm not.'

So he did it: wrote and produced a completely new first episode. The new opening scene showed a young doctor and a very attractive nurse kissing on a hospital operating table. There was a bottle of champagne in a bucket in the foreground. The dialogue left no doubt as to what they'd been up to.

I scratched my head. I hadn't meant it to be that strong. I think it was Reg Watson's 'get even' present but he says:

We had a doctor called Craig Rothwell who had a hobby of seducing nubile young nurses and drinking champagne on the operating table. That's all it was.

REG WATSON

The series was set in the Albert Memorial Hospital. Where was the Albert Memorial Hospital?

We hoped it sounded as though it was in Melbourne, to balance the fact the show was being made in Sydney. The Melbourne versus Sydney feeling did exist—probably still does—and we tried to eliminate it whenever we could.

Later we used the same device in *Sons and Daughters,* with one of the two main families in the show living in Melbourne and the other in Sydney.

At the same time Nine commissioned *Young Doctors,* the network had ordered a continuing drama from Crawford's: *The Sullivans.*

Nine only wanted one serial, but reckoned they had a better chance of a winner if they ordered two shows.

Maybe one would work.

Both shows were transmitted outside the ratings survey period.

Lynton Taylor phoned me and gave me the bad news.

I spoke to my assistant, Di Ayres.

'Di, call Reg Watson and say I want to have lunch with him today. Don't give him a reason. Just get us in somewhere nearby. You be the driver.'

I waited for Reg Watson in the basement car park of Grundy House. As he walked towards me I knew I had to tell him right away.

'They've gone with *The Sullivans. Young Doctors* is through.'

He staggered back as if I'd shot him in the chest. There was not much talk as we were driven to Chatties in nearby Chatswood. We sat opposite each other. Reg looked at me. 'I don't know what else I can do. I really thought it was working.'

'So did I.'

'I'll leave, Reg. There's nothing more I can do.' There was no resentment in his voice.

'I won't accept that,' I said. 'Let's stick together until we get the break we deserve.'

On the weekend I thought of nothing but *Young Doctors.*

By Monday night I had made up my mind. I called Kerry Packer at his home.

'Yes, son, what's on your mind?'

'You know I've always accepted the referee's decision, but not this time.

I reckon *Young Doctors* is working. I can feel it.'

'Do you really mean that, Reg?'

'Yes, I do.'

There was an eternity of silence on the line.

'I reckon you're right. I think it's working too. Call me at eleven on Thursday morning.'

When Thursday morning came I was running a meeting on the verandah of our house on Pittwater. I remember John Fowler was there. He'd been general manager at ADS 7 in Adelaide before joining us. Lynton Taylor, who had been his program manager for years, was now working for Kerry Packer. Joy was somewhere in the house packing because we were leaving for Hawaii and the USA later that day.

My mind was not focusing on the discussion. I was thinking about the call I had to make. At 11 am I left the meeting and I phoned Kerry's office. There was a delay putting me through.

It was Kerry's voice. 'You're two minutes late, son. Too bad.' Then he laughed. 'No, it's good news. We've decided to keep *Young Doctors* going.'

I didn't know what to say and blurted out, 'I'm leaving for Honolulu in a couple of hours'.

'Have a good holiday. You deserve it.'

I was ready to break up. It was a miracle. I walked back to the verandah. John Fowler and the others looked at me questioningly. I nodded. There were tears in my eyes and, I fancy, in the eyes of those around the table. We had worked so hard and now we had a reprieve.

The wrap party for the series was in progress at Eric Porter Studios. It was a pretty miserable affair. The cast and crew all believed the show was finished. Suddenly Lynton Taylor turned up, unannounced and unexpected.

'Sorry to interrupt but I've got some news you might be interested in.'

There was silence in the studio.

'*Young Doctors* is going ahead.'

The silence continued for a moment. Then there was cheering and laughter.

The wake became a riotous celebration.

Over its run, *Young Doctors* featured thirty-five doctors and about twenty-eight members of the nursing staff. Was there ever a hospital with a staff ratio like it? Some actors were in it when it started and still there when it ended. Gwen Plumb, Lyn James, Alfred Sandor and Tim Page, for instance. Seasoned performers who never let us down.

But it was the young and good-looking actors who attracted the audience. Well, that's a bit of a stretch. Some of the male *Young Doctors* were pop stars, hardly actors. But the audience lapped it up.

I played Dr Robin Porter in the Young Doctors *for the last couple of years it aired. My love interest was played by Eric Oldfield. I remember being out to lunch with him one day and a woman came over and told us about her brother's illness, asking us what to do about it. We were polite and said we were sorry but we couldn't help.*

'But you're both doctors,' she replied, amazed.

JOY CHAMBERS-GRUNDY

I remember going to St Vincent's Hospital to visit a friend. A couple of young nurses bailed me up.

'Aren't you the guy who makes *Young Doctors*?'

I admitted that I was.

'Well, let us tell you it's a load of rubbish.'

Pause.

'But we wouldn't miss it.'

They giggled and moved away.

After *Young Doctors* finished its run, Nine executives would say to me, 'You know, we should never have taken it off'.

Network executives have to make tough decisions—whether to stay with a show or let it go. But it's no consolation to a producer to hear that kind of remark.

Young Doctors ran for 1396 episodes before finally closing in 1983. It was

Australia's longest-running serial until it was overtaken by another Reg Watson hit, *Neighbours*.

Young Doctors, the little show that became a massive hit, did not win a single award over its long run. The audience loved it.

I was simply entertaining people, and that's all I ever wanted to do.

THE RESTLESS YEARS

It was still the 1970s. I was looking for a producer to give our company a bit more life, a bit more experience, especially as we were planning to try our hand at comedy.

Bob Crystal recommended Howard Leeds who had been executive producer and head writer for *The Brady Bunch, Different Strokes, The Ghost and Mrs Muir*. He developed hit series like *Facts of Life* and *Silver Spoons*. He had written for *Barney Miller, Bewitched*, the *Phil Silvers Show, The Dick Van Dyke Show* and so on. He had even produced and written specials for Red Skelton, Bob Hope, Jack Benny, Dean Martin, Frank Sinatra, Lucille Ball, Fred Astaire, Mary Martin and many more.

He arrived in Sydney to work for us in 1976 with his latest wife; I think he had been married a few times.

Class of '74 had ended in disaster because of the Control Board's interference but I wasn't prepared to let go of the concept. I contacted Ron Casey at Seven in Melbourne, who had been threatened by the Mother Superior, and he and Ted Thomas, who had become general manager of ATN 7 in Sydney, came to a meeting in my office. I convinced them that a similar idea played later in the night as a one-hour series rather than a serial drama, had a lot of potential. I called it *Glenview High*.

Howard Leeds produced the first episode and it certainly had style. He used a lot of techniques that were comparatively new to us. But somehow the show didn't really work; whether it was because Ron McLean's scripts lacked the warmth of Reg Watson's work, or whether it was because of the American influence, I don't know.

It wasn't much of a start for Howard.

Next I came up with an idea which I proposed to Ian Holmes who was then running the Ten network.

'How about an Australian *Carry On*-style special, like the British movies? We'll get together the most popular comics in Australia, both men and women, and put them into a TV movie.'

Yes, they were all in it and so was Joy, who was appearing in *The Celebrity Game*, a charades show on Channel Ten Sydney at the time.

So here I had an American producing a show that was based entirely on English comedy with mostly Australian actors. It was a mishmash, but in spite of everything *All at Sea,* the TV movie, got a twenty-one rating which these days would be a hit but back then was just okay.

Howard had struck out again.

He had made a comedy pilot in America years before which was based on the concept of a beautiful woman who was, in fact, a robot. We did an Australian version, *Million Dollar Baby*. Jimmy Hannan was the star and was pretty darned good, but Ian Holmes rejected it and it went nowhere. I previewed it recently and thought it was funny, clever and well directed. Jimmy Hannan was ideal as the unsophisticated, bumbling guy who had a fixation on a woman who was not really a woman but a robot.

Howard Leeds was with me from 1976 to 1978. In spite of his colossal CV, I was not able to capitalise on his obvious talent during that time, although *Glenview High* was to lead to our next major success.

Ian Holmes was still running Channel Ten Sydney and told me he wanted a serial drama for prime time and had something like Jane Austen in mind.

I walked around all weekend hoping something would come to me and finally rang Reg Watson and asked him over to discuss it. I told him I had this idea about a group of kids leaving school.

'And we follow them for the rest of their lives. What do you think?'

'Could work.'

'And we call it *The Restless Years*.'

'Might even be good.' Reg Watson grinned at me.

I always like it when he agrees with me. The only thing wrong with our relationship has always been that we have the same first name. It's never been a problem for us—we always know which of us is speaking—but it's certainly been a problem for others. So these days I call him Reg and he calls me RG.

We were both right. *The Restless Years* was a hit. I'm not sure it had much connection to Jane Austen, but it ran from 1977 to 1981.

Joy played the role of Rita Merrick, the Madam. She had gone to the audition wearing a black curly wig, very different from her own blonde hair. When Peter Skelton at Channel Ten saw the audition tape, he said, 'This girl is good but it's funny because she really reminds me of somebody'.

Joy made her acting debut in *The Restless Years*, then later joined the long-running *Young Doctors*. Her longest running role was fourteen years as Rosemary Daniels in *Neighbours*.

She was never late, always early. Didn't wear expensive clothes and, most importantly, always knew her lines. She was Joy, not Mrs Reg Grundy.

The cast and crew always accepted me as an actor. I am grateful for that. I was treated the same as everyone else and that's how I wanted it. In fact, for many years on Neighbours, *most of the younger cast had no idea I was married to Reg. I recall one of them finding out and she came to me in the canteen and with a look of awe said, 'Joy, is it true? Are you really married to Reg Grundy?'*

JOY CHAMBERS-GRUNDY

At least one of her off-camera experiences in *The Restless Years* was as bizarre as her on-camera storylines.

I was attending a Restless Years *function one night and had taken the black wig I always wore—as Rita Merrick—to be set at the Kings Cross hairdressers who were credited on the show. They fitted and styled the wig for me and I walked out looking exactly like Rita. I did not have to go far to go to my parked car which was perhaps two hundred yards away.*

Suddenly two women in very short minis appeared out of a doorway in front of me. Their profession was obvious.

'Rita!' one shouted.

A Restless Years *storyline going to air at the time featured Rita having difficulty controlling some of her 'girls' so I was a little apprehensive. I needn't have worried.*

'We're on your side,' said the first one. The other woman poked me in the shoulder. 'You pay their wages. They should bloody well do what you say.'

I said, 'Thank you, I appreciate your attitude', and hurried off to where I'd parked the car. I hoped they weren't following because my yellow Jag would only confirm that I was Rita.

It was my first experience of the way people sometimes can't distinguish between the actor and the character. It sure makes you wonder.

Joy Chambers-Grundy

The Restless Years was remade by Grundy in the Netherlands as Goede Tijden, Slechte Tijden and in Germany as Gute Zeiten, Schlechte Zeiten. Both mean 'Good Times, Bad Times', although a more accurate translation would be 'The Best of Times and the Worst of Times'. The Dutch and German shows are still running, still rating and still carrying the Grundy name.

So Class of '74 begat Glenview High which begat The Restless Years. They appealed to the demographics advertisers wanted to reach. I never gave that a thought.

KEEP THROWING PUNCHES:
A SALESMAN'S WAY

My grandfather, John Grundy, was a mildly spoken, mild-mannered young man who earned his living as a Singer sewing machine salesman in Albury.

When he drove up to a house in his sulky pulled by a grey mare, he made sure that he opened the front gate slowly, then turned around and gently closed it. You never knew when the lady of the house might be peering through the lace curtains at you.

It was good manners and good business. He sold a lot of sewing machines. With his winning ways and his sartorial splendour he became known as Flash Jack, an unusual nickname for a Salvation Army officer.

The art of selling has been a large part of my life too. I don't know how much I absorbed from Grandfather Grundy but, as a salesman, I have certainly tried to close any metaphorical gates left open and, even today, you will rarely see me without a suit and tie.

My formal education ended when I left school at fifteen but my education about life has never stopped.

Some people have described me as a compulsive perfectionist, and maybe that's so. I will accept that I am a workaholic. I guess these days Joy is the same—she writes masterly fact-based fiction, and all our offices or studies are side by side. The proximity works for us—we like to be together.

It's true that I have never had a day off. How can you take a day off from life? But I guess, in my case, it means that there has never been a day when I wasn't trying to achieve something, make some sort of progress.

I don't see it as a virtue or as a sin; it's just the way I am, the way I want to be.

In my effort to do better, I didn't read the Greek philosophers or the other great thinkers. Rather, I turned to populists—writers whose simple advice had appealed to millions of people. Maybe it gives an insight into my attitude to television. I had no desire to win awards, or be admired by elitists, but simply to entertain. I wanted to look at television through the eyes of the average person and most of the time I seemed to be able to do that.

The truth is that Elmer Wheeler, Dale Carnegie and another down-to-earth American, Benjamin Franklin, were the people who influenced me.

Elmer Wheeler coined the phrase 'Sell the sizzle, not the steak'. I kept that concept in mind whether I was trying to sell a show or sell advertising time.

And that's not the only trick of the trade.

Ian Kennon, who was managing director of Channel Ten in the late 1970s, said to *Sunday Age* journalist Roff Smith:

> *Quite simply, Reg is the best salesman I've ever known. One of the great tricks of successful selling is to get your potential customer to agree with you on a few points. Reg has that knack. He came into my office, we had a cup of coffee and he began to discuss the concept of the show.*
>
> *By the end of the discussion, when the contract papers came out, he had you in the position of feeling like a fool if you said no. After all, you'd been agreeing with him all afternoon.*
>
> IAN KENNON

'Yes' rather than 'no' responses make it hard for the buyer to say 'no' when the crucial invitation to buy is made. It seems that many of the program managers and heads of networks knew that I used this technique, yet it seemed to go on working anyway.

I was selling ideas, of course—intangible concepts—and if those concepts had failed when turned into TV shows, then the 'yes' technique was of no value. The Grundy track record of many more successful shows than ones that failed legitimised my sales approach.

A little imagination helps.

In 1969, Bruce Gyngell was on the early TAA flight from Sydney to Melbourne. So was I, but Bruce didn't know it.

'Morning, Bruce,' I said, as he walked down the aisle towards me. 'Believe you're sitting in this one.' I pointed to the vacant seat beside me.

'How the hell did you organise this?'

'Well, your secretary and my secretary were having a chat the other day and your secretary …'

'All right, all right. What do you want?'

'No, Bruce, it's not what I want; it's what you need.'

As the aircraft started to descend we shook hands. I had sold him another show.

Dale Carnegie wrote two books that sold millions of copies and are still read: *How to Win Friends and Influence People* and *How to Stop Worrying and Start Living*. Joy's read them, and when I'm worried about something Joy keeps reminding me: 'Stop worrying and start living'.

These titles, which became catch phrases, are clichés—overused figures of speech. But why are clichés used so frequently? Because they are often the most succinct, most appropriate expression to use.

I sold a lot of advertising, and influenced a lot of television executives to buy my shows, because of those clichés and the intrinsic commonsense ideas behind them.

And I was influenced by that great American, a man for all seasons, Benjamin Franklin. He came up with a way to improve himself by preparing a list of thirteen of his weaknesses which he wished to turn into thirteen virtues. Each week, he concentrated on one 'virtue', noting each time that he deviated from it.

At the end of thirteen weeks, he started all over again and tried to improve on his performance in the previous cycle.

The virtues could be as simple as …

Be punctual.

Don't argue.

And so on.

For years I practised the technique and hopefully benefited from it.

And then there was Edward de Bono, who coined the phrase 'lateral thinking'—finding a solution by looking at the problem in a different way.

I've been described as being a lateral thinker. I hope I am. I certainly try to be.

And I've always tried to remember these maxims:

'Your first ten words are more important than your next 10,000.'

'People seldom want to walk over you until you lie down.'

'Our main business is not to see what lies dimly at a distance but to do what lies clearly at hand.'

'Live in day-tight compartments.'

'Don't sell the steak, sell the sizzle.'

And, of course, 'Keep throwing punches', which has become a catch phrase of mine, I suppose.

It was way back in the early 1950s when I started using that expression. Bernie Stapleton, the chief at 2SM, had used it and I had thrown it back at him to get the okay to fly to Johannesburg for the Carruthers fight. I wanted to become someone of consequence, but was often as nervous as hell.

In spite of my anxieties, I settled down and by 1964 was making sixteen half hours of television a week. Then I lost the lot, but I kept 'throwing punches'.

I got another chance at QTQ in Brisbane and moved on from then. Things picked up so much and we were having such success in Australia that I decided to take the plunge and get into American television.

I kept flying to America and returning to Australia time after time with my tail between my legs.

I asked myself, 'Why am I doing this? I'm established in Australia now. People know me. Yet I'm beating my brains out trying to hit the jackpot in America.'

And whenever I decided to throw in the towel, I remembered: 'Keep throwing punches'.

The knockbacks in America were enormous. But I knew that no matter how tough it was, I would never break through if I stopped trying.

Even though *Prisoner*, our Australian women in prison drama, was sold to KTLA Los Angeles in the late 1970s, it took me ten years to convince the US networks that I had the ability and knowhow to produce locally made American television for them. A decade is a long time, but it was worth the effort.

BLANKETY BLANKS

One of the greatest American game shows of all time was *Match Game*, which ran for twenty years. Robert Noah, who joined me after I set up my American production company, had been executive producer of *Match Game* through all those years.

I had always wanted to make it in Australia but knew that the host would have to be an extraordinary performer with a great comedy sense and wonderful timing. There was only one in Australia who sprang to mind, and he had never hosted a game show.

I had seen Graham Kennedy perform many times as the star of *In Melbourne Tonight*. His television personality and cheeky comedy style had captured the Melbourne audience.

He gave his advertisers a hard time. I was at GTV one night when he produced a bag of chips during the show, emptied the contents onto his desk, smashed it all into a mound of tiny pieces, poured it back into the bag and displayed the bag with a tiny bulge in the bottom.

'See? That's what you get for your money.'

The chip-maker didn't complain. Sales actually went up.

On another occasion, holding a can to camera he said, 'Campbell's tomato soup, with just a hint of cardboard'.

It appeared he could do almost anything and get away with it.

But he couldn't.

In 1975 he was fired from *In Melbourne Tonight* over the infamous crow call incident. His crow call certainly did sound like the notorious four–letter word and people had objected. It wasn't the first time he'd done it either but on this occasion he was jumped on by the Broadcasting Control Board and banned from live television indefinitely.

In the 1960s Graham appeared briefly in one episode of the *Ampol Big Game*, a Grundy show which I personally produced in the same studio where he had made his name. Graham played himself that night, wearing a specially tailored St Kilda Australian Rules outfit. He was on camera for about thirty seconds. In spite of the brevity he was the best thing that happened in a terrible series.

As well as having him in mind for *Match Game*, I wanted to use him as a panellist on *Celebrity Squares*, a game show hosted by Jimmy Hannan, which featured all the usual show-biz suspects seated in a large construction of nine squares.

Celebrity Squares ran on Nine so I rang Lynton Taylor, my friend and the Nine programmer, to see if Graham would be acceptable to the network as a host after being taken off in Melbourne. Lynton said the crow call was GTV business and nothing to do with TCN. TCN was producing a network show and GTV could like it or lump it. So yes, Graham was acceptable.

One of the other panellists on *Celebrity Squares* was Don Lane, who'd taken over as the host of *In Melbourne Tonight* when Graham had been fired. Not surprisingly, Graham wasn't fond of him.

Celebrity Squares was produced by Tony Connelly, who says:

On recording days, we used to have lunch at TCN in the little boardroom and Don said, 'I want to do the Match Game'. *I pointed out that he was already doing* IMT *and* Celebrity Squares *and didn't he think he might be a little over-exposed? 'No,' said Don, 'I want to do it.'*

Kennedy came to me later and said, 'What the fuck's the Match Game?'*

TONY CONNELLY

Tony reported back to me and we sent off a tape to Kennedy. I just knew he was right for *Match Game*, which would have a new title if I produced it for Nine.

Kennedy was a difficult, temperamental man. It wouldn't be easy to sign him up but it was worth a try. I invited him for a day on the boat. We flew him up from Melbourne and made sure he got first-class treatment. He was met at Sydney Airport by my uniformed chauffeur and driven to Bayview in my 1972 green Rolls Royce. A beautiful car.

He was clearly impressed. So were we.

He was immaculately dressed, resplendent in cream trousers, a polka dot scarf around his neck and a double-breasted yachting jacket with brass buttons adorned with gold anchors. He looked a treat, if a touch overdressed for a casual Sunday afternoon cruise.

I bet he's had this gear tailored just for today, I thought.

Graham knew and liked Tony Connelly, the proposed producer of the coming show, so Tony was aboard the boat with Joy and myself. We explained the format to Graham and Tony said, 'Graham, if you do the show, it'll go through the roof'.

I added, 'We'll use the best comics in Australia—anyone you like. How about Stuart Wagstaff, Noeline Brown …?'

Joy said, 'What about Ugly Dave Gray? Maybe you could do a spot with him.'

Graham looked interested.

I asked for his thoughts about the show. We all hung on his every word. I poured him more champagne. He finally said yes.

I approached Ian Holmes, who had become the CEO at Channel Ten in Sydney. Ian knew Kennedy's pulling power. He had been at GTV 9 during the heyday of *In Melbourne Tonight*.

He knew the show had a good chance and he was easily sold.

'It's a marvellous idea, Reg, but I wouldn't want to call it *Match Game*. Don't want the word "Game" in the title. You're supposed to have all the bright ideas. What do you think?'

I was a step ahead of him. 'Well, when the host asks a question of the players they all have to fill in the blank, so how about *Blankety Blanks*?'

Ian laughed. 'That's it.'

We shook hands.

Blankety Blanks went to air in 1977. It was vaudeville/music hall stuff. And Australians laughed their heads off.

Before the show started, Ian Holmes called me.

'I want to run an idea past you. What if I put *Blankety Blanks* in at 7.30 pm? If it works, we'll disrupt the other networks' hour shows, and the rest of the night will be ours because the audience will stay.'

'I can't answer that, Ian. I make shows for everyone.'

'Yes, I know. But imagine you didn't. What would you think then?'

'In that case, I'd probably say it was worth a try.'

We already had *Celebrity Game* at 7 pm, the charades show Joy was in, and now we had *Blankety Blanks* at 7.30. But the *Blankety Blanks* ratings, while good, were not quite good enough.

Ian and I were on the Hawkesbury cruising along in *Carolyn J* one beautiful Sydney weekend. As we approached Cottage Point he became serious. 'I'm worried about *Blankety Blanks*,' he told me. 'I'm going to have to end the 7.30 experiment.'

'Give it time. *Blanks* will pick up.'

'I'm not cancelling it.'

'You'd be mad to.'

'So what do I do? Should I move *Celebrity Game* to 5.30 and put *Blanks* in at 7 pm, or do I put *Blanks* in at 5.30 and leave *Celebrity Game* at 7 pm?'

'No contest, Ian. *Celebrity Game* should go to 5.30 and *Blanks* should move to 7.00.'

Ian smiled. 'Exactly what I'm going to do. Just thought I'd try you out. You passed the test.'

The changes were made. *Celebrity Game*, the charades show, went to 5.30 pm. Joy was happy that at least it had not been cancelled and no doubt so too were the other regulars: Joe Martin, Johnny Pace, Harriet and host Mike Preston.

At 7 pm, *Blankety Blanks* was a sensation. I'm told Dave Gray and Graham Kennedy had been disappointed with the early ratings in the later slot, and declared they'd make the comedy more important than the game. Many people believe that's what happened.

Recently I looked at a few of the 7.30 shows and compared them with a number that went to air at seven o'clock. The comedy was exactly the same. Terrific. Graham and Dave didn't realise that it was the move to 7 pm that made the difference in the ratings. It was the perfect timeslot for it. Guess that's why Ian and I made the decisions and they got the laughs.

Kennedy appeared to break the rules, but did not. He was meticulous in regard to the format. He simply overlaid the game with his own brand of outrageous humour.

In 1978, Graham Kennedy received the treasured Gold Logie and said: 'I want to thank me for having faith in the Reg Grundy Organisation'.

Graham was the heart of *Blankety Blanks*. Without him we really didn't have a show, so we tended to get a little nervous when contract renewal time came round.

Which brings me to Harry M. Miller, the talent agent and entrepreneur, and to Computicket, a name that's likely to haunt poor Harry for the rest of his life.

I was in London with Barry Weston who was one of my senior people at the time. I asked him to fly home via South Africa because a couple of guys there were interested in doing a joint venture with us. While he was in Johannesburg, Barry noticed computer devices printing out theatre tickets on almost every corner. This popular service was called Computicket. Barry thought it was a good idea and registered the name 'Computicket' for us when he got back to Australia. We approached a number of theatre companies but none were keen and we lost interest, though we retained the name.

A while later we were making *Blankety Blanks* and it was time to renew Graham's contract. Harry Miller represented him, so Barry Weston went to see him, taking along a new contract.

The contract offered something reasonable for the times but Harry was not pleased. He pointed out that the ratings were going sky-high and he had in mind an extra $1000 plus two round-the-world airfares. I said I'd have to go back and consult.

I got back to the office and my secretary was white faced. 'Harry Miller was just on the phone. He's furious. I think he wants to kill you.'

I had no idea what it was about, but had her get him for me.

'What's the problem, Harry?'

'You bastard. I've invested a million bucks in Computicket and now I find you own the name.'

'That's right.'

'Well, I want it and I'm prepared to make an offer.'

'That's easy,' I said. 'There's a contract for Graham on your desk. Just sign it.'

And he did. He got Computicket and we got Kennedy.

BARRY WESTON

I think we got the better end of the deal.

In 1983 we played host to a group of BBC executives on *Carolyn J.* They said they were starting a new show based on the American *Match Game*, which of course was our *Blankety Blanks*.

'We've come up with a clever title; we're calling it *Blankety Blank*.'

How original, I thought, but kept my mouth shut. The sun was shining, the water was sparkling. No need to spoil the day. And to be fair, the BBC was not using my title. Not quite. They'd left the 's' off 'Blanks'.

Anyway, it wasn't the first time I'd been imitated.

I have had a moustache for most of my adult life. A couple of times I've shaved it off, and surveyed the great expanse of my upper lip. I remember doing it one New Year's Day, and Joy looked at me and said, 'I don't know you'. That was enough. I immediately started growing it again.

Swine flu is contagious and so it seems was growing a moustache back in those days.

Hair on the upper lip started to sprout among the higher echelon executives. Bill Mason and Ian Holmes fell into the trap and so did Andrew Brooke, who was one of my top producers and who would spend years in Europe with Grundy Worldwide and eventually run Grundy in Australia.

Around that same time in the 1970s, even Jog—who had moved on from the organisation years earlier—grew a moustache in remembrance of the good old days.

But there were renegades who bucked the system: Kerry Wright, Mike Murphy and one other.

'Look,' he said, 'having the same bloody first name is enough.'

Reg Watson was that man.

When Kennedy tired of *Blankety Blanks*, Ian and I agreed there was no point in the show continuing. Who could follow Graham Kennedy? There was no one.

We had made 500 hilarious episodes.

There may not have been any at all if Don Lane hadn't said he wanted to do it, and Graham hadn't overheard him.

DOCUMENTARIES

Englishman Ted Morrisby arrived in Australia with a great reputation as a BBC documentary maker.

In 1973 his first assignment for me was to produce a documentary based on a real-life story.

Wreck of the Batavia was the true story of the Dutch ship which was wrecked in the seventeenth century on the Abrolhos Islands off the West Australian coast. It featured Jeronimus Cornelisz, a Dutch East India Company official who set up a reign of terror in which many of the survivors were murdered.

Ted went to the Abrolhos Islands to make it and as I looked at the material as it came in, I became more and more concerned. I got in touch with Bruce Beresford, who was already a pretty hot director at that time, and he flew to the Abrolhos Islands and took over. He did a great job, with the exception of one scene where there were a number of women frolicking in the sea completely nude. The problem was that they had white marks on their bodies where their bikinis should have been, and this was supposed to be 1629! A little Max Factor would have taken care of that.

Edwin 'Ted' Morrisby took credits as producer and writer.

Ted later told the press that he had created many things that he did not create, and he also said he had been a great asset to me.

Ronnie Biggs is remembered for his role in the Great Train Robbery of 1963 when 2.6 million pounds were stolen. It was a huge robbery for the time and made all the English papers and the world's press.

In 1964 Ronnie was arrested and sent to Wandsworth Prison for thirty years. Fifteen months later, with three other prisoners, he used a rope ladder to climb over the wall and land beside three waiting escape cars. In spite of massive police surveillance he managed to leave England and cross the channel to France, where he had plastic surgery to his face and acquired new identity papers.

He then travelled to Australia and got a job as a stagehand at GTV 9 Melbourne where we produced many shows. It is likely that Biggs was a stagehand on one or more Grundy productions without us realising who he was.

Finally he made his way to Brazil, where he lived for thirty-two years.

By about 1977, Biggs was looking for money. He'd been on the run for years and had spent most of his share of the proceeds from the robbery. Bill Bemister was an English investigative reporter who had lined up Biggs and his wife and approached us to make a documentary. I gave Ian Holmes the thumbs up and he signed the project over to Barry Sloane, a freelance director/producer who had worked with us before.

And so the adventure started. And nearly stopped.

Brazil was the problem. I don't really know why, but I think it's safe to assume that although there was no extradition treaty between the two countries, Britain would have been putting a lot of pressure on Brazil to get Biggs back. Nobody wanted him turned into an international star.

Before landing in Brazil, Barry came up with a false name for the project— *Brazil the Beautiful Country*—to throw off the Brazilian authorities.

The shooting began.

Barry had to be careful so he often hid the camera in a paper bag when shooting in public to avoid the risk of being arrested. Getting the film out of Brazil was also dangerous. It was done piecemeal by using various sources. Often dummy film cans were left in hotel rooms for authorities to find and seize, which they sometimes did. Code words were used in communications with Australia.

'Weather' meant Biggs. 'Summer cold' meant trouble with authorities. 'Happy birthday' meant film had left for Los Angeles.

Sloane and his crew finally flew to London in the hope of getting an interview with Detective Chief Superintendent Jack Slipper, the famous Slipper of the Yard, who had been relentlessly chasing Biggs for years.

One night Barry returned to his hotel in London to see a man coming out of his room. The stranger said, 'I wouldn't go ahead with the film if I were you.' And disappeared.

They didn't get the interview with Slipper. They never found out who the mysterious man was, either, although I wouldn't mind betting he represented the British authorities in some way. MI5 perhaps?

Overall, there had been almost as much drama and tension in making the documentary as there was in the Great Train Robbery itself. Back in Australia we were on tenterhooks worrying and wondering whether our film team would end up in gaol—or worse!

Confessions of Ronald Biggs had been a coup, a ninety-minute documentary for Network Ten. Sloane and cameraman Tony Wilson and sound recordist John Oakley had spent two and a half weeks with Biggs. There's an entry in my diary to say that the cost was $100,608.

Biggs got nothing—that would be illegal. Any payments that may or may not have been made could have been to his wife and son.

That was another matter.

Bruce Beresford and Bill Anderson, the same William Anderson who is now a respected Hollywood cutter, were working out of our North Sydney office making commercials. During that time Bruce wrote and directed *Poor Fella Me* for the Grundy Organisation, tracing the effect of white settlement on the Aboriginal population.

Bruce introduced me to Peter Weir, who gave me the manuscript of *The Cars That Ate Paris*, which I read … and passed. It was Peter's first full-length feature film and became an underground cult classic, a low-budget black comedy about the inhabitants of a small country town who deliberately caused fatal car crashes and lived off the proceeds. It was a minor success in cinemas but proved very popular on the then-thriving drive-in movie circuit. The drive-ins came and went in Australia like a summer storm but they were red-hot business for a few years, with the unofficial slogan of 'You can drink, you can smoke, you can even slash the seats'. They disappeared almost overnight, driven out of business by the VCR and high land values.

The following year Bruce directed *Barry McKenzie Holds His Own*, which was fully funded by me.

Bruce Beresford worked on three scripts for me in our new north shore apartment which we never got around to furnishing before selling: *Cowra Break Out*, *Black Out Murders* and *Smithy*, based on the life of Sir Charles Kingsford Smith—all dramatised documentaries.

I remember sitting with Bruce Beresford and Ken G. Hall in our tiny theatre in Grundy House, watching the movie *Smithy*, which KG had directed.

I looked at the two of them. The past and the future.

Finally, we made none of those three documentaries. Others produced their own versions. They all failed to break even at the box office. I saved a lot of money.

Bruce talked to me about *Breaker Morant*. He was $50,000 short. I thought about it, but decided I needed every penny for my own productions. *Breaker Morant* became one of the best Australian movies ever made.

We made a documentary called *Killers of the Great Barrier Reef* for Gold Key (USA). It's not on the Queensland Tourist Bureau's playlist of all-time greats, but the theme of animals as cold-blooded killers out to get us is becoming familiar in many pop docos.

I still remember the scene where a scientist is standing in the water, discussing jellyfish. 'You've got to be careful with these little blokes; they can give you a painful … Ouch!'

We didn't make many documentaries, but the few we did were pretty good.

ON THE INSIDE: PRISONER

I had always been leery of systems that predicted the rating value of a television show. They invariably relied on information given by people who had been shown a sample episode.

In my experience, they lied about what they watched.

At cocktail parties when people were introduced to me they would often say, 'Oh, are you the man who makes those television shows?'

And after I had graciously acknowledged that I was, they would continue, 'Well, actually I don't watch much television. Only the news and sometimes a good documentary'.

I'd smile agreeably as they gave me a blow-by-blow rundown on all the shows they'd viewed the previous night.

And then I met an Englishman named Mike Firman, who had come up with a way to analyse the elements in a television show. If a drama rated highly it indicated that another show with similar elements had a chance of doing well. It was amazingly accurate. He called it TAPE (Television Assessment Production Elements).

Mike and I hit it off. I used TAPE to assess many of our ideas and the association was very successful.

One Sunday in the 1970s, *Carolyn J* was hanging off a mooring in Refuge Bay, just round West Head from Pittwater. Mike Firman, Joy and I were having lunch. The sun was shining, the water was like glass. All's right with the world, I thought. But of course someone else had used that line before.

'So, Mike, what do we do for an encore? *Young Doctors* is doing well and we're all confident that *Restless Years* will work. What's next?'

We threw around a lot of ideas and then one of us said the magic words, 'women in prison'.

As I am telling this story and dear Mike Firman has long ago left this planet, it would be easy for me to take the credit for the idea. Well, it had to be one of us. So, as Mike and I often came up with the same ideas, let's call it a draw.

Mike was having his say. 'There's something that appeals to the mass audience about women in confinement. What must it be like to be locked up without men? How must a woman feel who is confined and can't be with her children?'

We talked on and on.

First thing the next morning I called Reg Watson and Ian Holmes and talked up the idea.

'Let's get something down that we can show the networks.'

Later, Reg Watson and I put our heads together. Reg said, 'I agree it's got potential, but what about longevity? I reckon I can get thirteen weeks out of it and that's all.'

Even he got it wrong sometimes. *Prisoner* was to run for seven years and 692 episodes.

Reg Watson went to Corrective Services and asked if they could put him in touch with a woman who had spent a long time in prison. They introduced him to Hazel, who lived in Villawood.

Reg says:

We pull up outside these one-bedroom units and there is everybody's grandmother standing at the top of the stairs. She waves and we go in and she is immaculate, all ironed and starched.

'Hazel,' I say, 'is there anything you don't want me to ask you?'

'You can ask me anything you like.'

'Well … um … what did you do?'

'I didn't do anything. I was completely innocent.'

'Well, what did they say you did?'

'They said there were these shearers and there was a misunderstanding and they were poisoned.'

And then she says: 'Oh, please excuse me, I haven't offered you a cup of tea. And I've made you some cakes'.

REG WATSON

Reg reluctantly had the tea and cake and on the way home he said to the young female researcher who was with him, 'What do you think? Do you think she's innocent?'

'Oh, yes, I'm sure she is.'

'So do I. I think she's totally inno— … aaargh …'

He grabbed his stomach and collapsed. Horror from the researcher, much mirth from Reg.

Watson sent a car for Hazel and brought her to the office to see the initial episode. At the first break, she said, 'Well, you've got it right so far'.

Hazel's stories were solid gold but there were some Reg Watson couldn't use. This one, for example: 'When women wanted sex they would use toilet rolls to block the toilet and the plumber would know what he was really going inside for'.

It's true that Reg didn't use this in *Prisoner,* but he used a similar idea in *Dangerous Women*, the syndicated series we produced in Los Angeles. A young handsome electrician was often called to the prison to fix a fault in the wiring. And that's not all he fixed.

Reg wrote an opening two-hour episode and prepared an outline for sixteen (not thirteen) episodes. I remember reading that stunning first script under a banyan tree on the big island of Hawaii. I was back in Sydney before the pitch of *Prisoner* was made to the Ten network.

Peter Skelton remembers:

The meeting was at the Menzies Hotel above Wynyard, with execs from all the affiliates present including Wilf Barker who was then sales manager of ATV 0 in Melbourne. Like most meetings it droned on through the day and was mainly about how great the sales departments were doing. But around three in the afternoon 'new program proposals' came up on the agenda. This was my particular area and my recommendation was usually accepted without much question, although often some anti-Sydney comments from Melbourne people could be expected.

Peter had been certain he'd get a pilot commitment from the network.

He turned up at our home in Bayview that night to break the news to me. I was shocked because we had believed it was a done deal. So, of course, had Peter.

He said, 'Are you prepared to leave the concept with Ten for three months? If you do, I reckon I'll get it through.'

The next day we talked about it at the office and decided to take a chance and leave *Prisoner* with him.

Not everyone was as confident of that first script as I was and after the executives at Channel Ten had read it they came down with a bad case of cold feet.

Reg Watson and producer Ian Bradley, who had worked his way up from being the floor manager on *Young Doctors* and was to make many fine shows for us including the drama *Embassy,* were called to a meeting at Channel Ten in Melbourne. They were told that Ten planned to give the pilot script to some American woman who was supposed to be a hot shot on soaps.

Reg Watson wasn't impressed.

So Reg Watson's scripts were used and Ian Bradley produced them and the show got off to a whopping start. Later Reg Watson was to be followed by Godfrey Phillips as executive producer.

I was realising the importance of music in my TV shows and *Prisoner* was no exception.

If you hear the *Prisoner* song from another room you know you've missed the show. 'He used to bring me roses, I wish he would again'—a beautiful, haunting melody written by Allan Caswell and sung by Lynette Hamilton. Yes, that song was played at the end of each episode. Not at the beginning. Except for one special episode when the song itself was the storyline.

But if you're a *Neighbours* fan and you hear the theme from another room, you know the show's about to start.

We wrote individual themes for all of our dramas and a lot of our game shows. The talented Peter Pinne, who was later to run our South American operation, composed the appealing *Sons and Daughters* theme and many others in collaboration with Don Battye, another very capable Grundy producer. 'Sons and Daughters' came out as a single in Great Britain in 1984 and the record reached sixty-seven in the Top Seventy-five.

Prisoner pre-production happened with my knowledge but without my presence. I was out of Australia by the end of February that year. As usual, Joy and I were living in the air, flying between LA and New York, New York and London, and LA and Sydney while I tried to establish myself with the heavy hitters.

PRISONER: CELL BLOCK H

I was still throwing punches, trying to get a foothold in local American television, when *Prisoner* went to air in Australia in February 1979.

It was Tom McManus, not I, who landed one right on the button. Tom had been in charge of international sales for NBC for many years and had now joined me. Mike Firman from TAPE had suggested to me that we should try and sell *Prisoner* to KTLA, an independent television station in Los Angeles, and Tom followed up.

When he called to tell me an American station was buying the Australian tapes, I was beside myself.

It took a while, but KTLA Los Angeles eventually took twenty-six episodes to start with and only the title was changed to avoid confusion with Britain's Patrick McGoohan classic, *The Prisoner*. As Bob Crystal says, 'They wouldn't let the title fly in the United States. It was too close to McGoohan's drama. So Reg Watson came up with *Prisoner: Cell Block H*. H was for Hell.'

KTLA was owned by Gene Autry. Famous in the 1940s, 1950s and 1960s, Autry—along with Roy Rogers, whom he despised—invented the singing B-movie Western. He was billed as 'the Singing Cowboy' in the ninety-three movies in which he starred. I half expected to find his horse, the legendary Champion, stuffed and occupying the boardroom at KTLA. No luck.

Autry wasn't in the room either, but he might just as well have been. One of his silver mounted parade saddles was behind glass; there were rugs and drapery in the bright colours of the desert, heavy Western-style furniture, and several classic Remington bronzes. Remington was the famed creator of Wild West bronzes who said, 'Cowboys are my cash'.

I was there to talk to general manager Tony Cassara and programmer Greg Nathanson. The money for *Prisoner* was not huge—only US$5000 an episode—but I was able to negotiate a payment based on its rating performance.

'Let's use Arbitron,' I said.

Arbitron and Nielsen are the two US rating systems, and I knew that KTLA always rated better on Arbitron. Greg Nathanson was impressed.

'I love you. How could you possibly know that?'

Homework.

Tony and Greg had great confidence in the show and in July, just three weeks before it started, they put the whole station behind it. They even had a lit billboard on Sunset Boulevard and Van Ness Avenue showing images of the women prisoners in the show, twenty-four hours a day.

The big day for the first transmission was 8 August 1979, at eight o'clock.

It's hard to believe even now but *Prisoner* outranked two major networks—NBC and CBS. Running on a local independent station in LA, it more than doubled the ratings of KTLA with an audience of two million and a remarkable 25 per cent share of the seven-station market.

Someone from the US ABC network rang KTLA to enquire: 'What the hell did you guys have on last night to get a twenty-five share?'

We celebrated with a cheap bottle of champagne Bob Crystal bought at the local drug store.

The *Australian* newspaper called our American success 'the greatest overseas breakthrough since television began in Australia'.

But not everyone back home thought the move into drama was the smartest thing I ever did.

TV Times, in reviewing the show, quoted Lyle McCabe: 'If Reg Grundy had stuck to game shows he'd be a millionaire by now'.

One way or another, we did well out of KTLA, but not as well as Gene Autry. He sold it two years later for a reported $245 million, said to be the largest single station sale in US history.

Tom McManus, who'd made the original *Prisoner* sale for us, had some advice for me.

'Reg, you're off to a great start, but if you keep going you'll need a tough guy to do the deals for you. I reckon I know just the man.'

A few weeks later Joy and I had lunch with Tom and his Australian wife Jan, and were introduced to Dick Barovick and his wife, Joan. The setting was Windows on the World, a restaurant on the 106th and 107th floors of the North Tower of the World Trade Center. Looking out across Manhattan I could see helicopters and small planes way below, moving across the landscape.

It was a remarkable experience entering the elevator at street level and moving through space to the two top floors. It's hard to believe that later they were wiped off the face of the earth.

I had under my arm a presentation for that Stirling Silliphant feature movie, *The Brown Out Murders*. It looked pretty fancy and I thought it might catch Dick's eye. After all, we were hoping he'd be my legal representative in the USA. The lunch was wonderful in spite of the exorbitant prices and we all seemed to hit it off. Windows on the World became a regular luncheon place for us on our early visits to the Big Apple.

Our first real meeting was in Dick's office. He was one of the senior partners in a New York law firm and occupied the corner suite. Dick was a super-charged guy and on my first formal visit he accidentally upturned his ornate wheeled chair and found himself on the floor.

He got up and ignored it, and carried on talking.

In spite of Dick's abrasive style he knew everyone who was anyone in the television business and he certainly opened doors for me. Years later, when he was CEO of Grundy Worldwide, my international television production and distribution company, I called him from LA as I did on hundreds of occasions. During the conversation Dick said, 'I've got a great idea for a television program. It's called *Mother and Son*'.

I said, 'What's it about?'

'That's for someone else to work out. Do I have to do all the work in this company?'

The coincidence is that we did in fact license rights for the Australian series *Mother and Son* which John O'Grady had commissioned and produced for ABC Australia. We made versions in Chile and, after we'd sold the company, further Grundy versions were made in Denmark, Turkey and Greece.

Dick Barovick and his wife were close friends of Tom and Jan McManus, who in turn were close friends with Larry Fraiberg, who had run the

Metromedia stations for John Kluge. At another time, he headed up the Group W stations and WWOR, a TV station in New York. Larry would win a Peabody award in 1985, the oldest and most prestigious honour in electronic media. At one time he was referred to in the business as the 'broadcaster's broadcaster'.

Larry bought a number of my shows and scheduled them at unusual times. He took a chance on me and had success with my shows—I'll never forget that.

So here was this small group in New York who were like an encyclopaedia of television and who were a great help for me in this new and massive market. Dick Barovick never really connected with our other executives. He was tough and grasping perhaps, but he did do very good things for Grundy Worldwide even though our friendship ended when I sold the business.

On the fateful day of 9/11—11 September 2001—Joy and I were back in Bermuda. The phone rang. We switched on our TV and watched the tragic events unfolding live before our eyes as the terrorists flew into the towers. Of course the people in the Windows on the World restaurant all perished—seventy or so staff members and seventy-six guests.

We were remembering the many happy hours we had spent right there. It was horrific to see people jumping out of windows and the buildings tumbling to the ground.

The Tom McManus story didn't have a happy ending either. Tom had been diagnosed with prostate cancer and Jan and he discussed what action they should take. The decision: do nothing and enjoy the projected five years he had left.

Tom and Jan had a small cottage in upstate New York and Tom invariably rented a cheap car when they decided to go up there as, like many New Yorkers, he did not own a vehicle.

It was between Christmas and New Year and the roads were icy and slippery. A van coming towards them skidded across the road, slamming into their car. Ironically, Jan died immediately. Tom almost lived out the five years he had been told he had, but was not the same man without his Jan.

We attended the services for both of them in New York State. We had lost two marvellous friends.

We miss them both.

GRUNDY AND GOODSON

Back in the early days in Australia I hired a young woman who had been working for an insurance company. I realised that Pam Ferguson was born to be in production and she was soon travelling Australia as my PA and contestant coordinator.

The years went by until one day she said, 'Reg, we've had a wonderful time together but I'm moving on. I want to go to New York'.

She wasn't leaving the game show business, though. In New York she got herself an interview with the Goodson Todman Company. She met Mark Goodson, the king of American game shows, and his right hand man, Giraud Chester, better known as Jerry.

She showed them a list of the shows she had worked on. Mark turned to Jerry Chester.

'Most of these are our shows. How much do we get for them?'

Jerry replied, 'Nothing.'

Pam had blown my cover. She got the job and over time no doubt recounted many of our Australian adventures to her new bosses. I was unaware of any of this. But then the day came when I crossed swords with Jerry Chester.

Jerry had been vice president of programming at ABC and at NBC. He knew his stuff. I reckoned this could be a tough meeting so I had Dick Barovick and Ian Holmes with me. I knew I was legally in the clear as I had not needed to pay for TV rights in those early years, but now things had altered and obviously I would do what was necessary.

When we entered his office Jerry barely acknowledged us. He pointed to a sofa at one end of his office. He stayed behind his vast desk at the other end of the room. There were no handshakes.

I opened the firing.

'Jerry, I'm sure you know just how much regard I have for you and Mark. We have a great respect for your shows.'

'Yes, we've noticed that,' remarked Jerry sarcastically. 'Now what do you want?'

'World rights to your shows.'

Jerry nearly exploded. 'You are here in America competing with us, and you want our shows?'

'Jerry, we're like a fly on an elephant's back.'

'Not so,' said Jerry, and proceeded to give a detailed rundown on the game show situation on the three American networks.

Ian Holmes tried, in his quiet way, to soften the situation and Dick Barovick, who knew Jerry, did his best. We got nowhere. The meeting broke up.

When Ian returned to Sydney he sent Jerry a letter saying how much we had enjoyed the meeting. He didn't get a reply.

I eventually caught up with Jerry again in his New York office in the Seagram Building, a skyscraper at 375 Park Avenue between 52nd and 53rd. This time it was just the two of us, and that made all the difference.

I said, 'Do you miss being on the buyer's side? Like when you were at the networks?'

'Not really—I guess I was a little different to most network guys. Never went to the studio when a pilot was being made.'

The usual procedure in America was for network executives to sit in the studio passing notes to the producer as the rehearsal proceeded, and to continue making notes as the three pilot episodes are recorded.

'That wasn't my way,' Jerry went on. 'I looked at the material when it was sent to me in my office. Wanted to see it for the first time as the audience at home sees it.'

I was amazed. 'Jerry, I'm the same. In my case, tapes are sent to me as the recording day progresses. I didn't want to be in the studio seeing all the inevitable problems.'

That first abortive meeting was forgotten. Jerry and I were to become the best of friends. And as time passed, Mark Goodson gave me the right to make any of their formats in Australia.

Jerry would phone: 'Got a new show, Reg. Want to take a look?'

He always took me into the same room and left me alone. I'd give my opinion. I remember one in particular. 'Enjoyable but not your best. And why have you used one of your old game show themes for the pilot?'

He shook his head.

'You're too much, Reg. Mark's got to meet you.'

The day came for the meeting between Grundy and Goodson. Jerry Chester, Mark Goodson and myself sat at a table in the Four Seasons restaurant, which was also in the Seagram building, the same Park Avenue building in which they had their offices.

We talked about television. Particularly game shows.

Some time after that lunch Pam Ferguson suggested that Jerry and his wife visit us in Bermuda for the weekend. Jerry was unsure, but Pam talked him round.

The weekend was a great success. Joy was, as always, the stunning hostess, and Jerry and I talked non-stop.

As I drove them back to the airport Jerry said, 'You know, Reg, if Mark had done what you did—gone out into the world—he could have been bigger than he was'.

'Why didn't he?'

'Too frightened. Too afraid he might fail.'

I smiled to myself, remembering the guy who'd thought he was too old and too scared to have a go at television after watching Brian Henderson on that Mother's Day Special. But I'd made a go of it, and 'kept throwing punches'.

Jerry returned the Bermuda compliment. We were their guests at a dinner party at their apartment in New York. Sitting at the table were some of the producers who had helped to make Mark so famous. And wealthy.

Jerry had served as a juror in a 1968 murder trial in Manhattan, and had written a book, *The Ninth Juror*. He lent us his only copy. It had won him an award.

By now Mark was showing all our versions of their shows to his production staff.

The Better Sex was a Goodson/Todman format for CBS—we were making it in Perth. I sent a tape to Bob Crystal for him to show to Mark Goodson. Goodson was taping a segment of *Price Is Right* at CBS. They were on a break and Mark, through the loudspeaker, asked his entire crew to come to the booth and watch the Australian version of *Better Sex*.

> *Mark was saying, 'This Australian show is better than ours. Their colours are better and their production is better. And I was right about the colours of the set. We should have used those shades. You should look at all the Grundy shows and get some ideas from them'.*
>
>   *I left the control room with a wide grin on my face ...*
>
>   BOB CRYSTAL

It was all leading up to the inevitable.

I wrote a personal letter to Mark Goodson proposing that Mark and I form a new company: Grundy Goodson or Goodson Grundy.

It never happened.

Mark replied saying he saw me as the only game show producer that he truly admired and if he ever joined forces it would be with me. He ended with the 'but' excuse.

So the amalgamation never occurred.

The last game show I made for NBC was *Time Machine*, a format Bill Barr, a writer on *Sale of the Century*, brought to us. It didn't work, although Mark Goodson said he loved it. Few did.

Mark Goodson died aged seventy-seven in 1992. We flew from Bermuda to New York for the Memorial Service, which was held at the Museum of Television and Radio. Mark's three former wives spoke fondly about him.

Within weeks I was seated at a table in a room at the 21 Club discussing the possibility of buying the Mark Goodson Company. I was amazed when I discovered that it was financially smaller than mine.

FLYING HIGH: CONCORDE

Two days after that first meeting with Jerry Chester in 1978 Joy and I flew to London on the Concorde, which had started its New York service the previous November.

Because I was trying to set up local production companies around the world I was averaging thirteen international flights a year and many internal ones both in America and Australia. We seemed to spend half our lives on aircraft. Concorde made a big difference. Three and a half hours across the Atlantic instead of eight by conventional aircraft—it beat the trams I travelled in to report each day when I was in the army, from Double Bay to Rosehill.

Concorde was better and faster than anything commercial, and although the fare cost a whole lot more it meant we could get to London and be back in New York the same day.

How could the bloke who used to report the Easter Show cattle results for 2GZ now be flying Concorde? We shared those Concorde flights with many famous people, including Rupert Murdoch, Rex Harrison (who left the plane in a wheelchair), Henry Kissinger, Edward Koch (Mayor of New York), Ted Heath (the British ex-prime minister) and many others.

Joy asked Heath how many MPs there were in the House of Commons. He said he didn't know. That did not impress her. 'I bet Mrs Thatcher would have known,' she said when she came back to me.

Illusionist David Copperfield and model Claudia Schiffer sat in front of us on one flight, eating hamburgers which they had brought aboard and which he quickly made disappear. This was more surprising when the food aboard was supplied by the famous Roux brothers. Strangely enough we had seen Copperfield's show the night before at Wembley Stadium. I could have asked him for his autograph but he seemed to have his hands full.

We used to fly the short-lived Singapore-Bahrain-London run as well:

two four-hour flights instead of more than fourteen hours. Dame Joan Sutherland and Richard Bonynge sat behind us once and Joy took her Aunt Millie on that leg and then on to New York in the early 1980s. Apparently when she returned to her home on the Gold Coast after her world trip, Aunt Millie was heard to ask another very elderly lady at morning tea one day, 'Have you flown on the Concorde, dear?'

On one occasion we bumped into Bruce Gyngell at Kennedy while waiting to be loaded onto Concorde. He was busy taking photographs although I had never before seen him with a camera.

'New hobby, Bruce?'

'No, boy, serious stuff. Have a look at these.'

He produced a stack of photographs. I flicked through them. They were all out of focus, every one of them.

Bruce was known to be slightly eccentric. Everyone who knew him was aware of his interest in alternative lifestyles and had heard the enthusiastic lectures about the advantages of a macrobiotic diet and the size and shape of the stools it produces. I certainly wasn't going to say anything about out of focus photographs, and handed them back without comment.

'Notice anything?' said Bruce.

'Don't think so.'

'Have another look, Reg. See? They're out of focus. You ought to get into this. This really smart guy put me on to it. He's worked out that looking at out of focus shots is a great aid to meditation. He's right, too.'

Despite these eccentricities he was right up there with the best programmers I met anywhere in the world.

On 15 April 1990 we were again about to take off from Kennedy Airport. It was Easter Saturday and there were only seventeen passengers on board. We were told that Concorde had been cleared to fly through the New York security zone rather than around it.

I turned to Joy. 'Maybe we'll set a new record.'

And we did.

Concorde's record London to NYC crossing took two hours, fifty-four minutes and thirty seconds. We had just crossed the Atlantic faster than anyone else in all of history. I wonder what Columbus or Captain Cook would have thought.

The world's first supersonic airliner, Concorde had a cruise speed of 1350 mph. That's the muzzle velocity of a 0.303 bullet. With all four Rolls Royce Olympus engines on full throttle, Concorde had the equivalent horsepower of 10,000 Mini Minors.

Our captain on this record-breaking flight was—wait for it—Captain Britton. Appropriate enough.

We were to fly Concorde with Norman Britton on a subsequent flight. The captain was waiting to get into the rest room and I was ahead of him.

'Captain's privilege,' he said as he stepped in front of me.

'We were on board when you broke the record, Captain Britton.'

He grinned at me. 'Bet you don't know my nickname.'

'Yes, I do,' I replied. 'You're "The Animal". The British Airways staff told us that same night.' He laughed, put out his hand and said as he disappeared inside the WC, 'And don't you forget it'.

I haven't.

In 1996 Captain Leslie Scott established a new record with Concorde's fastest ever transatlantic crossing on 7 February. The New York to London flight took two hours fifty-two minutes and fifty-nine seconds. We had lost the title by just one minute and thirty-one seconds.

And how did the Concorde flyers feel after the last flight ever?

One of them, on the BBC news, summed up the feeling we all had: 'Like taking your favourite dog to the vet to be put down'.

I must confess I had the same feeling when I sold Grundy Worldwide.

But that was a while off yet.

THAT'S SHOWBIZ

I've been lucky to have enjoyed wonderful relationships with the vast majority of people I've worked with throughout my life. But sometimes good relationships can hit rocky roads.

My idea of having Lyle McCabe and Bill Mason as joint managing directors wasn't working. Ian Holmes had been right when he said it was a bad idea.

In any case, Bill was leaving Australia to set up Grundy game show productions overseas, so Lyle held the reins in Australia.

I didn't realise Lyle was planning to walk out on me.

I remember the day when I called our group together to farewell him. I am always emotional in these kinds of situations and there were tears in my eyes as I wished him well. One of our staff was a Jewish lady. She said, 'RG, are you sure you're not Jewish? We always cry at farewells.'

He was leaving for health reasons, yet, in a couple of weeks, was able to form a small production company with John Collins, a smart operator but in my opinion a poor producer.

Nevertheless, Lyle had said some good things about me now and then.

From the beginning the thing that most struck me about Reg was his logical mind and organisational skill. He could solve quite complex problems by breaking them down into their component parts and dealing with them one part at a time.

LYLE McCABE

He was soon to discover that it was easier running someone else's production company than succeeding with his own.

Lyle made a show that went to air in Queensland. The *Courier-Mail*, Brisbane's daily paper, wrote that Grundy had made some terrible shows but that this latest one was 'the worst show Grundy has ever made'. Kerry Wright, our skilful legal counsel, had represented me as early as 1970 when he worked at Diamond Peisah Solicitors. It was Kerry who informed the *Courier-Mail* that the show was not a Grundy production but a Lyle McCabe production. The *Courier-Mail* coughed up $20,000 to settle the matter.

And then there was Tony Barber.

He was doing a first-rate job as host of *Sale of the Century*, having originally been hired to host *Temptation* and then *Great Temptation*. He had only appeared whistling in a cigarette commercial prior to being found by us. Tony learned quickly, and was soon right up there with the best game show hosts.

During the run of *Great Temptation*, Barber left our employ and was paid directly by the network.

I had made big changes to the original American format *Sale of the Century* and later when I remade the show in America NBC executives agreed that I had greatly improved the show.

Tony had shown a strong interest in the original American show.

Later while he was hosting *Family Feud* for us he flew to America to try and buy the rights to *Sale of the Century*. He didn't bother to first find out who actually owned them so came home empty handed.

Tony Barber eventually published his autobiography, which I have not read. I'm told he spoke ill of me, which is surely a case of biting the hand that feeds you.

I could have taken him far if only he had let me help him up the ladder.

Performers come in all shapes and sizes but few acknowledge the people who help them on their way. There are exceptions though, and I'd like to mention a couple.

Anne Haddy, the fine actor who played Helen Daniels in *Neighbours*, was one. Incidentally, Helen Daniels was the mother of Joy's character, Rosemary.

Gwen Plumb, who appeared in every one of the 1396 episodes of *Young Doctors* as Ada, was another. She was one of Australia's most talented and versatile actors. Gwen was recorded as saying: 'Thank God for Reg Grundy who gives us the work'.

Tony Barber could have learned a lot from Gwen.

DAME NELLIE

Joy and I were home for Christmas in 1978 but flew out before *Prisoner* went to air in February. I'd already seen the early episodes and I loved everything about them.

I was sure we had a winner. Even the press had been reasonably kind although *TV Times* did say the show 'could be described as *The Young Convicts* or *The Restless Lags*'.

Before leaving Australia I'd told journalist Gerald Lyons that filmed drama would be my major interest in 1979.

'We've got an eight by one-hour series on Dame Nellie Melba coming up and another on Sir Charles Kingsford Smith. They'll both be on film.'

Neither project was anywhere near ready to go. They would cost a bundle.

I was especially keen on *Melba*, the story of the Australian opera star. I'd seen the Jack Hibberd play, *A Toast to Melba*, and optioned the rights. Michael Lake, Grundy head of production, had come up with a budget. It would cost well over one and a half million. I'd have to find production partners somewhere if I were to get it up. And I'd need a writer.

The year before, I'd met David Butler in London. He'd written major mini-series for Lew Grade: *Marco Polo*, *Edward the Seventh* and *Jesus of Nazareth*—a Christian writing the story of a Jew for a Jew.

'*Melba*. I love it. I'll give it all I've got.'

Looked like we had the man for the job.

I commissioned three scripts at two thousand pounds each plus five hundred pounds for a repeat. In time, I got a first draft of episode one and returned it with director Bruce Beresford's notes.

Months went by. Dead silence from David Butler. His agent, Mark Westaway, explained that David was unwell. A bad case of shingles. The message had that 'she'll be right on the night' feel. I could only hope. And in the meantime I needed to get the money.

I thought England was the place to go looking, but since I hadn't met any English television executives, I didn't kid myself it was going to be easy. I was soon to find out just how high the hurdle was.

I approached the BBC first. Bill Cotton was heading up BBC Entertainment and sat behind his desk in the low light of his office around seven at night and listened to my pitch. Polite but not really interested.

Later, I realised that light entertainment was his specialty. He had discovered the *Two Ronnies,* got *Dad's Army* to air against great resistance, and understood what ordinary people wanted to watch. *Melba* was not his cup of tea.

I was to have a wonderful relationship with Sir Bill Cotton and regret that I didn't spend more time with him before he died.

Maybe I'd have better luck at London Weekend. The British Independent Television Authority had issued a license to Thames Television to broadcast throughout London and the southeast of England from Monday to Friday.

At 7 pm on Fridays, London Weekend, another licensed broadcasting company, took over on the same frequency, closing down at one minute to six on Monday morning when Thames took over again.

Bizarre.

I thought I had a chance as London Weekend had gained its licence by declaring that they would present highbrow arts and drama productions. But by the time I sat in Brian Tesler's office in 1979, light entertainment had become the order of the day. If only I had made the *Melba* pitch ten years earlier.

Lew Grade at ATV, where Reg Watson had made *Crossroads,* was different. He too loved popular entertainment but had made a splash with historical mini-series. He'd started in show business by winning a Charleston competition at the Albert Hall in the twenties and becoming a professional dancer. Now he owned ATV in Birmingham, the most powerful member of the ITC Entertainment Group, the group of stations that would become the ITV network in Britain.

Lew was a great salesman. He had surprised the American networks by selling *Jesus of Nazareth* in the USA for a record-breaking 12 million dollars. The Americans were dazzled by his showmanship and entranced by the fact that a man with the grand title of Baron could also be a champion Charleston dancer, judged so by no less than Fred Astaire.

I should have thought of it earlier. It was obvious that a sale of *Melba* to Grade was a real possibility. It was a great concept and I had David Butler, the man who had already written some of Grade's highly acclaimed mini-series.

'All my programs are great,' Lew said. 'Some are bad, but they're all great.' A producer after my own heart.

But he passed on *Melba*.

Perhaps if I'd had finished scripts to show instead of just an opening episode and, eventually, a first draft of a second it might have been different.

I continued to chase David Butler.

My English lawyers, Denton, Hall and Bergin, wrote to Kenneth Ewing at Fraser and Dunlop: 'We are concerned that our client, Reg Grundy Productions Pty Ltd, has not yet received remaining scripts under agreement dated 22 November 1978. Though we realise Mr Butler has not been well earlier this year, it is now some three months since either ourselves or our client has heard from him and the delivery date for the last script under the agreement has passed'.

Meanwhile, we'd been looking for production partners and a deal had been stitched together with HTV, Harlech TV, which operated in Wales and the west of England, with a budget of $300,000 an episode.

Back in Australia Ian Holmes had the local networks interested in a pre-sale and was hoping for $100,000 an episode for Australian rights.

It was going well.

If we only had those scripts!

Not a word from David Butler. He couldn't be found, even by his agent. We read in the trade press that he was writing another project for NBC called *Marco Polo*. And that he might be writing a novel. Butler's agent was sympathetic but couldn't control his client, who had clearly given up on *Melba*.

Kerry Wright wrote to him and we formally sacked him, and decided to start all over again with Australian writer Jonathon Hardy. We lined up Joan Carden to sing as Melba and set a date of March 1983 to film the music sequences.

It didn't happen.

Every project has its moment when it sounds fresh and exciting to potential co-production partners and networks alike, and *Melba* was starting to look a little tired. Too much time had passed, the gloss was off the gingerbread, and it became impossible to keep all the deals in place.

We'd had T-shirts made with a picture of Melba on them.

We've ended up with a single one of those, which Joy occasionally wears to the gym.

▲ I don't normally dress like this. Joy and I are at Buckingham Palace in 1983, after receiving an OBE from the Queen. What a memorable day!

▲ With Reg Watson and Bob Crystal in Los Angeles in 1979. We're on Sunset Boulevard outside KTLA, which had taken up *Prisoner: Cell Block H*. The show's opening episode out-rated two networks.

▲ Bill Mason with us. The man who produced Grundy game shows round the world. From Australia to America to Britain to Europe to Asia. We had more winners than losers. No wonder we're smiling.

▲ That's an Emmy I'm holding, and a prestigious one at that. I received the Founders' Award in New York in 1996 before an audience of over 1000 people.

◀ Sir Llew Edwards, Chancellor of Queensland University, presents me with an Honorary Doctorate in 2003. They let me keep the fancy wardrobe.

▶ Leaving St Paul's Cathedral, London, after renewing our vows in the OBE Chapel, a privilege granted to members.
© *Grahame Bateman*

▼ The Grundy family—some of the people who helped me on my way. There were many more.
© *Grahame Bateman*

▼ My boat *Boadicea* – she caused quite a fuss in Sydney. I stayed out of sight. We liked this cartoon and it hangs in our New South Wales home. © *Rod Clement*

▼ A moment of leisure. Catch and release trout fishing in New Zealand. © *Chinni Mahadevan*

▲ On safari in South Africa. No guns, just cameras. © *Joy Chambers-Grundy*

▼ 'The Wildlife of Reg Grundy' exhibition opening night at the Art Gallery of New South Wales with the great Australian boxer Vic Patrick. It was his last outing. © *Grahame Bateman*

▲ With my darling Joy on board *Boadicea*. © Grahame Bateman

MY SUITCASE OR YOURS?

I always did my best to make the most of all opportunities, especially in America.

I never missed the annual NATPE conference.

NATPE stands for the National Association of Television Production Executives. It's where much of the business of television gets done; all the major players are represented there. If you want to sell a show, find a co-production partner or get into syndication, NATPE's the place to be. It is held in various places: Las Vegas, Los Angeles, San Francisco, New Orleans, Miami Beach to name a few.

In 1979 it was in Vegas and Hector Crawford turned up. The first time ever.

I needed to be noticed and thought I might do that by introducing two-up to Vegas. I arrived with an elaborate presentation and lots of kips and silvered pennies to use as giveaways.

I soon discovered Vegas needed another game like it needed diphtheria.

I had a second idea. I prepared a brochure showing various locations and establishments. A Kentucky Fried Chicken outlet, for instance, or a tram. Conventioneers were asked to decide which were in Australia and which in America. My aim was to show that Australians and Americans were pretty much the same. I offered a big prize—a tour of Australia.

It was won by Frank Biondi who was then assistant programmer at Home Box Office. Grundy staffer Steve Kibler, a congenial American who was trying to get a movie up for us called *Bondi Blue*, took Frank and his wife around the country later in the year. Steve gave them a hell of a good time, including a day out on the Grand Banks.

Later, Frank Biondi became Head of Universal Pictures, Universal Studios and MCA. I had first met him at HBO when the company was just starting out. I offered to make telemovies for him in Australia. He said no.

At the end of the convention Joy and I flew back to Los Angeles. We started to unpack our bags, beginning with one of our Hartman suitcases, and saw a script lying on top. On the front of the document were the words 'CRAWFORD PRODUCTIONS'. The bag was exactly the same as mine, but obviously it was Hector's.

The Devil was whispering in my ear: 'Read the script. Read the script'.

Instead, I closed the bag and called the Bel Air Hotel where I knew Hector was staying.

'Hector, it's Reg Grundy. I've got your bag and I hope you've got mine.'

There was a long pause.

'Just a minute.'

I waited. Then Hector was back.

'Yes, I've got your bag.'

I laughed and Hector seemed to be between laughing and crying.

'Hector, I didn't read it.' He knew what I was referring to.

'Oh, of course, I know you wouldn't do that.'

A few years earlier, in 1974, I had entered the drama field and between the two of us Hector and I were making more television in Australia than anyone else. I called him and suggested we should get together. He arrived at Bayview in a government car. Joy and I took him out on the Grand Banks and we had a pleasant day—again on the Hawkesbury. I suggested we should combine our efforts.

On his return to Melbourne he sent me a polite letter saying he preferred to remain independent. So that was that. He continued to relax on his houseboat, and Joy and I continued to enjoy ourselves on *Carolyn J.*

Although Hector and I were successful, we were very different animals.

Nigel Dick, who had been General Manager of GTV 9 and was later on the Crawford board, says:

Hector had a very different attitude to Reg's with a very different approach to television. He made pretty good dramas but was not good at the game shows. He'd made some in radio so we gave him a go but they didn't work out at all. Reg always knew what the networks would go for.

I remember Hector once said, not unkindly, when talking of Reg's success with serials: 'Reg Grundy casts pretty people'.

NIGEL DICK

In 1996 I was at the International Emmy Awards at the Hilton Hotel in New York.

Frank Biondi, who had won that trip to Australia, gave me a generous introduction when I accepted the Founders Award Emmy that night. Part of the citation for my Emmy was: 'for accomplishments of an individual whose work is recognised throughout the world'.

Backstage, Frank reminded me of my offer to make movies for HBO.

You were ten years ahead of your time. You were right, we were wrong.

FRANK BIONDI

After the ceremony our party of about fourteen went to the Peninsula Hotel bar. We were a little too excited to go straight to bed. Jack Chambers carried the Emmy for me. We all sat at a long, low table and ordered a round of drinks.

When the time came to pay, Joy called the waiter over. I asked for the bill. The waiter returned to the bar and instead of coming back with it, the barman came over. 'Your check's been paid, ma'am.'

'Oh, by whom?'

'An Australian gentleman who was at the bar. He said to tell Mr Grundy he was so proud to be Australian tonight it was the least he could do.'

'Where is he?' we asked. 'We'd like to thank him.'

'Oh, he left; he just wanted to pay for you, that's all.'

There are some people out there who continue to rejuvenate your faith in humanity. Whoever you were, we hope you read this so we can thank you now.

JOY CHAMBERS-GRUNDY

GRUNDYS AT SURFERS PARADISE

It's obvious that pictures and sound have been my life but occasionally we've strayed into greener pastures. Mirages almost every time. When we strayed we mostly lost money. Sometimes large lumps.

Grundys at Surfers Paradise—GASP—was an indoor fun fair and a massive example of the shoemaker stepping away from his last. It had been a long-drawn-out affair getting it ready and I was dubious to say the least, but when we finally opened on a long weekend we made a lot of money.

'How long has this been going on?' Ian Holmes and I said to one another.

The answer was, not for long.

The location was terrific, right in the heart of Surfers Paradise. But it wasn't on ground level—customers had to ride an escalator to the next floor up. The layout reminded me of the upper level floor in a department store. A former executive from Disneyland, Skip Palmer, was appointed vice president of Grundy Leisure and was responsible for running the entire area, including the tiny pizza food outlet, Chuck E. Cheese.

Chuck E. Cheese was a computer-generated rat from New Jersey who led a troop of puppet characters in a cabaret every few minutes from the walls of the pizza parlour. It was one part of the complex that I thought might actually work. Chuck E. Cheese was doing fine in America but failed to be a hit for us.

Grundys at Surfers Paradise started bleeding money and by March 1983 we were looking at a walk-away loss of six million.

Should we have asked people to pay to enter the fun fair? After much discussion the answer was no. We were between the devil and the deep blue sea.

There was one person who had the carnival know-how which GASP needed, and that was Jimmy Sharman, who had the Dodgem concession. Sharman was a legend who had travelled Australia with his boxing tent and his famous cry: 'Who'll go a round or two for a pound or two?'

Sharman wanted to turn the whole thing into an internal fairground, something like sideshow alley at the Royal Easter Show. Should we have allowed him to operate as he wanted to? Well, we should at least have listened a lot more closely to what he had to say. GASP was too quiet, too neat. Not enough fun, especially for children.

When time came to renew our lease we were bleeding at the rate of some two million dollars a year. If we walked away we were committed to leaving the place as we found it. There would have been make-goods, which would have cost us millions.

So the whole lot was sold to a new owner for one dollar.

As the years went by I was spending most of each year overseas opening up production companies. Sticking to my last.

However, once I sold Grundy Worldwide I seemed to forget about that. Backing a stage musical probably wasn't the smartest thing I ever did.

We bought half the global rights to the musical Sisterella *with promoter Kevin Jacobsen for two million.*

 It was a huge flop and write-off. Those are the risks you take. A global hit could be worth fifty million but if it doesn't work you lose the lot in set and first run costs. That's what we did when Sisterella *failed in Melbourne in around 1998. So you can blame me for recommending that one. I will put my hand up and say* Sisterella *was probably the worst investment we ever made.*

TIM HUGHES

In fairness to Tim Hughes he also pulled off some huge successes for us. Tim had been with me since he was first hired by Sue McIntosh when he was nineteen, except for a brief period when he ran the Sunshine TV Network in Queensland, in which we had the major shareholding anyway.

Tim was responsible for the grand success of our radio enterprise, the largest regional network in Australia: RG Capital Radio. And he was instrumental in selling our 20 per cent stake in regional television station Mackay TV to Chris Skase—we made three million dollars, which was more than the whole TV production business made in Australia that year.

Tim ran RG Capital for us from 1995 until 2002.

Then there was the project at Seal Rocks off Victoria's Phillip Island, which wasn't too good. Seal Rocks has Australia's largest colony of fur seals and the idea was to open a restaurant with cameras supplying live images of the seals.

We did it and I visited several times and was struck by one obvious drawback: the seals stank to high heaven. I'd photographed and dived with seals off Mexico's Baja Peninsula. They didn't appear to smell at all but those at Seal Rocks were really ripe. We eventually sold out at a substantial loss.

The only one of these adventures to be really successful was the Sydney Entertainment Centre at Darling Harbour. It returned a profit on a very moderate investment. Our co-shareholder in Arena Management, the company which managed the Sydney Entertainment Centre, was Kevin Jacobsen. We sold our interest to Kevin for three quarters of a million dollars.

Arena went into receivership in August of 2009.

SALE IN AMERICA

By 1982 I was still a long way from being on the American A list, but at least people were no longer saying 'Reg who?' when I called.

I was feeling optimistic enough to extend my *Sale of the Century* deal to cover the US. Just in case.

Dick Barovick, my New York lawyer, negotiated a new deal with Al Howard and Al was happy to do business with us. And why wouldn't he be? He was to get $100,000 a year for the three-year run of the agreement plus $2500 a week if *Sale* was produced in the US and $1500 a week for anywhere else in the world.

I was optimistic but a year later I was still trying to become an 'American' producer.

And I was sure *Sale* was still my best chance.

I kept knocking on doors and at last I got an appointment with someone in 'daytime' at CBS Television City, in Los Angeles. Bob Crystal drove me through the security gates. Before me was the famous white building. Not just any white but what was known back then as television white.

I found myself in a room big enough to be a boardroom. There was just me and the woman from daytime programming whose name I have long forgotten.

I'd had one of the Australian episodes converted to NTSC videotape—in Australia we use the PAL format—and ran it for her. The show looked great—exciting and involving. The final credits rolled. Judgment time.

'Entertaining, no doubt about that, Reg ...'

She didn't actually say 'but'. She didn't have to, her intention was clear.

I leaned forward and politely asked, 'But?'

'I liked it, I really did.' She hesitated and then said, 'But I don't think it's got legs'.

Foolish woman. If she'd known the history of the show she would never have made that statement.

The original American *Sale of the Century*, the very different show to mine which Al Howard had owned, had run for almost four years in America from September 1969 to July 1973.

And then there was the Australian track record: number one in the National Top Ten with regular audiences of almost two and half million, and the most successful game show ever made or shown in Australia.

Not bad for a show without legs.

I walked out of the building feeling the frustration of it all. I knew I had to shrug it off. I reminded myself of the old salesman's tale.

A guy had been trying to sell life insurance without much success. One day he read a piece of advice which was to change his life: keep a record of all the house calls you make for a month whether you make a sale or not. Then divide the amount you have earned by the number of calls you have made. Now you know what a call is worth.

Then when you leave a prospect who has turned you down, say to yourself, 'I just made another 17 dollars'.

My problem was that I had made many 'house' calls and so far hadn't sold anything. So until I did, the formula didn't apply.

As we drove away from the white building, I said: 'Bob, let's try NBC. What have we got to lose?'

Earl Greenburg was in charge of daytime programming at NBC. We had a number of unproductive meetings with Greenburg.

One stands out.

Earl Greenburg's office door was open. We walked in. He was not at his desk. He was relaxing on a sofa with his arms around a huge stuffed teddy bear.

'Well, hullo,' he drawled, not bothering to disentangle himself.

At least he was awake. He gave us a wan smile, then looked in my general direction.

'Nothing to say to you guys at the moment. No decisions before the new chairman arrives on 1 July. Give me a call when next you're in town.'

I was fuming as we drove past the Hollywood Bowl.

'Bobby, he wouldn't know a game show from a hole in the wall. Why do we have to deal with these bastards?'

On the first of July, Grant Tinker became the new Chairman and CEO of NBC and confirmed the brilliant young Brandon Tartikoff as head of entertainment and programming. At thirty-one, he was the youngest man ever to be given a network to run.

I sent a telex to Bob Crystal.

'Go after Earl.'

Bob followed orders and upset the temperamental Greenburg.

On 25 August I sent another telex.

Too bad Greenburg's feathers are ruffled but without some pressure from us my hunch is that he will do nothing. There is no doubt in my mind that the first aim of any station or network is to have the highest ratings in its market.

With NBC's low daytime ratings, if Sale of the Century *delivered bigger ratings and a greater share Greenburg would be a hero even if the total audience were made up of ninety-year-olds.*

Remember, Bob, it's sometimes necessary to upset people to get what you want. Keep throwing those punches.

I encouraged Bob to keep after Earl the Pearl throughout most of 1981, bombarding him with Australian ratings and other success stories.

On 27 August I telexed Bobby again.

Now that you've got Greenburg's attention—why don't we get him to like us? Try to cultivate him? Find out if he likes big lunches with plenty of wine (or whatever) and serve it up to him.

You're the man to do it. Get out your Dale Carnegie and go after him.

In December, Grant Tinker fired Greenburg!

'Why am I knocking myself out like this,' I thought, 'when I could be back in Australia basking in the success we are having there?'

There was better news ahead.

Dick Barovick was on the phone to me.

'I've got you a breakfast meeting with Brandon Tartikoff for eight thirty next Friday. He'll meet you in the Palm Court at the Plaza Hotel in New York.'

Brandon Tartikoff!

I certainly knew who he was. Over the previous two years he'd turned the network around, taking it from last to first with groundbreaking shows like *Hill Street Blues*, *Cheers*, *Family Ties* and *St Elsewhere*. And there were more to come with *Miami Vice*, *The Cosby Show*, *The A-Team* and *Seinfeld*. What a programmer.

'Reg, getting to meet Brandon is like getting to see God. Make the most of it.'

I intended to.

It was 26 February 1982. We had flown into New York and were staying at the Sherry-Netherland Hotel on the corner of 59th and 5th Avenue, diagonally opposite where I was to meet the golden boy of television.

I entered one of the two Italian Renaissance-style panelled elevators and was taken down to the foyer by the uniformed, white-gloved operator. I walked through the small ornate marble and bronze lobby onto 5th Avenue.

Right across from me was the magnificent Plaza hotel.

Standing on the sidewalk was Danny Kaye wearing woollen socks snugged into open sandals. He was flagging down a cab.

Was seeing Danny Kaye a good sign or a bad sign?

I worked my way through the traffic and stood in front of the famous hotel.

I could clearly remember the day when I couldn't afford to be eating at the Plaza, or to be staying at the Sherry for that matter. But I wanted to have a presence, to be able to say to Brandon that I was staying at the Sherry-Netherlands.

I was early, determined not to let him get away.

I took a seat in the Palm Court, an elegant room which had been a part of the Plaza since it opened in 1907. It had been used for scenes in many books including F. Scott Fitzgerald's *The Great Gatsby*. To think they gave me a table. Maybe it was Brandon's name that got me in.

Brandon entered and looked around. I pointed at myself.

'Reg Grundy?' he asked. 'Brandon Tartikoff.' He dropped his leather satchel to the floor beside his chair and sat down.

I had a feeling I was going to like this man.

We talked easily about television and the time went quickly. Maybe we ate little because we had so much to say. Or, thinking back now, maybe there was a reason why Brandon only picked at his bagel.

As we finished our coffee he said, 'I'm thinking of bringing back game shows between ten and midday. They used to be there you know'.

'Yes,' I said, 'I'm a student of American television. Grew up watching American shows. And I've made a hell of a lot of game shows, some of them based on ones that played in those morning time slots.'

We were on the right subject. I figured I was in with a chance.

'There's a game show I'm making in Australia right now which is a massive hit. Networked. Stripped at seven o'clock at night. I've made a lot of changes to it and I reckon it's pretty good. It's *Sale of the Century*.'

Tartikoff blinked. He recognised it.

I went on. 'Yes, you'll know it. Had a fair run on NBC starting back in 1969. Look, I realise you must be terribly busy, but I'd like to send you a tape.'

'Okay.'

'I'd appreciate it if you'd find time to look at it. I mean you, personally.'

I didn't want someone like that CBS woman making the decision.

'Send it to me and I'll see what I can do.'

It was only later that I discovered Brandon was being treated for Hodgkin's disease, a lymphatic cancer. He first had it at the age of twenty-three, then went into remission. Now it had returned; it was to kill him at the age of forty-eight.

I later heard that he was undergoing chemo and it was a closely held secret that he was wearing a wig and had false eyebrows taped to his face. If the report was true he must have been wearing the 'disguise' at breakfast that day.

I hadn't even noticed.

I walked down the steps outside the Plaza where, four years later, they shot the memorable 'That's not a knife' scene from Paul Hogan's movie *Crocodile Dundee.*

Even if the crew had been shooting the scene right there and then I wouldn't have noticed. For ten years I'd been struggling to get into the American market. I had kept throwing punches and at last someone might be about to give me my chance.

Within the week Brandon was on the phone.

'Reg, I like it a lot. The changes you've made have improved it out of sight.'

He continued.

'If I decide to go with a game show block next year there's a chance your show could be in the line-up. I'll get my daytime people to call you.'

That was it.

I slumped back in my chair and rubbed my eyes. Sometimes my emotions well up in me. And this was one of those times.

It would be a long wait before I got the news from NBC, until I knew whether or not I was in business in America.

Lucy Johnson, a warm, capable woman, had taken over as head of daytime at NBC. I was to have many meetings with Lucy and her assistant Nelson Davis. Just recently she had this to say.

Putting anything to air on daytime television was a very different proposition to any other time—especially twenty-five years ago. The habit-forming pattern in the audience is what you counted on because it was a Monday to Friday experience. Most people were either morning viewers or afternoon viewers. So whenever you took something off the air you had to feel secure that what you put back on would warrant the change. The rest is instinct and experience.

Drama had been tried for a very short time in the morning. It had failed.

It was time to try something else. We decided to create a very strong game show block. Good, strong classic shows.

LUCY JOHNSON

Lucy said, 'We all love your show, Reg, but there's just one thing.'

There always is.

'We love it but it's so Australian. How could we make it more, well, American?'

'Oh, I thought we'd find a great American MC, use only American contestants and we'd feature American prizes and only questions suitable for the American audience. Do you reckon that might do it?'

I hadn't intended to be sarcastic but it certainly came out that way.

Happily, Lucy didn't seem to mind. She laughed.

'Yes, I suppose you're right. Let's do some run-throughs.'

This was new to me.

'But you know the show. We'll deliver exactly what you've seen except that it will have American elements not Australian ones. I promise you nobody who talks funny like me will ever be seen or heard.'

'Oh, I suppose you're right. But we always do extensive run-throughs of new game shows.'

'I really don't think it's necessary. In this case.'

The meeting ended. The score was nil-nil.

I called Bill Mason in Hong Kong. He was there producing our first game show to be made outside Australia. It was *Dat Sou But—Sale of the Century*, Chinese version.

'Bill, I've told them we're making *Sale* in Hong Kong and Lucy Johnson and her team are thinking of dropping in on you en masse.'

'For Christ's sake, don't let them come here. The studio roof is leaking and the toilets are holes in the ground.'

'Okay, Bill. Got it.'

We both burst out laughing.

It was a long, long year as I waited for the decision.

I was in our apartment at the Wilshire hotel, getting ready to leave for Sydney to celebrate Christmas, when the phone rang.

'Reg, it's Nelson Davis, NBC.'

'Hello, Nelson. Nice to hear your voice.'

'I reckon you'll think that in a minute. *Sale of the Century* is in our New Year schedule. Congratulations.'

I was rubbing my eyes again.

I was about to become the first non-American ever to make a show in daytime for the mighty NBC network.

Sale of the Century on NBC went to air on 3 January 1983.

I know two people who got it wrong: the woman at CBS who said it didn't have legs, and the Hollywood reporter who wrote, 'Of the four new game shows that started on NBC last Monday there is one that will disappear after thirteen weeks … *Sale of the Century*'.

At the end of the first thirteen-week cycle the other three game shows were cancelled. The one remaining in the schedule was *Sale of the Century*. It was to run for six years.

And then there was another who had not believed in *Sale*: Earl Greenburg. But he didn't count.

The only one who really mattered was Brandon Tartikoff.

He was a wonderful man. He was tough, he was all the things you're supposed to be as a leader, but he had a twinkle in his eye. He was extremely smart, passionate about the business, and at that particular time, very ill but no one really knew much about it. We all sensed that something was going on but it was not talked about. He was extra brave for going through traumatic medical procedures in those couple of years yet still showing up at work and making the big decisions. He was a very special person.

LUCY JOHNSON

In 1996 I received the International Emmy Founders Award in a glittering ceremony at the Hilton Hotel in New York.

I had sold my first American production to Brandon Tartikoff when he was diagnosed with cancer. And it was in 1996 that he again suffered a recurrence of Hodgkin's disease. In spite of his illness, when Bobby Crystal approached him, Brandon found time to make a warm video congratulating me on the Founders Award. He was to leave this world on 27 August 1997.

I had sold my first show in the UK to Michael Grade at the BBC. He too was asked to say something. His secretary replied that he was too busy.

New shows are always difficult to set up, doubly so in a foreign country. If I didn't want to get bogged down in the sort of detailed planning that would be necessary, I was going to need help in getting the American show to air. No one knew *Sale* better than Bill Mason, who'd been making it back in Australia in one form or another for nearly a decade. I pulled him out of Hong Kong and set him to work in LA.

There was some initial resistance when I first walked into an American studio to make the show but not nearly as much as I was later to find at the BBC.

In the late 1950s America had been shocked by the quiz scandals and so they were very nervous about us doing something that might cause them a problem. So I divided the office space in two with doors and electric gates between the two halves. The producers weren't allowed to talk to the contestant coordinators and vice versa and any contestants who came in for auditioning were not allowed in the area where the questions were written.

The crew was very wary and I remember once when I was on the floor I said to the director that I wanted to change the display on one of the tables. So I walked over and picked up a cup to move it six inches and all hell broke loose. 'You can't touch the cup.' 'So how do I go about moving the cup?' 'You have to contact the scenic designer.' So we contacted the scenic designer who had to contact the head props man and the head props man had to contact the junior props man who was out having a cup of tea.

As time went by they became more and more used to the fact that we knew what we were doing and they let me move the cup.

I found that the cameramen over there, at least on the crew I was given, were quite elderly. They were about sixty-two or sixty-three years old, compared with the cameramen I was used to in Australia and Hong Kong who were only twenty-two. When I said that they had to zoom in to the Fame Game *board on air, well, you don't do that, you don't zoom on air.*

BILL MASON

American Ray Ellis, the celebrated record producer, arranger and conductor, wrote the theme for *Sale of the Century* and for all our American shows, including the famed Reg Grundy Productions fanfare at the end of each broadcast.

Ray had conducted the last recording session for Billie Holiday. He told me he was reluctant to do the Holiday session because of her condition. Drugs had ruined her. When the session was done he knew he had become part of musical history.

The legendary Glenn Miller had toured Europe entertaining troops during the Second World War. Ray had played tenor sax in the band.

It's no secret that I like to sing and during the time I was associated with Ray Ellis, Joy spoke to him about me cutting a record. They started to set up the session in Hollywood with top professional musicians. But yes, you might have guessed it, I backed out.

It's hard to believe, but I visited the US set of *Sale of the Century* only once. I preferred to have the rehearsal tapes sent to me by runner. Before tape rolled for real, I was able to call Bill Mason or Bob Noah in the control room and give them my notes.

Bob Crystal says, 'The runner was a boy named Kevin Kopelow who by night was manager of a Numero Uno Pizza place. Today he's one of the top producers for Nickelodeon.'

Kevin wasn't the only bright young talent to use Reg Grundy Productions as a stepping stone to a show business career. There were plenty of them over the years.

Leslie Crawford was our receptionist before becoming associate producer on *Sale of the Century* for three years, then moving on to both the *Johnny Carson Show* and the *Jay Leno Show*.

And what about Caryn Lucas? She was a girl Friday on *Sale* but was soon producer on *Time Machine* and then wrote many episodes of the sitcom *The Nanny* plus the hit movie *Miss Congeniality*.

Sharon Sussman helped us develop *Monopoly*, *Scrabble* and *Small Talk* and later made her own hit show for MTV called *Singled Out*.

George Vosburgh produced *Sale of the Century* for several years but was then stolen by Merv Griffin to take over *Jeopardy*.

Burt Wheeler took over from George as *Sale* producer and stayed with it to the end when he joined Sharon Sussman in Wheeler Sussman Productions to successfully make a range of television series. They are still good mates of ours.

Los Angeles is full of such stories—and such ambitions. Sue McIntosh, who is now managing director of RG Capital and a special friend, was our Chief Financial Officer in Los Angeles for years before she moved to Europe. When she advertised for a bookkeeper in LA, she was swamped with applications. Few of them could keep books but all included ten by eight glossies with their showbiz CVs.

Anything to open a crack, if not a door, into a show business career.

And Reg Grundy Productions wasn't a bad place to work, apparently.

I'd been there for about six weeks when I walked into Bob Noah and said, 'Bob, where's the person who screams?' Bob was as surprised as I was. 'You know something? There isn't one.' I'd never worked at a place where there wasn't someone browbeating you every day—screaming at you. But Grundy's was simply a pleasant place to work.

BURT WHEELER

Burt had been working on *Sale* for a while before I met him.

Nobody ever introduced me to RG. Finally I thought, 'Nobody's going to do this', so I ran into him one day in the hallway and said, 'Hi, Mr Grundy. You don't have the faintest idea who I am but I'm Burt Wheeler and I'm the head writer on Sale of the Century'. *He looked at me for a moment and said, 'Of course I know who you are and you're doing a fine job on* Sale'. *He couldn't have had the faintest idea who I was but he made me feel like a million dollars. It was like, 'Thank God you're here, Burt. The show would die without you'.*

BURT WHEELER

Despite ratings that weren't all that brilliant to start with, I was convinced *Sale of the Century* was a world-beater and I wasn't thrilled about sharing the cake with Al Howard. Nothing wrong with Al, but being of a 'sole trader' mentality, I'd rather own the show outright. I instructed Dick Barovick to buy him out.

But Dick was reluctant. 'It'll cost a lot of money,' he grumbled. I told him to do it anyway, but nothing seemed to happen.

Sale had been running on NBC for a few weeks when I called Dick from Australia.

'Have you done it?'

'No.'

'Just do it, Dick.'

'Well, that's clear.'

Dick was right about it costing a lot of money. It took a quarter of a million to buy the copyright but it was probably one of the best deals I ever made. NBC paid us an above-the-line fee of $35,000 compounding by 10 per cent each year over six years. That adds up to, well, a lot of money.

So why was Al Howard prepared to sell out his share?

Well, he knew that American game shows ran in thirteen-week cycles and most didn't get picked up for a second cycle. That could have happened with *Sale*. All over in thirteen weeks.

I took the chance. Al took the money.

We made *Sale of the Century* in a number of countries including the UK. I tweaked the format from time to time but the Fame Game remained an important element.

Here's a Fame Game question which was not used because it refers to an actual contestant on the show. See if you can identify him.

'Before he became a millionaire TV star he was struggling to get some face time on air. He made his first TV debut on a game show called *Sale of the Century* on Sky 1 in England in 1990 at the age of thirty. His only goal was to win a Fiat Uno. Unfortunately, he won kitchen utensils.'

A fellow contestant on that same Sky 1 show who uncovered some footage while clearing out some old boxes in storage said:

Watching the video now I remember thinking he was quite posh and handsome. He had a good sense of humour but I would never have put him down as a future superstar.

The main thing I remember about him is he couldn't answer one of the questions. He didn't know who Saddam Hussein was. But I suppose in 1990 a lot of people would have been the same.

BARBARA HUMPHREYS, QUOTED IN THE *SUN*, 13 APRIL 2007

And that Fiat Uno?

Simon Cowell doesn't need it now!

PUNISHMENT

The success of *Prisoner: Cell Block H* in America made us the producers of the month. We were living through that special time that a producer enjoys when he comes up with a massive hit.

It wouldn't last long and I was making sure we milked the cow.

Tony Cassara and Greg Nathanson at KTLA—both good guys with a real understanding of the TV business—were hanging on my every word.

I said, 'I think we've proved that it's possible to create and produce a show in Australia that can work in America. We've done it with women in prison; let's pilot a series focusing on men in prison. It'll be tougher than *Prisoner* so let's call it *Punishment*. You put up the money and we'll make the pilot in Sydney. Lower costs than here, with the same look and style.'

'How much lower?' That was Tony Cassara.

'We'll do the pilot for $150,000.'

Tony raised an eyebrow. It was a good price. He probably wondered how I could be so sure about the cost when a script was yet to be written.

I was able to lock in the price fairly confidently because Reg Watson had already written a script about men in prison called, not surprisingly, *Men in Prison*. A bit of a rewrite and it became *Punishment*.

'And while we're on a roll, let's make a pilot right here in your studios for a teenage serial that will knock their socks off.'

We had a deal.

The Two Reggies, not to be confused with the Two Ronnies, got going.

Reg wrote a marvellous opening episode.

I insisted that he read it to them. 'We'll order some grub from Nate 'n Al's and you fire away.'

Nate 'n Al's was the well known delicatessen on North Beverly Drive in Beverly Hills. When Bobby Crystal ran Doris Day's music firm they used to go there all the time. In those days Hollywood types like Groucho Marx, Harry Ruby the songwriter, and especially comedy writers, hung out there.

Reg Watson looked at me. 'Sure you wouldn't like me to direct and play all the roles as well?'

'No, Reg, just read the thing.'

I figured that if we provided food from Nate 'n Al's then all Tony and Greg had to do was munch and listen and we'd have a chance of pulling it off.

We did.

The serial drama, *Starting Out*, was recorded in KTLA's own Golden West studios with locations mainly on Sunset and Hollywood Boulevards. Reg Watson was in charge. Station people said they'd never worked on anything that was so professionally made.

Unfortunately, *Punishment* was a different story. We were both in LA so we had to leave it to Alan Coleman to produce the pilot.

Reg gave him strict instructions on everything but in the end the style and tone of the pilot bore very little relationship to Reg's script.

Ex-ABC producer Bruce Best had nothing to do with the pilot but became executive producer on the series.

Jenny Sharpe and I did the whole series. We were the script department. As far as I know I was producer and exec producer. I had zero input from anybody on any level. There was no feedback on the scripts and when the finished show started to appear there was a deafening silence from all quarters.

Basically I was given the show and left to it. Maybe my ferocious ABC style scared them.

I can well believe it wasn't particularly commercial.

BRUCE BEST

So here were the two Regs in LA while in Australia a pilot was being made which seemed to ignore Reg Watson's concept and a series was being produced by a former ABC producer who was given no instructions by anyone.

The day came when I had to screen both pilots at KTLA. Reg Watson was back in Australia by then.

It was set up in Tony Cassara's office. As always there was not a scrap of paper on his desk—cleanest desk I ever saw.

I screened *Punishment* first.

In spite of a guest role by a young Mel Gibson and some other fine performances, the show was dying before my eyes. It was far too sombre—not what they were looking for.

There was silence at the end of the screening.

I stepped into the void.

'Perhaps we should see both pilots and then we can discuss.'

I took the silence to mean they agreed.

The pilot episode of *Starting Out* opened briskly.

I was watching Tony and Greg closely and could detect that they were relaxing. It was moving fast, a bright lively show with good performances.

Then it was over.

'It's terrific,' said Tony.

'I love it!' exclaimed Greg.

I reminded them, 'We've only got one episode'.

'Maybe we can record four more and trial it for a week.'

The talk went on.

Over the weeks which followed, *Starting Out* was somehow forgotten.

And *Punishment*? It was as if it had never happened.

DANGEROUS WOMEN

We were back in Sydney, in the apartment at the Quay.

Prisoner had ended its eight-year run in Australia. But I was like a dog with a bone. I couldn't let go of the concept.

I picked up the phone and called Reg Watson.

'Reg, I've got an idea.'

I could almost hear him groan.

'No, listen. Five women leave prison. They set up a lodge by a lake and try to forget their past. They never do. What do you think?'

There was silence for a moment.

'Well, it's not the worst idea you've ever had. What's it called?'

How many times have I had to answer that question?

'Working title is *Five Women*. Yes, I know it's lousy, but we've got to call it something.'

When we returned to America, I approached Brian Frons who was running daytime for NBC. Maybe he would see its potential as an afternoon soap.

We had prepared a small 'taster tape' which largely featured the main character, beautiful Faith Cronin who had left her abusive mobster husband to create a new life. He had cut her up and she wore an ugly scar down her right cheek.

In the show she would have plastic surgery to remove the scar and give her a new identity.

The tape presentation ended with her turning to camera and revealing the disfigured side of her face.

'Oh, no,' said Brian Frons, 'I can't look! She's one of the ugliest women I've ever seen.'

I stopped the tape.

'Brian, that ugly woman is being acted by my wife. It's make-up.'

'Oh, Reg. Good God, the make-up is simply amazing. Of course I know Joy. She's a stunner. Sorry.'

'It's okay Brian, she'll forgive you. Just buy the show.'

He didn't.

I was determined to get it on air. I'll put up the money myself, I thought.

The voice of reason, Reg Watson, was saying, 'Are you really going to put up the money?'

'Maybe, maybe.'

I approached Larry Fraiberg who was running WWOR in New York.

I pitched the idea. He loved it. And agreed to invest in the first series.

Larry said we needed to stir up interest at NATPE, which was being held in New Orleans in a few weeks' time. Many of the syndication deals were made there. He arranged for Reg Watson and myself to make a presentation to KCOP and WWOR executives and particularly to the programmers.

Reg Watson went first and, in his calm manner, clearly intrigued them.

I reminded the group that prison movies mostly worked and that *Dangerous Women*, as it was now known, was a natural spin-off from *Prisoner: Cell Block H*, which had created a sensation when first seen on KTLA.

I was on a roll, getting wound up, when Larry Fraiberg walked toward me.

'Stop talking,' he whispered as he brushed past me.

I hurriedly mumbled my close and sat down.

That night we all had dinner together.

Larry said, 'Reg, I reckon you should never try to sell something that you've already sold.'

I remembered Bruce Gyngell had said the same thing when I sold him *Sale of the Century*.

I was underwriting the series of *Dangerous Women* and before the shows went to air we got commitments from stations in Los Angeles, New York and a few other key markets. Not enough to cover my production costs. The show would be running on a big deficit in spite of its minuscule budget.

Should I keep going?

I had a policy of never deficit financing a show. But this was different.

I decided to take a chance.

Bob Crystal talked to the board of AFTRA, the American Federation of Television and Radio Artists, to see if they would let actors work for an unusually low pay scale. Bob explained that if AFTRA wanted actors to be working it had to help out with our budget problems. Amazingly, they agreed and created a low budget scale for videotaped drama in syndication.

After the meeting, most members of the board gave Bob their resumes and photos in the hope of working on the show!

Next problem was to find a studio willing to do it for a price.

Glendale Studios was mainly used for commercials. The lighting grids in the sound stages were very low, but so was the price. We managed to fit our sets in, using the parking lot to build the exterior of the lodge where the women were supposed to be living and working. But what about the prison yard? Next door to Glendale Studios was a fire station. The chief agreed for us to use the exterior wall. We installed an iron gate in front.

And we cast some of the firemen as prison guards.

It was amazing that we were able to get a look so real when we were using a studio parking lot and a fire station's back wall.

BOB CRYSTAL

Roger Corman, who made a series of successful low-budget movies, saved money shooting without expensive items like permits and police protection. Hit and run filming; watch out for the cops, shoot from a moving car and hope the natural light will match well enough. Ron Howard directed his first movie for Corman that way. If it was good enough for Corman, it was good enough for us.

We shot our street exteriors in Glendale and in Hollywood.

The shows turned out pretty well and were promoted with two great pitch lines: 'Some are guilty. Some are innocent. All are dangerous, and 'Behind every good man there's a dangerous woman'.

Reg Watson announced that *Dangerous Women* was not a rehash of *Prisoner*, which had wowed audiences in Australia, America and Britain.

He did a satellite early morning pitch to stations all over America. He was relaxed and terrific. In contrast, our American head of sales, while a competent salesman, nearly had a nervous breakdown.

I was in New York when WWOR aired the first episode in prime time. It played beautifully. But I was horrified that there was no announcement at the end of the show telling the audience when the next episode would be broadcast.

I called Larry Fraiberg.

'It's a new show, Larry. How are people supposed to know when it's on again if you don't tell them.'

'Don't worry, Reg, I'll fix it.'

And he did.

Larry had a talk show in prime time hosted by Clint Holmes, which was floundering. We brought our cast to New York for a *Dangerous Women* special. It got the highest ratings that Clint's show ever had.

Dangerous Women kicked off in August 1991 on KCOP CH 13 in Los Angeles as well as WWOR CH 9 in New York and was due to run twice weekly.

I soon got a call from Evan Thompson, the boss at KCOP.

'I've decided to run two episodes back to back rather than one episode two nights a week. If we run both episodes on one night we can get behind it and promote it more.'

I was certain that was the wrong move. 'But it won't stand up over two hours, Evan, it's too long. I advise you against it.'

In the end he did it anyway. It didn't stand up and that was the end of *Dangerous Women* on KCOP.

But it was the midwest that really killed the show.

Broadcasters said, 'If we take *Dangerous Women*, viewers will threaten to boycott the advertisers who buy into the show. It's too hot. Midwesterners will be upset.'

In other markets such as Miami, Florida, broadcasters were pressing us in a different way.

'Make it tougher and sexier.'

What's that saying about a rock and a hard place?

Before its end, *Dangerous Women* had become the highest-rated drama ever to air on WWOR, the independent station Larry Fraiberg was running in New York. Gratifying, but not enough to stop me bleeding to death.

After fifty-two episodes and 8 million dollars, I reluctantly pulled the plug. I had funded the last twenty-six episodes on my own and the cash drain became too great.

It was really a terrific show, and probably ran before its time.

NEIGHBOURS

I've mentioned my experience with EST.

Joy had been sceptical about the whole thing but after I had completed the course she said, 'I must say I can see a difference in you'.

I think she meant for the better.

There was no doubt Reg had changed. He was bouncing out of his skin and that meant something, as he is pretty hyperactive at any time. But this impressed me so I succumbed to it as well. My sister and I took the course in Atlanta. My friend Carmen Ward and a number of other friends like Reg's marvellous secretary of thirty years, Di Ayres, did it too.

Joy Chambers-Grundy

Reg Watson was next.

RG came to me one day and said, 'I want you to do EST.' I said all right, and what it did for me—it showed the lack of communication between fathers and sons.

In many cases, guys got up and said, 'My father never told me he loved me.'

'Well, did you ever say you loved him?'

'Oh, no, we couldn't talk.'

I said to RG, 'I've got this idea for a drama about three families and the whole concept is about communication between the generations.'

Reg Watson

So *Neighbours* became that drama and we two Regs inserted a scene into the first episode to sell the EST message. It was about the only influence I had on the show because of my overseas adventures.

The scene went like this.

Max Ramsay has two sons—Shane whom he loves and Danny whom he ignores. There's a reason for that, which is revealed in a later episode.

One day Max Ramsay and Shane are at the Olympic pool. Shane is training for the high dive in the Olympics. Danny comes running up to his father who looks away from the pool to talk to him just as Shane makes the perfect dive behind his back.

Danny is berated by his dad.

'Look what you did. You made me miss it.'

One EST message would remind us that we are responsible for our actions. Max could have said over his shoulder, 'Just a minute', and seen the dive.

So Max Ramsay was responsible for missing Shane's dive, not Danny.

I imagine the significance of the scene was lost on the viewers but we two Regs got it.

The scene alone didn't make *Neighbours* a hit, but we reckoned it was a terrific moment in that first episode.

Reg Watson created a Ramsay Street community where the stories were simple and where the biggest question was whether Kylie and Jason should have sex before marriage.

When *Neighbours* went to air in 1985, the *Sydney Morning Herald* wrote, 'Occasionally there comes to television a soapie so charming in its simplicity that to pronounce it a winner seems inadequate. *Neighbours* is such a series'.

Mike Firman, the founder of TAPE, put it this way: 'The show's greatest weakness is its greatest strength—nothing much happens'.

Reg Watson says:

That was the basis, really. A boring idea for a concept but it changed the way we thought in serial drama. For example, we had a grandmother with no generation gap between herself and her grandchildren. In one of the opening episodes, the grandmother was painting and the grandson was sitting for her. He casually said to her, 'Grandma, when you and Grandpa were dating, did you have sex?' Normally, we would have her throw the paintbrush down and say, 'Look, I don't want to discuss this', but we went the other way and she discussed it with him very sensibly because he was now the same age as she was back then and wanted to find out whether she thought it would be okay to have sex.

REG WATSON

Neighbours needed a theme and Reg turned to Tony Hatch and Jackie Trent who not only created many hits like the chart-topping 'Downtown' but also wrote the theme for *Crossroads*.

Tony and Jackie gave Reg a fancy dinner when their *Neighbours* royalties hit £25,000. Reg Watson wasn't happy that the Grundy Organisation got nothing.

Neighbours started off well enough in Melbourne but was soon struggling in Sydney. The problem may have been the differing time slots: ATN 7 in Sydney ran it at 5.30 pm while Melbourne and Adelaide had it at 6 pm, all before the news; while Brisbane played it at 7 pm, after their news and current affairs hour.

It wasn't long before ATN 7 virtually gave up on the series and moved it to 3.30 in the afternoon.

Neighbours was cancelled by the Seven network after 170 episodes.

In an unprecedented move, and to the astonishment of the industry, Ian Holmes managed to sell *Neighbours* to Ten.

The Sevens had a board meeting and decided to cancel the show. Casey called me from Melbourne and so did Ted Thomas in Sydney. I thought Neighbours *had never had a real chance with all the varying time slots and that there was still plenty of life in it. I called Max Bostock at Ten in Sydney and Bill McKenzie who ran Ten in Melbourne and suggested the idea of them taking over the show and they showed interest.*

IAN HOLMES

Ian added that it might be possible to buy the permanent sets from Channel Seven in Sydney.

Strangely enough, they were soon destroyed in an accidental fire.

And what's more, Ted Thomas, general manager of Seven Sydney, was threatening to sue Grundys for selling *Neighbours*, a show which Seven had cancelled and no longer wanted but in which it claimed to have rights.

Ted was particularly unhappy about pilots he had paid for being used to sell to other networks once Seven had passed.

This led to what was to become famously known in legal circles as 'the *Neighbours* clause'.

The Neighbours *clause meant that you couldn't shop around a show that has been bought and paid for. That got the stable door shut but the* Neighbours *horse had well and truly bolted.*

KERRY WRIGHT

Neighbours was repackaged for the Channel Ten network with a more youthful approach.

Channel Ten Melbourne is based in the suburb of Nunawading. The show was produced there and had its second premiere in January 1986.

Ten aired our *Perfect Match* at 5.30 pm, followed by the hour-long *Eyewitness News* at 6 pm. *Neighbours* was at 7 pm, replacing reruns of *MASH*.

Ten's head of publicity, Brian Walsh, came up with a great stunt to launch the series. He hired a couple of flat-top trucks, erected dummy sets that looked vaguely like *Neighbours*, flew some of the cast up from Melbourne and parked the lot outside Channel Seven at Epping while he slipped the security guard $100 to let them drive in and out of the Seven complex.

At 7.15 am, Ten's *Good Morning Australia* crossed live via helicopter to capture the trucks with sets and cast moving out of Seven's driveway. Each truck had a banner reading, 'We're moving *Neighbours* to a new home'.

Reg Watson wasn't happy.

I really didn't like the cast being involved in an in-joke of this nature. I thought the idea had been dropped and the first I knew was seeing them leaving ATN on the trucks and waving to camera.

REG WATSON

The Ten version of *Neighbours* featured new sets, new characters, a good deal more humour and a younger look with relative unknowns—Jason Donovan, Guy Pearce and Craig McLachlan—joining the cast. Kylie Minogue appeared after a couple of months and one of the great television romances was born. Charlene (Kylie) and Scott (Jason) would marry on camera and achieve one of the highest ever ratings in the history of Australian soaps.

Wonderful messages arrived, including this one:

Obviously Australia loves thy Neighbours. *Warm congratulations from all at Crawfords. With kind regards, Hector Crawford.*

Joy became Rosemary Daniels in *Neighbours* and by now no longer had to prove that being the boss's wife had nothing to do with getting the role.

She had to audition just like everyone else.

Joy has fond memories of *Neighbours*. One of her stories gives an indication as to why some people thought I was dead or perhaps had never existed at all.

It was near Christmas 1989 and we were shooting scenes for the show in Manchester in England. The actors were Derek Nimmo, the English comic actor who specialised in playing ministers and priests, Ian Smith who played Harold and Anne Charleston who played Madge, his wife ... and, of course, me as Rosemary Daniels.

On the first day Derek Nimmo was boasting about how well he knew Reg, that he was a close friend. Ian Smith got quite upset and said to me, 'Joy, this is not fair. I've been working for Reg for over ten years and I've never even met him but Derek Nimmo knows him well'. I said to Ian, 'I've been married to Reg for nearly twenty years and I can tell you that Derek has never met Reg'.

Ian was insistent, saying three or four times as the days passed, 'If Reg is here why can't I meet him?' So towards the final day I said to Reg, 'I really think it would be a good idea if you came round to the castle, where we're shooting. There's only Ian, Anne and Derek and I know Ian will appreciate it'.

Reg did finally drop in and Ian soon realised that he had never met Derek. Ian was delighted.

JOY CHAMBERS-GRUNDY

For many years I was a member of Actors' Equity, having been a performer of sorts with my own show in the early days. So I had some feeling for performers but over the years, I rarely met actors in my own shows.

Why? I'm not sure.

I suppose it has to do with my practice of not going to studio to see the shows made. You get into a habit. And I'm a pretty private guy, really. It took me a long time to decide to write these memoirs.

But I do like actors.

Occasionally I visit NIDA and watch students at work in the television studio named after me. Whoever you are, when you graduate and get your first big break, I'll be the one cheering the loudest.

Many actors came out of *Neighbours* to achieve big careers. Here's Reg Watson talking about one of them.

We had great difficulty casting the father, Jim Robinson, and finally settled on second choice. We started recording the outside broadcast scenes and I wasn't happy with him at all. The scenes were coming in and they weren't good and I thought, 'Oh my God, this is going to ruin it. It just won't work with him'. Then his agent rang out of the blue and said, 'He wants more money'. I was able to say he'd broken his contract and we were able to fire him. But we were now in a position of having a show without a lead actor when, strangely, the phone rang and it was Alan Dale and he said, 'Why won't you give me work?' and I said 'You'd better come and talk about it'. I explained that I'd heard nobody would write for him because he had a reputation of being so vehement about people's scripts that he would throw them across the studio. I said, 'If I can have your personal assurance that this won't ever happen, we will try you out'. He said it wouldn't happen and thanked me very much and

I told him to get on the plane and fly down to Melbourne. We then reshot all the scenes to include him.

REG WATSON

Brian Walsh launched a marketing blitzkrieg which worked the younger stars almost to death. Every weekend they would leave Nunawading to fly all over the country for shopping centre appearances. They would get rapturous receptions but still the ratings were less than brilliant. Ten was seriously thinking of pulling the plug.

Walsh and the Grundy Organisation held a desperation meeting and Walsh suggested doing some filming in Sydney.

He is reported to have been watching filming on Manly Beach when he phoned Ray Miller, then editor of the Sydney *Daily Mirror*, to say that there were 'two kids in school uniform and, fair dinkum, they're having a sex scene down here'.

They weren't—but the resulting front-page headline, 'Shock Teen Sex on TV', seemed to do the trick and ratings started to rise.

Brian Walsh, who deserves a lot of the credit for the eventual success of *Neighbours*, soon became our head of publicity.

Neighbours became a critically important program for us. Not only because it would eventually produce distribution income of eighteen million US dollars gross a year, but also because it helped me to at last break into the UK television fortress.

We'd been making regular visits to London since our honeymoon in 1971 but I was never able to make any serious inroads.

Finally, BBC's program director, Michael Grade, visited Los Angeles and he and I had lunch at the Wilshire hotel in Beverly Hills. Mike Firman had put pressure on him to meet with me, even though it was clear that the BBC was not accepting outside producers.

I told him about our success with game shows and serial drama.

When I mentioned money he played a straight bat.

'I don't think we could afford it,' he said. That's code for, 'We won't let you in'.

I tried one more time. 'We have a serial in production. We'd be prepared to include an English family who had migrated to Australia.'

'That's a good idea.' He was visibly brighter.

It wasn't long before Bill Cotton, managing director of BBC Television, and Roger Laughton, controller of TV daytime, visited Sydney. We looked at a couple of episodes in Ian Holmes's office. They seemed impressed but the BBC mills grind exceedingly slowly and they didn't actually commit.

But it looked promising and *Neighbours*, although still shaky with ratings of twelve, looked like it might get a new lease of life.

The BBC took its time but at last decided it wanted a soap in its new daytime line-up and there were five candidates. Four of them were US productions. The other was *Neighbours*.

Ian Holmes was able to issue a press statement:

The Grundy Organisation has concluded agreements with the BBC in Britain for their purchase of the Grundy-produced serial drama, Neighbours.

Mr Holmes said, 'The BBC has purchased Neighbours *for national broadcast throughout their United Kingdom network. We understand they intend airing the drama in their new daytime schedule, five days a week'.*

The historic first episode was shipped by Visnews to Britain for editing 'to meet BBC requirements' (that is, to remove commercial breaks) and was transmitted at 1.30 pm on 27 October 1986. There was a repeat the next day at 9.05 am.

As far as the BBC was concerned, *Neighbours* was to be just a little low-cost soap to fill a slot in the afternoon schedule. It turned out to be a bit more than that, and soon had a loyal and apparently even royal audience.

Colin Stanley-Hill was the Australian court correspondent and once a member of the Queen Mother's staff. He received a phone call at 3 am one morning. 'It's the Palace here, Colin. What's happening on *Neighbours*? The Queen Mother is very interested to know what stage it's got to in Australia.'

In January 1988, BBC program controller Michael Grade gave in to general viewer demands and those of his sixteen-year-old daughter,

Alison, and moved *Neighbours* to 5.35 pm, with a repeat the next day in the old daytime slot.

Within a couple of months there were more people watching *Neighbours* in Britain than the entire population of Australia. The program was whipping *Coronation Street* in the ratings.

And the BBC was paying a fat dollar. By 1995, when I sold the business, it was US$60,000 an episode. Multiply that by the annual production run of 240 and it comes to US$14.4 million just for transmission on the BBC.

But that all came later. In the earlier years, keeping *Neighbours* on air was a continuing problem for us.

Ten steadily reduced the licence fee to the point where production could continue only because of the BBC sale. We made nothing out of it in Australia and had Australia been the only market, *Neighbours* would have ceased production. Dick Barovick and I took on the battle of keeping the British end alive.

We'd be in London saying to one another, 'We've got to get a commitment for another three years or the show will end'. Finally we offered a flat rate for the next three years with no increases. The BBC accepted the offer.

In the second half of the 1980s, Australian television hit tough times.

In 1987 the Ten network was bought by Frank Lowy through his company Northern Star. Frank Lowy is one of Australia's most successful businessmen, but TV was not for him. In 1989 he sold a controlling interest to Steve Cosser for $22 million.

At the same time Christopher Skase had bought the Seven network. Struggling under the weight of debt plus management fees to himself and other execs of 100 million in 1989 alone, Skase made an outrageous bid of 1.2 billion (raised to 1.5) to buy MGM/UA movie studios and film library in America. The bid failed and Skase's company Qintex went into meltdown.

Receivership threatened both Channels Ten and Seven and they were having trouble meeting their monthly commitments. This was the time to make them an offer they couldn't refuse.

I called Ian Holmes.

'Ian, this is a one in a million chance to buy back the rights to all our shows on both Seven and Ten.'

We paid $5.5 million, most of it to Ten, and recovered all rights both networks held in Grundy programs.

Ten and Seven had had 35 per cent of the end rights to shows as profitable as *Neighbours*, *Prisoner* and *The Restless Years* to name but three, and now we owned 100 per cent of all of them.

With *Neighbours* alone returning $15.1 million gross in 1994, it was one of our best ever deals, right up there with buying world rights to *Sale of the Century*.

That was the genius of Reg Grundy. While everyone else was in retreat, he decided to go forward. It was an extraordinary move and a turning point for the company. I think we got the 5.5 million back in just one or two sales.

JIM HENRY

Other opportunities presented themselves over the years.

At one point, Ten's share price was down to about 20 cents.

I approached Frances O'Brien, who was our company secretary (I never called her by her Christian name).

'I think we should put all our money into Channel Ten. What do you reckon, Miss O'Brien?'

'Mr Grundy, that's not the business of this company.'

That was that. One never argued with Miss O'Brien.

But I knew we would continue to make shows for Ten. So I did finish up putting a fair whack into the network.

Sometimes it's better to go with your own instincts than rely on someone else's view.

At the same time as we bought the rights to our TV shows back from Seven and Ten, Bruce Gordon bought Crawford Productions. Not quite as profitable a deal as ours, though. Years later Bruce said, 'I bought Crawfords and have successfully managed to lose a million a year ever since.'

I guess that's show biz.

Twenty years after *Neighbours* began, it was being screened in about sixty countries to an estimated audience of over forty million. Fans from all over the world were making the long pilgrimage to Melbourne to visit the real-life Ramsay Street and the television studios where the show was made. Not bad for a show 'where nothing much happens.'

It's hard to work out the secret of the whopping success of *Neighbours* in Britain. It's easy to suggest that the bright, sunny show was a pleasant contrast to gloomy Britain, or that viewers responded well to the classless world and to the core theme of young people communicating with older people. And it is well known historically that British audiences are loyal.

All that may be true, but the most engaging suggestion is that little *Neighbours* offers 'an attainable *Dallas*'.

You don't see my name on *Neighbours* any more. When Fremantle bought the company it replaced my name on all the programs we had made.

A number of countries in Europe did not.

Grundy Light Entertainment in Germany run by Ute Biernat, the very impressive CEO.

Grundy Productions, Spain, where until recently Emanuela Spinetta, a good friend, kept the flag flying.

Grundy Productions, Italy, also run, until recently, by Emanuela.

Grundy/UFA was and still is the drama joint-venture company in Germany responsible for producing a number of hugely successful soaps, where we enjoyed a great relationship with the charismatic Wolf Bauer.

Magyar Grundy/UFA is a subsidiary of Grundy/UFA, producing TV programs in Hungary and other places.

So the Grundy brand goes on, even when my name has disappeared in my homeland.

VALE BOBBIE

Sale of the Century was going well and I was getting used to the idea of being a producer of American game shows … in America.

I liked the feeling.

But as the business grew I was away from Australia for most of the year.

Many times, Joy and I tried to persuade my mother to come with us but she had a fear of flying and missed the chance to experience my success first hand.

In 1983, Joy arranged for Audrey Driver, a registered nurse, to become my mother's companion, moving into the Double Bay flat with her—the same flat I had lived in until I married.

Audrey had to manage a strong-willed woman who sat regally in her lounge chair each day and watched her son's shows. I don't think she missed too many, although, in 1983, she would have needed a nimble finger on the remote to watch them all. There was *Prisoner* and *Perfect Match* on Ten, *Waterloo Station* and *Sale of the Century* on Nine, plus *Runaway Island*, *Sons and Daughters*, *New Price Is Right* and *Wheel of Fortune* on Seven.

An impressive run, but there were to be even more prolific periods in our production history.

It was difficult to get Bobbie out of her throne in her small living room but sometimes she and Audrey ventured out for lunch in Double Bay or even as far as Doyle's at Watsons Bay. They were driven there and back and always returned in time for her to settle into her chair and turn on the TV.

A ritual developed. At five each afternoon, Audrey handed Bobbie a whiskey and water. Much water, little whiskey. The one drink lasted for hours as she forgot to pick up her glass once the shows started.

I have always thought that even though Bobbie would never fly in an aircraft she was given one of the greatest gifts a child could bestow on a parent. Being able to sit and watch her only son's television shows every weekday and even sometimes on weekends for decades of her life.

Joy Chambers-Grundy

We had been in Australia for Christmas and had returned to LA on 3 January 1984 in time to celebrate the first anniversary of *Sale of the Century* on NBC.

The next day I got the news that my mother had fallen and broken her hip.

It seems she had walked over to the mantelpiece to straighten a small bust of me when she collapsed. It was distressing for Audrey who had left the room a moment before.

We were back in Sydney on the fifth.

Joy and I stayed at the Sebel Townhouse so that I could be near to my mother in St Vincent's Hospital, just five minutes away.

A week later, my mother seemed to be well on the way to recovery and was telling me that I should get on with my life. 'I'm all right, Bubby, as long as you phone me while you're away. Give me a kiss and do whatever you have to do.'

Bubby. Strange name for a sixty-three-year-old man but it had been her name for me since I was a kid. And whichever word she used—bubby, bubba or bub—it was a word of love.

Should I go or should I stay?

The doctors assured me that my mother was recovering. That she'd be okay.

We flew out to Vancouver, then Toronto and on to Bermuda, where we received the keys to our new home on the island's south shore.

At 6.20 am on 3 February, the phone rang. It was my personal assistant and dear friend who was to stay with us for thirty years, Di Ayres.

'Reg, I think you'd better come back. Your mum's asking for you.'

I had been calling my mother every day but now phone calls weren't enough.

We were on a 9.17 am flight back to Sydney.

Again we were at the Sebel to be close to my mother.

I visited her every day. I couldn't leave Sydney now.

Throughout her illness, my mother had accepted the pain without complaint. She was making a brave effort to recover but now she had to deal with pneumonia.

Nine days later, on Monday 27 February, she died.

Lillian Josephine Grundy had been the best of mothers to me and a wonderful, loving de facto mum to my one and only child.

On 29 February, we said goodbye to her. She was laid to rest in the cemetery at Mona Vale, minutes away from our Bayview home and a hundred metres from where Joy's lovely mother, May Chambers, had been buried six years earlier.

My mother had often come to Bayview to help Joy in nursing May in her last months. May Chambers died in our home, aged seventy-one.

Now both these unselfish, marvellous mothers were gone.

We visit them whenever we are in Sydney.

Even now, when I think of my mother, I regret the questions I didn't ask about our wonderful life together.

SCRABBLE

I was in New York staying at the Helmsley Palace. Dick Barovick was on the phone.

'Michael King wants to meet with you. How about tomorrow at eleven. Your suite?'

'The distributor guy? Okay, but better give me a rundown on him.'

'His dad started them off by selling the old black and white kids' series, *Our Gang*. The sons Michael and Roger lifted their game. They discovered Oprah Winfrey in Chicago. Michael's a good man for you to meet.'

Michael was right on time. 'Reg, nice to meet you. You're doing great. Congratulations.'

He wasn't wasting time.

'We've picked up the rights to *Monopoly*. We'd like you to come up with a TV version.'

What an opportunity!

Michael added, 'Of course, we're asking a couple of other producers to come up with a format as well'.

'Michael, I'm pretty independent. Never competed in a beauty contest. Done okay on my own.'

Michael got to his feet.

'Understand. Let me know if you change your mind. Could be another good move for you.'

I called Bob Noah in our LA office.

Bob had become a member of my American group in time for the start of *Sale of the Century*.

In the early 1980s it had become clear that I was going to need someone who was as connected to game shows as I was and there was no one better qualified than Bob Noah. He had a splendid game show mind—still does.

He'd created shows like *21*, *Concentration* and *Tic Tac Dough* and had worked for all the big American game show producers including Goodson-

Todman and Heatter-Quigley. He had impeccable credentials so I went after him. He took some getting but finally gave in and we respected each other and worked happily together for a decade.

Between us, we might be able to give this *Monopoly* thing a good shake. Worth a try anyway.

'Bob, even if we do take it on, there's no guarantee we can come up with a speeded up version that'll work on TV.'

But I couldn't walk away from it. I had to keep throwing punches.

'What the hell,' Bob Noah said, 'let's have a go. What have we got to lose?'

The problem was to create a version of *Monopoly* in which we were certain to have a winner in less than half an hour.

We reckoned we had found a way.

We had an elaborate tabletop game board built and the King brothers with their CEO and Michael's wife Barbara came to the run-through in our office at 9911 Pico Boulevard, Beverly Hills.

They loved it, even played at the table themselves after the formal presentation ended.

But we had a problem. In order to get a winner in a limited time we had introduced a new element that was not part of the traditional *Monopoly*.

Kingworld was worried that Parker Brothers, who owned the rights, would not accept the changes and so they finally didn't go with us—they turned to Merv Griffin, who had made it big with the US version of *Wheel of Fortune*.

His interpretation included Mister Money Bags, the little man in the Top Hat—the *Monopoly* symbol. Ours didn't. His show lasted twelve weeks on ABC.

A few years later CBS bought Kingworld for about three and half billion dollars.

We'd put a lot of effort into *Monopoly* and were disappointed to miss out, but there are two great board games in the world and we had more luck with the other one.

Not that it was easy.

Scrabble was a monster of a thing to adapt and I remember saying, 'You can't just put *Scrabble* on television, because who'd watch it? It'd be worse than watching chess'.

Bob Noah and I played around with it for ages and finally decided to use just two letters as the basis for each game. From that we created a marvellous show which really wasn't *Scrabble* but looked like *Scrabble*.

We had a board which looked exactly like a *Scrabble* board—same colours—and even people who played *Scrabble* believed it was *Scrabble*.

Scrabble might have been difficult to adapt but it was one of the easiest formats to sell. In fact, I hardly had to sell it at all.

I hadn't pitched it to anyone when we had a call from NBC to say that although *Sale of the Century* was doing well, the shows around it were disasters.

'We need something,' they said. 'Have you got anything?'

Of course we had something. But I could see a problem. Our *Scrabble* was bright, amusing and involving and you could play along at home, just like *Wheel of Fortune*. What would NBC think about that?

Bob Noah and I discussed the odds.

'Reg, they'll pass if they feel it's too like *Wheel of Fortune*. After all, they're both based on letters of the alphabet.'

'Yeah, or they may go for it because it's like *Wheel*.'

NBC's two senior daytime executives, Brian Frons and Jake Tauber, came to our offices on Pico Boulevard late one afternoon to see a tabletop run-through.

At the end of the run-through, Tauber said, 'Got a room?'

We knew what that meant. It meant they wanted to go somewhere away from us to discuss matters, alone. We were in with a chance. If they hadn't liked it, they'd have been out the door.

They weren't gone long and Brian Frons was smiling when they came back.

'We like it,' he said.

He took a breath and continued.

'And do you know why? Because it's kinda like *Wheel* and should work well in the slot after *Wheel*. Let's make a pilot.'

So we did. But first we needed a host.

I was in Sydney hanging off a phone line while Bob Noah and Bob Crystal ran the auditions in LA. No one was thrilled with the results.

Then I remembered Chuck Woolery. Chuck had been host of *Wheel of Fortune* but came second in an argument about money with owner Merv Griffin and quit in 1981.

Bob Noah said, 'Chuck's a great idea.'

Brian Frons was disappointingly dubious but agreed to talk to Brandon Tartikoff. Brandon said, 'The audience loved Chuck on *Wheel*. Why won't they like him in *Scrabble*?'

The program launch for *Scrabble* was in the Rainbow Room at Rockefeller Center. We flew into New York and it was the usual razzle-dazzle with large quantities of drink and finger food. The pilot was played and apparently enjoyed.

I met Chuck Woolery for the first time. 'Hi,' he said. 'I just wanted to meet the man who pays my salary.'

And it was a pretty good salary too for those days, soon to reach $7500 a week. Happily for us, our deal with NBC said that the network paid everything in excess of $2500.

And there was an elderly man who sat nodding and smiling as he watched the show. He was Alfred Mosher Butts, who had invented the game in the 1930s. And what did he say to me?

'Very nice, Reg. But it's not *Scrabble*.'

It was on one of our trips to New York that Tom McManus, who ran international sales and distribution for me, arranged for us to visit Jim and Sheila Cruthers or, to be precise, Sir James and Lady Cruthers.

Cruthers turned the first sod when Perth's television station TVW 7 was being built. He became the chairman and managing director.

Their apartment was in the Museum of Modern Art tower, looking down on the Sculpture Garden.

Sheila opened the door and, as she heard our knock, she was thinking, 'Reg isn't young any more so I've got a pretty good idea what his wife will look like'. She later said she couldn't believe that instead of being an elderly lady, my wife was a stunning young blonde.

Sheila was very active in New York creating an awareness of Australian art and the walls of the apartment were covered with fine examples. I didn't know much about art collecting and neither did Joy, but we decided to start learning and buying.

Sheila and Jim's son John Cruthers is now the curator of our Australian art collection.

Jim had become personal adviser to Rupert Murdoch in New York—a deal which was made on one piece of paper which they both signed.

He called the next day and said, 'Rupert would like to meet you'.

I got a cab and headed for the *New York Post*. I told Rupert how economical it would be to make *Prisoner* in America. If I'd convinced him, I think he'd have taken it on and he wouldn't have cared about the cost of the show.

Eventually he said, 'Is your driver still waiting downstairs?'

'Oh, no. I'll get a cab.'

Probably it's imagination, but it did seem to me that Rupert blinked. I might have been the only person ever to come to a meeting with him who didn't have a limo waiting downstairs.

Not that I cared.

I had two networked shows on NBC five days a week. That's ten shows, each carrying a credit for Reg Grundy Productions.

The guy with the funny accent had finally arrived.

ROGER EASTGATE HOLDEN MIRAMS

Roger Mirams had an amazing life in the industry.

He was official photographer at the 1956 Olympic Games in Melbourne.

I was there as a broadcaster covering the events for 2CH, but we didn't meet until many years later.

Roger was a one off—a wonderful producer with a zest for life who had bacon and eggs for breakfast every day and drank 'rooster's blood' (red wine) every day of his life.

In 1971 and again in 1972 he produced *Sky Force* with Ron McLean as writer—a groundbreaking series backed by Paramount.

Later, both Ron and Roger would finish up working for me.

Way back when we lived at Bayview I invited Roger to come and have coffee with me. After the small talk I looked at him and said, 'How would you like to eat on a regular basis?'

'Sounds good.'

'Then why don't you come and work for me?'

Roger joined me that very day.

He produced a large number of excellent international co-productions for children under the Grundy banner. They included: *The Lost Islands* (1976), *Secret Valley* (1980), *Runaway Island* (1982), *Professor Poopsnagle and His Flying Zeppelin* (1989) and *South Pacific Adventures* (1990).

Most of Roger's projects were directed by Howard Rubie. The cameraman on *Professor Poopsnagle* was Ray Henman, who had manned a turret lens camera in the studios at TCN 9 when I first appeared on TV.

Roger was the oldest producer in our group but I fondly called him our youngest producer.

Yes, he loved life. He was full of ideas and enthusiasm.

And that turned out to be a problem.

On the first day of a shoot he would invariably want to change something.

Roger's deals were extraordinarily complex. He would sell a show to Spain and then happily accept that he must use a Spanish actor. No problem. The Spaniard might end up playing an English admiral even though he barely spoke English. But he was in the show.

Productions often started before Kerry Wright, our legal counsel, could sort out the deals and eventually Roger was told that he couldn't start shooting until Kerry had signed off on the legalities and Sue McIntosh, our Chief Financial Officer, on the financials. Roger never took a blind bit of notice and always started when he wanted.

But he wasn't a producer who lived high on the hog. Every possible penny was up on the screen.

Kerry Wright admired him for the way he battled on, saving money by crossing Europe by second class rail and avoiding hotels whenever possible. When in Monaco, for instance, he stayed in Kerry's spare room.

We all loved Roger. And we all miss him.

Ian Holmes, who was running the Australian operation, saw a lot of Roger and has particular memories of him.

Roger's first house on Mackerel Beach, Pittwater was one of those Canadian pre-fab log cabins which he put together himself. He never had any money, spending it all on his films. There was no road access but he had a mate who owned an amphibious Duck and that's how he got all the materials across Pittwater. He had a grand piano over there too and no doubt it got there the same way.

Roger sold that house and built another which he named 'Roger's Last Erection'.

He loved entertaining families and kids and often had gatherings on holidays like Australia Day. The house was up a steep incline and he'd installed a chair lift. Kids loved it especially when they were bombed with water balloons as they made the climb. There were arms reaching up out of the ground, skeletons dangling in the trees and if you visited the guest bathroom there was an arm reaching out of the toilet bowl.

Roger thought like a child which is one of the reasons kids liked his shows so much.

IAN HOLMES

We were not in Australia when he died in early 2004 but we had our memories.

Joy and I waving to Roger as he played his trombone on his front verandah overlooking Pittwater and hoisted the skull and crossbones to indicate he was home as we sailed to West Head in *Carolyn J*.

And the day Roger married Irene. We were taken with other guests across Pittwater on the Palm Beach ferry, a jazz band playing all the way. The minister marrying them on the beach was barefooted, as we all were. It seemed the right way to celebrate two people coming together who were determined to enjoy every moment of their lives.

Roger's shows never made any money and his co-production arrangements produced endless headaches.

But he sure was a joy to have around.

TIME MACHINE

Michael Brockman was heading up daytime at ABC in Los Angeles when Bob Noah, Bob Crystal and I had lunch with him.

Over a Cobb salad Michael said, '*Name That Tune* has been one of the great game shows of all time. Do you reckon you fellas could come up with a format based on music but that isn't *Name That Tune*? Sandy Frank owns *Tune* and the last thing I want to do is negotiate with him'.

Sandy was a one off—an aggressive salesman who wouldn't take no for an answer. His area was syndication, selling shows to television stations right across the country.

Stories about him are legendary.

In the 1970s Sandy is flying across America. He feigns a heart attack. The aircraft makes an emergency landing close to the city where he has an appointment with one of the local broadcasters. Sandy makes a miraculous recovery and gets to the television station right on time.

Sandy phoned prospects when the spirit took him. He never calculated the time difference, so sometimes a prospect's phone would ring in the early hours of the morning.

One suffering broadcaster decided to make Sandy break the habit. He recorded a message and phoned it in to Sandy every morning for seven consecutive days. 'Hi, Sandy, it's Bill Williams. It's 7 am here in New York. What time is it in LA?'

It would have been 4 am.

Next time Sandy needed to call Williams, he made sure he checked the time first.

Are the stories true? Maybe. Well, it's fun to think so.

Bob Noah and I looked at each other across the table. We knew we had a problem. While there had been many *Name That Tune* reincarnations they all suffered from the same problem. A tune that could be identified by a grandfather may not be recognisable to his son and most certainly would not be known to his grandson.

So the show had a massive demographic problem.

In the 1970s and 1980s producers tried to overcome it by limiting the tunes to rock and standards, thereby pleasing no one.

We had to create a show where knowing the title of the tune was irrelevant.

After weeks of work we came up with *Keynotes* and ABC funded a pilot.

We thought it turned out well. Better than well, in fact.

But ABC turned it down.

We believed they were clearly wrong. So we made another pilot for NBC. Again it was turned down. Later, we produced the show in England and Australia but it never reached the heights we'd hoped for it.

Bob Noah and I had worked together over the years doing run-throughs of game show ideas we invented. Some resulted in shows which found an audience in America, some became big hits in other countries, and some failed to make the cut.

Time Machine was one show that bombed in America and failed to see the light of day anywhere else in the world.

Bill Barr was a staff question writer for *Sale of the Century* and he persuaded us to watch a run-through of a game show he had created. Normally we didn't look at other people's formats, but Bill was a popular figure in the Grundy group and we made an exception.

Bill had called his idea *Time Machine*.

For the first time, Bob and I sat watching someone else's run-through.

The concept was based on nostalgia and working out price tags from the past. Bob and I liked it, and persuaded NBC to come to a presentation at the Sheraton Universal hotel in the Valley.

By the end of the run-through it was obvious that Brian Frons and his off-sider Jake Tauber liked the show.

'It's good,' said Frons, 'but we don't want contestants sitting behind desks. Think *Price Is Right*. Give us some action and movement and we might be interested.'

We knew that *Price Is Right* had been a big hit in the late 1950s and early 1960s with four contestants sitting behind a desk.

Then, in the 1970s, Bud Grant, president of CBS programming, had persuaded a reluctant Mark Goodson, whose company owned *Price Is Right*, to come up with a more modern version in which contestants came out of the audience. And there were no desks.

History was about to be repeated.

But we had a concern. Yes, we could make the show with a modern *Price Is Right* look, but should we make a show that featured pricing? A typical question on *Time Machine* might be, 'How much were theatre tickets in 1947?'

Wouldn't we be too close to *Price Is Right*?

We decided to throw out the pricing and in doing so we threw the baby out with the bathwater.

We worked hard to come up with games that had numerical answers but were not dollar values.

NBC was having a network meeting in Los Angeles and wanted us to do a slap-up run-through of the new style *Time Machine* for visiting NBC executives.

There was no studio available so we rented Francis Ford Coppola's Zoetrope Props Bay.

It was a long, fairly narrow area and we hung a drape lengthwise dividing the area into two walkways. Then we set up miniature cardboard sets along the walls which ran the length of the walkway and back. At the far end, the curtain fell short of reaching the wall so that our mobile audience could walk round the curtain and down the other side while watching more games being played.

Robert Wright, soon to become president and CEO of NBC, was there along with Brandon Tartikoff, president of programming. With them were John Agoglia, executive VP of business affairs, Ray Timothy, president of NBC owned and operated stations, Steve Sohmer, executive VP and writer, married to Deidre Hall, one of the stars of *Days of Our Lives*, and John Miller, head of publicity and creative advertising.

It was the most illustrious audience we ever had.

Bob Noah was the MC and I was the producer as I led our portable audience from one set to the next.

It went very well and the executives were taken to an area that we'd set up with a circle of chairs, all illuminated from above. Their conference was brief and they soon started to make their exit but not before I fronted up to Brandon Tartikoff.

'Brandon, we've based this show on the certain knowledge that the audience attention span is getting shorter and shorter and that's why the format has a series of games, all of them brief. We want to grab them and then move on before they get bored.'

Brandon nodded in agreement. 'We'll get back to you.'

Later that day, NBC ordered the show. It must have been one of the fastest program buys of all time.

Just as we had for *Sale of the Century* and *Scrabble*, we brought Bill Mason over from Australia and turned him loose on *Time Machine*.

He did a slap-up job. The set alone cost a million dollars.

But it was obvious from episode one that the show wasn't working.

Right to the end we were making changes, even cancelling production for a week while we tried to get it right. But nothing could prevent it from being a slow-motion train wreck.

Time Machine lasted nineteen weeks.

Why nineteen and not thirteen?

The network didn't have a replacement ready and, in any case, keeping the show on air for a further six weeks helped write off the cost of the set.

HOT STREAK

The fact that we'd made pilots of *Keynotes* for two American networks and they'd both turned it down was irritating but not discouraging

After all, before Bob Noah joined me he'd made three pilots of his show *Sabotage*; one for each network—ABC, CBS and NBC. All three said no.

I'd seen his pilots and liked the show. So after we'd been together for a while, we came up with the idea of transforming the *Sabotage* format and trying to sell it again.

By 1983 we'd greatly changed the show and called it *Party Line*. NBC ordered a pilot which had elements of *Laugh-in* mixed with the original *Sabotage* format.

It went well. We liked the pilot.

NBC turned it down.

In those days, when an established game show producer came up with an idea he called one of the networks and set up a time for the daytime programming people to see a run-through.

Bob Noah and I came up with an idea, which we called *Back Seat Driver*.

In response to our phone call Jackie Smith, head of ABC daytime, duly turned up at our offices.

It was the worst, most embarrassing demo in which I had been involved. As usual Bob Noah acted as host and I played the silent producer. Bob realised it was dying but valiantly struggled on. Whenever I could I caught his eye and smiled reassuringly.

He knew it was terrible and he knew that I knew.

It was just rotten is what it was.

BOB NOAH

At last it was over.

Usually if the network people didn't like the idea or felt that it didn't suit their schedule, they were quick to leave. This time Jackie lingered.

Here was my chance.

'Jackie, if you're not in a hurry, I'd like to screen what we believe is a wonderful show we made for one of your competitors. I think it would be just right for your schedule.'

Noah was looking at me and shaking his head.

To my surprise Jackie said, 'Let's see it'.

So I ran *Party Line*, the pilot that NBC had just turned down.

When it was over Jackie said, 'I like it. Let's do a pilot'.

Bob was still shaking his head.

We reworked it again, drastically changed the format and this time called it *Hot Streak*. It was fast, sometimes funny and invariably exciting. It was the best version so far and ABC loved it.

I talked to Bob Noah about a possible host.

'There's a guy in England, big star, who I think would be perfect. I'm going to send Bob Crystal over to try and get an option on him.'

Bobby flew to London and over afternoon tea at Harrods got a verbal agreement from Bruce Forsyth.

We lobbied the network but it took time to get their okay. In the meantime Bruce, who was holidaying in Puerto Rico, had become impatient and returned to Britain.

Finally the network agreed. Now we had to get Bruce's formal commit-ment. It wasn't easy but eventually he agreed to our offer. Bruce Forsyth would host *Hot Streak*.

He came to LA with his beautiful wife, Puerto Rican Wilnelia Merced, who had represented her country and become Miss World.

A Rodeo Drive outfitter offered to supply Bruce's suits.

We were on our way.

The program was to be a daytime strip, Monday to Friday, and it was the tradition to record a week's worth of episodes in one day. Bruce was appalled.

'I can't do more than two shows in a shift.'

We talked to wife Winnie who talked to Bruce and persuaded him to give it a go. The studio audience loved him; the applause and laughter were the best we had heard in any studio. During the day, Bruce got better and better and, when the five shows had been recorded, said, 'Why don't we do this in England? It's terrific'.

Later in London we showed them how.

Hot Streak went to air on 6 January 1986. It lasted just sixteen weeks—sixty-five episodes. New people were programming ABC's daytime and, as so often happens, the new broom swept clean.

So a format originally called *Sabotage* had been made three times, then remade first as *Party Line* and then as *Hot Streak*. Soon there was to be a sixth version: *Ruck Zuck*.

In January 1988, *Ruck Zuck* premiered in Germany and ran for almost thirteen years.

At last we'd got it right—in another language. All along we'd known it was a good show.

Selling television productions isn't easy.

But I seemed to be getting the hang of it.

MY MATE EDDIE

I first met Eddie Williams around 1948 when I was calling the fights for 2SM. He owned radio station 2BS in Bathurst and was part-owner of 2DU Dubbo with Wally Grant. They took the fight calls on relay. Ed called in to 2SM one day to say hello. We hit it off straight away and when I switched to 2CH he followed me, rather than staying with 2SM.

Eddie had been mayor of Bathurst at one time, earning the title of 'the flying alderman' because of the way he drove his old Holden around town and because he competed at the local speedway on his motorbike.

Eddie invited me to Bathurst to appear on his Friday night radio sports show, which was called something like *In Bathurst Tonight*.

An hour before it went to air Ed said, 'Come on, Reggie, we better go and get the prizes.' We cruised around Machattie Park, stopping outside a greengrocer's shop where the roller shutter was halfway down.

'Buddy, it's me, Eddie. We've come for the goods.'

Up went the shutter. Buddy and Eddie shook hands.

'This is Reg Grundy. You know, the fight caller? He's the guest star tonight.'

That was news to me. I mumbled something and got out of the way.

'We've got some good stuff for you this week, Ed.'

He rolled off such words as bananas, cauliflowers, potatoes, beetroot and other fruit and vegetables, which were transferred in cartons into Ed's Holden.

We got to the station and I watched anxiously as the needle on the long play vinyl disc of the show going to air got closer and closer to the middle of the disc.

We shouldn't be here. We're due on air in a handful of minutes, I kept thinking.

Eddie was letting me do the worrying, as the needle was about to reach the final groove.

'Maybe we should go down,' I mentioned as casually as I could.

'Okay, Reggie, if you want to,' replied Eddie.

If I want to. I was a bundle of nerves.

Down we strolled to the small theatre in the basement of the 2BS building. It was a full house. I was in the front row as Eddie strolled out on stage just as the red light started flashing: 'On Air'.

Eddie did his opening spiel and the show got under way. Local sporting celebrities came and went, then Eddie reappeared.

'Now's the time for the highlight of our show, *Buddy's Sports Quiz*. And to present this week's question is the man we all listen to calling the fights. From 2SM, all the way up here from Sydney ... Reg Grundy!'

'Come on up, Reg.'

Eddie had not briefed me on this.

He was looking straight at me.

'Okay, Reg, what's tonight's sporting question? Bet it'll be on boxing. And for your information the jackpot didn't go off last week so tonight we're adding a galaxy of fruit and vegetables from Buddy's greengrocery.

'All right, hands up anyone in the audience who wants to have a go.

'Okay, Bill in the second row, come on up.'

It took a while but Bill finally got there. Meanwhile, the audience happily chatted amongst themselves.

'Quiet, quiet. Let Reg ask his question and see if Bill takes out the jackpot.'

I mumbled some question about who was middleweight Empire champion. Bill came up with the right answer and there was much applause as Eddie listed the fruit and vegetables Bill had won.

Later that night I saw a man slowly pedalling around the park with cartons and crates attached to his bicycle. It was Bill, who had become Bathurst's latest radio star.

The next day was Saturday and Ed took me to the races where 2BS was covering the whole card. No broadcast box—just the two of us sitting in the stand with the gear around us. Ed was both the engineer and the race caller.

With one race to go he turned to me. 'Ever called a race?'

I remember sinking down on the bench pretending not to be there.

'Come on, Reggie, there're only three nags in this last one.' He called in to the station.

'Cross over now,' he said down the line.

'Well, listeners. We've got a great surprise for you. We've got a guest caller for the last race. You probably heard him on 2BS last night. Okay, Reg Grundy, it's all yours.'

I struggled to give a sound picture of the three nags milling around waiting for the starter's signal.

And then they were off.

Out of the blue I recalled that one of the horses was called Rag Doll. Ed whispered to me that the other two were Here's Luck and Surprise Package.

Rag Doll immediately went to the front with Here's Luck close behind and Surprise Package running last. That's how they started. And that's how they finished. I just said those three names over and over again until they crossed the finishing line.

On the way back in the car, Ed turned on the radio. We were just in time to hear the studio announcer saying: 'And now, here is a replay of the final race at today's meeting with guest commentator Reg Grundy'.

I listened to the playback as I repeated the three horses' names until at last the race was over. The announcer was saying, 'Well, that's one of the finest race calls any of us are likely to hear, from that great sportscaster, Reg Grundy'.

Eddie flashed me a grin. 'Told you you could do it. You were terrific!'

Many years later Eddie was laughing with me about that weekend.

'They weren't bad days were they, Reggie?'

He was about the only person who ever called me Reggie. He was ten years older and often lengthened it to 'my boy Reggie'.

On a later visit I took along a guy who was doing some writing for me at 2SM. Let's call him Joe.

Ed took us out to a dirt track he'd made in the bush. We put this guy Joe on Ed's motorbike, gave him a push, and started him travelling around the circular track. There he was, sitting up like Jackie, going round and round, resplendent in tweed jacket, tie and all.

And then Joe started waving at us as he went by.

It was Eddie who finally woke up. Joe was waving because he didn't know how to stop the bike. Ed grabbed him the next time around. He had a bit of a fall but as Ed said, 'Better than watching him starve to death on my bloody bike'.

Suddenly, it was twenty-five years later.

It was one night in our home in Bayview in the 1970s about a year or so before we got a silent line. Joy answered the phone and came to me. 'There's a lady called Sophie on the phone. She says her husband Ed Williams is an old friend of yours. Have you ever heard of him?'

'Eddie Williams?' I was delighted. I took the phone.

'Hello, Reg, I'm Sophie. Ed would love to catch up with you. You know he's a member of the Broadcasting Control Board now?'

Eddie on the control board. I couldn't believe it.

'Is Ed home now? Could I speak to him?'

'Oh, would you mind?'

As if I would ...

'Hello, Reggie.'

It was the same old Eddie Williams. The cheerful voice that I had not heard for years. It was a renewal of the friendship we'd had and now it would continue until Ed died.

More years passed and we were living in Bermuda when Eddie was on the phone yet again

'Reggie, I've got some great news. At least I hope you'll think so.'

This could be anything, I thought.

'Yes, Ed.'

'We're coming over to be with you.'

'To Bermuda? That's wonderful. How long will you be staying?'

Ed laughed.

'Reggie, we'll be staying quite a while. We're moving to Bermuda for good. I want to be near you.'

Joy and I were delighted. By now Joy and Soph were the best of friends. Still are. It was the start of a wonderful period in our lives and, I believe, for Ed and Soph as well.

I've always been a workaholic but it wasn't long before Ed had me out on the golf course for a game every week. It didn't matter how much I protested, Ed would say, 'Reggie, I'll pick you up at ten o'clock'.

There was no point in arguing and deep down I was pleased that Ed wouldn't let me off the hook. It meant four hours with a man I loved. Often it was both Ed and Sophie and that meant Joy and I would make up a foursome.

I was a very ordinary golfer but compared to Eddie I was a pro. Eddie was never going to improve because after every swing he would say something like, 'I know what I'm doing wrong'.

And he'd change his grip, his stance or his swing, which meant if he went around in, say, 105, he would have made 105 adjustments to his swing.

But with Eddie, it was not about winning—it was always about letting me and Joy win. On a par three, Joy would be certain that she had hit her ball into a bunker, only to find when she got to the green that there was her ball sitting pretty.

There was much laughter playing a round with Ed. Often, as I was about to swing, he'd start waggling the head of his club until I stared him down and he'd say, 'I am motionless', which was almost worse.

On the green, if his ball was on the far side to me and it was my turn to putt, he would realise that he was in my line of sight and instead of quickly moving away would slowly move crab-wise to one side.

In spite of all this, the happiest hours of our week were on a golf course with Ed and often with Sophie.

We were in Australia, at the Gold Coast, playing golf with John Ayres, my long-time assistant's husband, when an official trundled out to me as we stood on the fifth green.

'Mr Grundy?'

'Yes.'

'I'm afraid I have some bad news for you.'

He paused.

'Mr Eddie Williams. I believe he is a friend of yours?'

'Yes.'

'Well,' he paused again, 'Mr Williams has had a heart attack. He's passed away.'

Joy and I cancelled the rest of our visit back home, jumped on an aircraft, and headed back to Bermuda. We couldn't miss out on saying our goodbyes.

The church was packed. Everyone loved Eddie. I was one of the pall-bearers and gave the eulogy with tears in my eyes.

And what were the circumstances of his death?

Sophie and Ed had an apartment on the edge of Hamilton, the small capital city of Bermuda. And right near the tiny residents' carpark was a patch of green. That's where they found him lying, with his driver at his side.

Maybe he had been practising his swing and maybe, just maybe, he finally got it right. And that was too much for his wonderful heart.

He couldn't have made his exit a better way.

THE PACKERS

It was a day in the 1970s.

'Mr Packer on the line.'

'Put him through.'

'Morning, Kerry.'

He was not interested in small talk.

'Listen, son. I want you to do me a favour. I want you to lend me fifty thousand.'

I felt like I was a contestant on one of my own game shows and the MC was saying, 'You have ten seconds to give me your answer'.

I heard myself saying, 'Kerry, can I get back to you?'

'Today?'

'Yes.'

Kerry Packer, Australia's richest man asking me—me—to lend him fifty thousand dollars.

The Packer name has always been synonymous with wealth and power.

There were three Packer men. I had dealings with two of them—the sons of Sir Frank Packer. I only saw Frank once. We did not speak but I felt his power a few times when I was starting off.

On one occasion he ordered that my production credit be removed. 'Reg Grundy Enterprises Production' became 'A TCN Production'.

Bruce Gyngell, who was programming TCN 9 at the time, said, 'Forget about it. Frank will, and then you'll get your credit back'.

And that's exactly what happened.

In March 1966 I met Kerry Packer for the first time.

It was in Bruce Gyngell's tiny glassed-in office in the general staff area.

Kerry was saying, 'Son, I've got a show I want you to make for me'.

I was thinking: I'm much older than him.

'It'll be promoted in the *Sunday Telegraph*.'

Later I learned that Sir Frank had put him in charge of promotions there.

'Ken Howard will be the compere. I want you to produce the show. You'll record it on Saturdays. It's a kind of quiz show, called *Tele-Auctions*. You start the week after next.'

'But, err,' I started to speak.

'If you're wondering what to call me, it's Kerry.'

'Well, err, Kerry. I reckon Ken Howard is the best race caller in the world but he wouldn't know much about doing a game show.'

'You can teach him.'

Kerry was moving to the door.

He looked back over his shoulder and mentioned a ludicrously small amount of money for me to produce the show.

'Kerry, I can't possibly make it for that.'

'Okay, son, we'll get somebody else.'

'But Kerry, truly. I simply can't do it for that.'

I tried two or three times. No luck.

Bruce said, 'Let's leave it for now. We'll let you know if we want to discuss it further'.

If only they had known how much I needed the show. Maybe they did.

I got the job and worked out a deal directly with Kerry Packer in his Castlereagh Street office. It was something to do with a percentage of the profits based on the *Sunday Telegraph* promotion. I created a simple quiz show to support the idea, which included a barrel containing coupons cut from the *Telegraph*.

At this distance, I haven't the faintest idea what it was about, but Kerry devoted seven full pages each week in the *Sunday Telegraph* to promote it.

Ken Howard was one of the best known Australians at the time—the man who had transformed race calling. He was a colourful figure with a signature expression. When a finish was close and he favoured one horse over the other it was always, 'It's London to a brick on'.

In Steve Cairns' marvellous book, *London to a Brick On: A Salute to Australian Race Calling*, he reveals that, despite his confident manner, Ken suffered badly from nervous tension and as a consequence his diet on race days consisted of one meat pie, a bottle of lemonade which lasted the whole day, and headache powders.

In the studio Ken Howard, one of the nicest men I ever met, was nervous and out of his depth.

Now we understand.

Joy came down from Brisbane every week to be the barrel girl. She was terrific, looked great on camera, and it was obvious Kerry was 'interested'.

Because Joy lived in Queensland she sometimes mispronounced Sydney suburb names. Lakemba became LAK-emba. Nobody seemed concerned except me.

Kerry always attended the Saturday show and whether it was to supervise or give Joy the glad eye, we'll never know.

Although I reckon I've got a pretty good idea.

'Kerry, I'm Reg's girl.'

Just as she'd once told Johnny O'Keefe.

One week Kerry said to Joy, 'Tell Reg I want to see him'.

'Kerry, he's busy producing your show. You'll have to wait.'

Kerry replied sarcastically, 'Well, then, tell him when he's got a minute I'd like him to spend that minute with me'.

Tele-Auctions was a nightmare for Grundy Enterprises. We had the task of finding the winning coupon. The coupons were spread out on every available area of our office floor. Each one of us would check the findings of the previous person. We could not afford to make a mistake. And fortunately we never did.

In 1970, Ken Hall retired as CEO of TCN and Clyde Packer, the elder son, became joint managing director with his father.

'It was a very equitable arrangement,' Clyde said later. 'I had the responsibility and he had the authority.'

In 1972 I received a 16 mm film of *Split Second*, a new American game show. I sent the film to Ron Haines who was programmer at Nine, giving him twenty-four hours to look at it. The next day I gave the film to Ian Holmes at Ten, warning him that the first broadcaster to call with a buy order would get the show.

I was lunching with Ian Holmes in Crows Nest when I was called to the phone. Returning to our table, I told Ian that Nine had bought the show.

The format was simple. Two contestants were required to answer general knowledge questions at great speed, the winner having a chance to win one of five cars. Five car keys were placed in a hat. The player selected a key, then tried it in one of the cars. If the engine started, the player won the car.

We planned to feature five cars ranging from a Mini Minor to a Mercedes-Benz.

Before the show went to air I received a call from Clyde Packer who started swearing at me, using the 'f' word over and over again. He said that he had been told that we would not be giving away a range of cars but, in fact, five Mini Minors. Someone had been whispering in his ear that I was conning him.

I explained that I had a wide range of cars. He fumed at me.

I said, 'Clyde, you're wrong, let me explain.'

He hung up.

I called back immediately.

His secretary said, 'I'm afraid, Mr Grundy, he's gone out.'

He clearly didn't want to take my call.

There was no follow-up from him or from me. The show went to air. It was moderately successful and it did have a range of cars.

So why did he abuse me?

Clyde was clearly uncomfortable in his role at TCN. His marriage of eleven years was over. Divorce proceedings had started. The relationship with his father was close to breaking point. I think he needed to take out his frustration on someone. The someone that day was me.

Later that year Clyde resigned when his father vetoed an interview with Bob Hawke.

Kerry moved in, taking over first the television operation then, when Sir Frank died in 1974, the whole media empire.

After Clyde left Nine I met him at a party and accidentally spilt coffee on his suit.

It really was an accident.

The following year I financed the movie *Barry McKenzie Holds His Own*.

Clyde represented Barry Humphries at the time so we invited him down to Bayview to discuss Barry's deal and the movie. Clyde had put on a tremendous amount of weight and we weren't sure that we had a chair that could safely seat him. So we put him on a sofa with me facing him on the matching sofa and a coffee table between us.

Wearing a caftan, he ate his meal from a tray.

The meeting went well. There was no reference to the past. Clyde went to America soon afterwards, set up a small production company, and married again.

When Kerry took over he was sometimes referred to as the 'idiot son'. The rumour around TCN 9 was that he had once fired off both of the telecine machines (film projectors) at the same time. Whether he did or not, we will never know.

Kerry quickly showed that he was master of the TV game. He was an avid viewer of television and had an instinct for what would work. He had a feel for TV that both his father and brother had lacked.

He had mood swings and wasn't always easy to get on with. Tough, enigmatic, blunt, at other times he could be sympathetic and understanding.

Bruce Gyngell eventually moved into the big office as CEO at TCN and was quickly at loggerheads with Sir Frank. He left Nine for Seven and eventually left Seven as well, and was in a sort of no man's land as an adviser to Kerry.

One day that voice was again in my ear.

'Hello, son. Got a minute?'

It needed no answer.

Of course I had a minute.

I got in my car and headed for Castlereagh Street.

Kerry was seated with a man from a leading advertising agency.

'We're discussing six o'clock. We've got a problem.'

The agency guy was spouting what I thought was a load of rubbish.

Kerry was getting impatient.

I cut in.

'Kerry, if you just give me the six o'clock time slot and leave it to me, how long would it be before I had a show that improved the ratings?'

'Ah,' he said, 'three months.'

He dismissed the other guy and said, 'Okay, do what you like'.

I came up with a game show. I think it was *Celebrity Squares* with Jimmy Hannan, but don't shoot me if it wasn't.

It did okay—certainly not a disaster—but it didn't have a long run.

Kerry's decision had indicated his faith in me and that meant a lot.

Much later we had lunch at the Dorchester in London where we were staying. He had a whole floor. I had a suite. He was brutal and blunt with the waiter, telling him the food wasn't good. We talked about cricket and his plans to modernise the game. There's a rumour I heard recently that says I was offered World Series Cricket before it ever got to Packer and that I'd passed. I think I'd remember something like that if it had happened.

In the early 1980s Nine received a script, *Taurus Rising*, from well known writer Tony Morphet. Nine liked the concept but felt that the Morphet group did not have the producers to make it.

It was offered to us.

Taurus was the name of a building being constructed by the central character's company. It was to be Sydney's tallest.

Reg Watson and I read the script and made many changes and decided that the title must go. Somehow we got so caught up in making the show that we never got around to changing it.

The show went to air in 1982. Few people watched it. I was surprised because I was very pleased with the first episode. Recently, Joy and I looked at it again and still thought it was good.

So what went wrong?

That damn title.

We understand titles like *Young Doctors, Sons and Daughters, Prisoner, Wheel of Fortune*. But *Taurus Rising*? I believe the audience didn't get it.

Before the show went to air Ian Holmes and I were called into Kerry Packer's Castlereagh Street office.

Kerry opened the batting.

'I'm changing the deal. I'm not getting enough out of the foreign rights.'

It was a long meeting and at the end of it Kerry had a bigger slice of the foreign rights and we had a higher production fee.

Clearly he hoped that *Taurus* might become Australia's *Dallas* with great overseas potential.

Eventually *Taurus* premiered on American cable. Some people did indeed think it was Australia's answer to *Dallas* and *Dynasty* and, what's more, that the big American soaps could learn a thing or two from us, especially that a good storyline is better entertainment than even the best wardrobe.

Kerry was pointing to the door. The meeting was over, or so he thought. I spoke up.

'Kerry, could I have a private word with you?'

Ian left the room.

I had lent Kerry that fifty thousand dollars some time ago. It had been a long wait.

'When am I going to get my money back?'

Kerry didn't as much as blink.

'What money?'

'The fifty thousand I lent you.'

He looked me straight in the eye.

'You mean the fifty thousand you *gave* me?'

'That's not how I remember it, Kerry.'

'Do you need the money? Are you broke?'

'Well, no, I'm not broke.'

He glared at me.

'Of course you're not. You make a bloody fortune out of me, don't you? Well, let me tell you something. When a man puts pressure on someone for money, it might be called a loan but it really means "give" me the money.'

'Understand?'

'Not really.' He can't be serious, can he?

He moved round his enormous desk and sat on the front edge.

'Son, I like you. I'd hate to see you have to beg so I'm going to break my golden rule and give you that money back.'

Did he really think he was doing me a favour?

'Thanks, Kerry. I'll try to remember the rules next time.'

'Don't be bloody annoying. Send someone round to pick up the money in the morning.'

'I'll do that.' I headed for the door.

THE PACKERS

293

'Just one more thing.'

He put out his hand and grasped mine.

'Good luck, son.'

No doubt about Kerry Packer. He was a hard man to read.

Ian was waiting outside.

'Ian, I've had a bust up with Kerry. We may never make another show for Nine.'

'Well, if we don't, we don't. We'll be okay.'

I was glad to hear that and respected Ian for his answer.

The following day Barry Weston, Grundy company secretary, drove into the city where he met with Kerry's man outside the *Telegraph* building and was handed a brown paper bag full of money.

Fifty thousand dollars.

In the Costigan enquiry much was made of Kerry's use of brown paper bags containing large amounts of money.

When asked why he wanted the money in cash, Packer had replied: 'I wanted it in cash because I like cash. I have a squirrel-like mentality'.

He was a gambler. In Vegas he was one of the 'whales'.

And did my demand for my money hurt my relationship with Kerry? Did he stop doing business with me?

Definitely not.

After *Taurus Rising*, we made six more series for Kerry including dramas *Waterloo Station* and *Possession*.

By 1984 *Sale of the Century* was in its second year on NBC and we had a pilot coming up for the game show *Scrabble*.

My mother had become very ill and I was in Australia.

On 6 March the first test episode of *Scrabble* was recorded at the NBC studios Burbank with pilots two and three being made the following day. The networks always ordered three pilot episodes and chose the best one to show to their bosses to get approval to schedule the show.

I needed to see one of those pilots.

Bob Crystal approached Russell Watkins, Nine network's representative in Los Angeles, to ask if they would send the pilot to Sydney by satellite.

He got the okay. Only Kerry could have authorised it.

The next day I previewed it in Len Mauger's office in the *Telegraph* building in Castlereagh Street. After it was over I thanked Len and was walking to the lift as Kerry appeared beside me.

'You're not going to try and sell that bloody thing to me are you, son?'

Clearly he had been watching in his office.

I grinned, 'I might', and got into the lift.

We didn't have the Australian rights but could have got them. It was another example of me letting an opportunity slip through my fingers.

In 1995, $5.4 million worth of gold bars and a Vegemite jar full of gold nuggets were stolen from Packer's personal safe.

Kerry was down $5.4 million but still had his empire.

In 1995 I sold Grundy Worldwide. I was up hundreds of millions of dollars but had sold the business I loved. Big difference.

Ten years later, in 2005, I heard that Kerry's health was deteriorating. I called him at the *Telegraph* building in Castlereagh Street and spoke to his secretary.

'Oh, Mr Grundy, Mr Packer is not available at the moment. Could you call back in an hour?'

I called back. 'I'm sorry but it's impossible for Mr Packer to speak to you now, Mr Grundy. He's in the lift going down to the gym in the basement and I can't get him till he gets there. Would you mind calling again in five minutes?'

This time Kerry answered the phone.

'How are you, Reg?'

'Kerry, more to the point, how are you?'

'Oh, I'm all right. Just trying to do a bit of exercise to keep me going. Reg, how far can you walk?'

No more did he call me 'son'.

I didn't know what to say and said, 'I suppose two miles'.

'Really? That much?'

'I'll be back in Australia in about a month. Why don't we have lunch?'

He said, 'Love to, let me know when you get here.'

I sent him a copy of my photographic book, *The Wildlife of Reg Grundy*, via our friend Lynton Taylor. Kerry was delighted to receive it. He was always fond of lions and had pictures of them behind his desk.

We came back to Australia earlier than we had planned to be part of the Sydney Opera House ceremony commemorating Kerry Packer's life.

Kerry was brutal at times, difficult, hard to deal with and dismissive. At other times, if he thought you had the talent or the 'touch' for television, he wanted to keep you around.

I guess I was one of the lucky ones.

THE BBC AND ME

In the 1980s and 1990s in LA, Bob Noah and I were continually working on game show concepts.

One that we liked had been shopped around and suddenly ABC was interested. We called the show *Run For The Money*.

We recorded three pilots on 6 and 7 June 1987. Total cost? Around half a million US dollars.

ABC bought some other show without even looking at our pilots. Same old thing. New broom.

I had just started my campaign to break into English television. Independent television production companies were non-existent in the UK so I realised I'd be fighting an uphill battle. But my timing was good. Maggie Thatcher's government had decided that there would be a 15 per cent cut in BBC in-house production to make room for independent producers.

I was in with a chance.

After the Melba fiasco I realised that I should be pitching light entertainment formats. Particularly game shows. At that time most English game shows started with a long comedy monologue from the presenter. Why doesn't he get on with the game? I'd think.

I'd had that 1986 meeting with Michael Grade at the Wilshire hotel in Beverly Hills when we had talked about *Neighbours* and game shows. Now was the time to follow up.

Soon Joy and I were flying on a regular basis from Bermuda to Kennedy Airport, then by Concorde to Heathrow.

The next morning I would be at BBC Television Centre, West London waiting to see Michael Grade. Michael, wearing red braces and red socks, would listen to my newest idea and show little interest.

Then one day he mentioned that the BBC had done a deal with the Super Channel, a satellite service, to provide English-language entertainment across Europe.

'They're looking for cheap, long-run formats ahead of the launch in about six months. Do you have a game show where we could use contestants not only from the UK, but from all the countries in the Super Channel footprint?'

Run for the Money was flashing in my head.

'Michael, we've got a show that was designed as a tournament with contestants coming from various parts of America. Why not European countries instead?'

Grade said the magic words: 'I could be interested'.

'We'll tape a run-through and send it to you with a written description of the format.'

Michael was cautious. 'I wouldn't get your hopes up. Don't hold your breath.'

We made the demo at Shulman's facility on Hollywood and Vine. Bob Noah was the host; he always did an able job. It was easier than having to explain the format to someone else. Bill Mason was producing from the control room.

Long ago, as I've said, I had stopped going to the studio when we were producing shows. Run-throughs were different. I needed to be there because we would have to experiment and make changes to get the format right.

I wanted to be away from the studio but still in the building. I was given the sales manager's office.

The set was a mock-up. No frills. Bob was doing his best but it wasn't coming to life. I picked up the phone and spoke to Bill Mason in the control room.

'Bill, it's flat. Ask Bob to talk to camera every now and then as if he's talking to Michael Grade.'

It worked like a dream.

A week later I was in London with Bill Mason. Joy had flown off to Australia without me for once, for a month's gig as Rosemary in *Neighbours*.

Bill and I ran the tape for Roger Laughton, the BBC programmer, and

Carol Wisdon, the programmer at Super Channel.

They liked it a lot.

I promised to send Roger a detailed paper on the format. Bob Noah wrote the draft and I reshaped it into a pitch document.

Years later Roger said, 'You know, Reg, that was the most elegant presentation I received when I was at the BBC'.

Carol Wisdon wanted to start taping in January/February 1987 in time for their launch. Roger and I agreed that March would be more likely. We named the show *Going For Gold*.

It was October before episode one was recorded. Bill Mason, by then running things in London with his wife Anne, had a torrid time of getting going.

To start with, they wouldn't let me into the control room. I was in a little room out the back with a monitor and a headphone talking to the BBC's executive producer saying things like, 'Stop. Move camera three across', and he's going berserk because he hates it.

With a quiz show, if the host makes a mispronunciation or someone gives an ambiguous answer, it's very important to stop tape immediately so you can clear that point up before you create a domino effect. So I'd say to the executive producer, 'Stop tape, please'. 'Could you stop tape now' … 'Hello? Stop tape!' And four more questions would go by and he'd say, 'Oh, just a minute, Bill wants to stop tape. Anybody see anything wrong?' Or there'd be a whizz pan and I'd tell him about it and he'd say, 'Did anyone see a whizz pan?' So they did this to me and I nearly went insane.

BILL MASON

Meanwhile, Bill Mason and Kerry Wright were also having trouble with BBC management. The Beeb just didn't know how to deal with us.

The problem was that the BBC had no mechanism for dealing with independent producers of game shows. The only boilerplate agreement in existence was one being used by Channel Four.

It was totally unsuitable for our requirements so many hours went into redrafting an agreement that reflected our copyright position.

BILL MASON

It didn't take hours, it took months, with lawyers on both sides bleeding over every clause and telexes flying like driven snow.

There seemed to be no end in sight but it all came to a conclusion at a landmark dinner at the White Elephant, a club in Curzon Street, Mayfair. It was 30 September 1987.

The BBC lawyers were still splitting hairs. Copyright was the big issue. Kerry had been locked in an all-day session with BBC lawyers. They wouldn't budge an inch and neither would Kerry.

Joy and I were dining with Kate and Bill Cotton at the White Elephant in Curzon Street when Kerry called me to say the deal was deadlocked.

'Kerry, call me back in five minutes.'

I returned to the table and Bill Cotton.

'Bill, the lawyers are stalemated over copyright. Can you and I agree on this? BBC gets the UK and we have the rest of the world?'

Bill leaned across the table and shook my hand.

'Tell your lawyer to tell my lot what we have agreed on.'

We said it together.

'Lawyers!'

So the end credits were …

UK copyright © BBC 1987

World Copyright © Reg Grundy Productions (GB) Limited 1987

The first agreement, dated 7 May 1987, was not signed until January 1988.

We were to receive £27,500 a week and a pre-production 'one off' of £60,000, non-refundable but recoupable over the life of the series.

How much profit was in that £27,500 a week?

Can't remember.

Going For Gold had a very good run. From 12 October 1987 to 9 July 1996. It was still rating well when they took it off.

But the French version, *Questions pour un Champion*, ran rings around it for longevity and, incidentally, was the beginning of our invasion of Europe. It started the following year in November 1988 and is still running in 2010. The French host has always been Julien Lepers.

It had an enormous following.

Many years ago we were spending a few days on our motor yacht in the south of France. Some of us were straddling a blow-up banana while being pulled along by one of our tenders.

Ian Holmes was in front. Joy was ahead of me.

Ian called to the deckhand to speed up. He did, but at the same time he swerved.

My head jerked forward, Joy's head fell back.

They slammed into one another.

Joy and I were thrown into the water.

I was surrounded by a pool of blood from a cut on my forehead and was trying to swim back to the boat.

A deckhand plucked me out of the water and ferried me back to *Idolwood II* where I was placed face up on the upper deck. Joy and concerned guests peered down at me.

Dick Barovick said, 'We better get him to a hospital.'

The English hospital was in the hills behind Cannes and so named, I suppose, because the French doctors and nurses could speak English. Joy and Dick explained to the doctor what had happened. Dick gave my name.

'Oh, oh, Monsieur, not the Grundy of *Questions pour un Champion*?'

I opened my eyes and smiled. Dick filled in the details.

Later, the twelve stitches were taken out at St Johns and Elizabeth hospital in London where we were always looked after by our friend, Dr Roger Hayward.

The head nurse warned me as she studied my forehead, 'Never let a doctor take out stitches'.

Then she added, 'I've never seen anything like this before. These stitches are perfect.'

I didn't tell her that it was a French doctor who had done his best stitching because my name was on the end of a French game show.

Run for the Money became *Going for Gold* which became *Questions pour un Champion*.

Run for the Money never got to an American audience.

That's television I guess.

I HAD AN IDEA ... PAROCHIAL INTERNATIONALISM

Going for Gold on the BBC was the first show we made in England.

Over the years we would make many more, not only in Britain but throughout Europe and the rest of the world.

From the beginning I had taken the view that we wouldn't simply license our formats to allow others to produce copies of our programs in their own markets but would ourselves, when the opportunities arose, make local versions of our own shows.

I believed that people all over the world were pretty much the same, so a successful show in one market had a good chance in another if it was locally produced and featured local people.

I came up with a slogan that I hoped would help us on our way: 'Parochial internationalism. Be local to be global'.

It may be commonplace now but it was a brand new thought then.

And suddenly there were a lot of opportunities to apply it.

Television in Western Europe was deregulated and privatised in the late 1980s. The number of stations more than doubled overnight and many of them were looking for low-cost, long-run shows.

It wasn't easy moving onto continental Europe where my experienced Australians had to work in languages they couldn't speak. We sometimes had to use interpreters and who knows what was being said. If the interpreter knew the station executive, he might well be saying, 'Why do we have to do business with these strange Australians?'

Sometimes we had a second interpreter to monitor the first interpreter.

It took a while for the Europeans to get used to the streamlined Grundy production methods.

Bill Mason remembers *Questions pour un Champion* and the very first problem.

We found an office in the suburbs of Paris and hired all French staff, mostly bilingual. We used an outside production company for facilities and it all came together fairly easily.

Julien Lepers was the host. I'd written the usual introduction—'Hello and welcome to the show'. I always kept it short so as to get into the show quickly. Out came Julien for the first time and started to read the ten seconds I'd written. He was still going about two and a half minutes later. I pulled him up and asked him what he was saying. He said, 'Well, I'm saying thank you for watching. My wife and I had a lovely weekend in the country and so on. It's the French way.'

I told him it wasn't the French way any more.

BILL MASON

Questions pour un Champion is still in production in 2010 after twenty-two years on French television.

Remember *Hot Streak*, the show turned down by two American networks?

Bill Mason who was head of entertainment for us in Europe had been talking to Wolfgang Fischer of Tri-Star about *Hot Streak* since 1986. His persistence was rewarded when it started on Tele 5 in Germany two years later. It ran until 1993 before switching to RTL.

Success breeds success. *Hot Streak* became *Ruck Zuck* in Germany and *Rap Klap* in Belgium. There was even a junior version in Germany called *Kinder Ruck Zuck*.

Parochial Internationalism was working.

Up until 1990 we had only made game shows outside Australasia but then we were approached by a representative of Joop van den Ende, a Dutch producer. He said, 'We've got an output deal with this new company, RTL, operating out of Luxembourg and which is going to broadcast into Holland and we need a soap. We'd like to license a format.'

Kerry Wright told him that we did not do format deals but we'd consider a joint venture.

It was called Grundy/JE.

We decided to remake *The Restless Years*. It would become *Goede Tijden, Slechte Tijden* (*Good Times, Bad Times*).

Reg Watson flew to Holland to set up our first serial drama in Europe. For six months he parked himself near Aalsmeer, rewriting the first 250 Australian scripts to adapt them locally.

Mike Murphy took over as producer. The show was a ratings triumph. The youth of the Netherlands embraced it.

It was time to celebrate.

We turned on a dinner for Joop and his people in the Gray d'Albion hotel in Cannes. Joop was then a Dutch producer only. By the end of the evening we had agreed to make more shows under the Grundy/JE flag.

In the spirit of the partnership, Mike Murphy passed over videos and scripts from *Prisoner* to his JE counterparts.

'You might be interested in doing this one with us.'

JE soon announced that they were doing their own version. Without us. We took them to court in Holland. They produced a woman who claimed that she had created the concept and had had no access to our material.

The Dutch judge ruled in her favour. Their version was called *Women's Wing*, not *Prisoner*.

It failed.

Later, Joop formed Endemol with Dutch producer/creator John De Mol. Endemol is a combination of their two names.

The Dutch are tough people to do business with.

A CEO of one of the companies we were negotiating with said to Kerry Wright at one stage, 'Kerry, do you think we Dutch are very arrogant?'

'I'm not sure I'd go that far,' said diplomatic Kerry.

'Well, we're happy to be that. We're called the Chinese of Europe.'

Good Times, Bad Times was going great guns in Holland and we were about to expand further.

I was in Bermuda when Mike Murphy called. RTL Germany had commissioned us to make them a version of the same show. They insisted we partner with a German company, UFA.

As the weeks went by more and more memos came from RTL station executives about their version of *Good Times, Bad Times,* called *Gute Zeiten, Schlechte Zeiten.* Not one of them was favourable. They were even threatening to withdraw the show before the first episode went to air.

Mike and his crew were holding their breath. So was I.

Again Mike was on the phone.

'We're number one in the ratings.'

The memos stopped coming.

Later we made another German serial based on *Sons and Daughters*. It was called *Verbotene Liebe* (*Forbidden Love*).

It seemed we couldn't go wrong.

Parochial internationalism had caught on and the plan to have Grundy production companies round the world was nearly complete. We were Grundy Worldwide Limited, consisting of completely separate local production companies in:

Australia

England

France

The Netherlands

Germany

Spain

Belgium

New Zealand

Hong Kong

Chile

Italy

India

Indonesia

Paraguay

Sweden.

We had our own distribution company, Grundy International Distribution, which soon owned a huge catalogue of drama and game show programming.

I announced: 'The expansion of our operations has been financed solely through internally generated resources and the company remains debt free.'

But how was I to monitor our progress in each area of the world? It would be hard to do unless I was awake twenty-four hours a day.

We did our best with MCI, the precursor to email, and to which we had been an early subscriber. But it wasn't enough.

We decided to have each leader send a monthly report to me. Then the reports would be combined and an edited composite would be sent back to everybody.

Joy agreed to take on the responsibility of combining the reports into one.

In 2003, Don Groves of *Variety* called me about receiving the Golden Nymph Award from Prince Albert at the 43rd Monte Carlo Television Festival. The citation read: 'For his concept of "parochial internationalism" and the contribution that he has made to local and international production'.

I passed on to Don one of the secrets of my good fortune.

'My philosophy has always been that you must be willing to fail. Just keep throwing punches. You're bound to hit something.'

Before this book is published there will have been a meeting of television heavyweights in Cannes. They will have discussed the idea that they should have local production companies throughout the world.

Ed Waller is editorial director of television publisher C21 Media Ltd. He writes:

What started in 1992 with Good Times, Bad Times *for RTL, based on Australian show* The Restless Years, *continues with shows like* Pop Idol.

These days intellectual property is valuable because it can further plans for good old global domination. Australian formats pioneer Reg Grundy probably owns the business model ... developed all those years ago with Sale of the Century *and* Sons and Daughters.

ED WALLER

By the time I sold the company all my dreams had come true.

And that slogan had made all the difference.

Parochial internationalism. Be local to be global.

IT'S NOT ALL ABOUT MONEY

I can't remember if I had any money when I was going to school. Maybe my mother handed me something for school lunch. But if she did, I don't remember.

I do know that I had everything I wanted within reason.

The first money I earned was that pound a week I got at David Jones. Not exactly a king's ransom.

Then there was the money in my army pay book. Not much when I started off as a private and not that much more when I graduated to being a sergeant.

Of course I had lots of money for a brief time when each week I went to the bank in the Sydney Showground just across from the Hordern Pavilion and picked up the pay for about a thousand soldiers.

But that lasted about one minute and twenty seconds as I crossed back to the Hordern Pavilion where all those men in uniform were pretending to be soldiers but, in fact, were accountants.

After the war, at 2SM, I received 7 pounds 10 shillings for working six days a week and long hours, and made a tad more selling time.

At 2CH I can't remember what I got.

I can. I remember Reg telling me in 1954 that he was earning 100 pounds a week. An enormous sum. I was getting 12 pounds a week.

JOHN O'GRADY

My entry into television made me feel good but I was still getting peanuts, although of course it increased when my three shows were stripped five days a week.

Like the Queen, I don't carry money. I have credit cards that are never used because I don't carry them. It's not deliberate. It's just the way it has developed over the years, but it has its consequences.

How can I get by like this?

If Joy and I go out, she picks up the tab. Or, if we are accompanied by a Grundy person, he or she pays.

Andrew Jenkins is one of our close personal staff and when he's with us he mostly carries the cash. He takes his responsibilities seriously.

The second thing we do when we arrive in a new place is to find the most convenient ATM in town. The first thing is to find the best coffee shop.

I have a list of the best of both all round the world.

I don't mind carrying the money. The hard part is the bookkeeping. The accountancy involved would tax Price Waterhouse Coopers and that's assuming I can get the receipts. It isn't always easy.

Once, in Brisbane, RG asked me for money.

'What do you want money for?'

'To buy a book.'

'Which book? I'll buy it for you.'

But this time he wanted to do his own shopping. 'I'll buy it myself thanks.'

I gave him $50.

He came back looking pleased with himself. He had his book but no receipt.

'Don't worry about it,' he said, 'I know the boss.'

ANDREW JENKINS

Sharon Sussman and Kevin Kopelow both worked for me in Los Angeles.

Reg had been to the mall alone one time and saw a pair of shoes that he liked and said that he'd hidden them behind a suitcase but couldn't remember which mall it was. Kevin and I had to go from mall to mall trying to be inconspicuous while we looked behind suitcases. We never found the shoes.

SHARON SUSSMAN

This surprises me as I don't ever recall being in a mall alone in my life, but if Sharon says it, it must be right.

On one occasion we were in Sydney when Joy's sister Coral and her husband arrived by ship from the UK.

We picked them up.

As I approached the Bridge I realised I didn't have any money for the toll. I asked Coral's husband if he had any money. He did, and paid the toll. He was surprised.

He had been told I was a millionaire!

And of course there have been many times when Joy and I have hosted dinners and one of our Grundy people has paid the bill with company credit cards. Every now and then one of the guests politely thanks the person who appeared to pay. C'est la vie.

Years later, after we had been living in Bermuda for sixteen years, we were attracted to a beautiful location with its own saltwater lagoon.

Sue McIntosh, who has handled our finances impeccably for decades, was in Bermuda for one of our regular meetings. She listened to our story and when we had finished she surprised us by saying, 'It sounds wonderful. Why don't you just buy it? We can manage'.

We did. We built a beautiful new house where we have a loyal little staff. Well, a loyal little 'family', as we like to call them: Maggie Moore, our assistant of over twenty years, who helped me enormously with *The Wildlife of Reg Grundy*; Derek Smith, our maintenance man; our chef, Alix; and Lucia, our housekeeper. Chinni Mahadevan, curator of my photographic library, spends a lot of the year there too and so do our assistants, John Watson (who was our purser on the *Boadicea* for years), Neil Freestone, Andrew Jenkins and from time to time Grahame Bateman, who is my wildlife buddy.

I have rarely been in a supermarket, but once about fifteen years ago in Bermuda the housekeeper was sick and Joy was out. Goodness knows why my secretary or somebody didn't go out to buy the few items needed, but somehow it was left to me.

I went into a supermarket in the parish of Paget. I had a note with the eight items written down but, as usual, I had no money.

I approached one of the ladies at the check-out and told her someone would come back and pay later but these were the things I needed.

She gave me a big smile.

'That's all right, darling, come with me,' she said.

I followed her round the aisles while she got all my items, put them in a bag for me and said, 'You pop back with the money when you can, darling'.

That's Bermuda I guess. Might not work in Australia.

Is it eccentric to never carry legal tender? Perhaps. But that's me.

I never gave money much thought. It was not the most important thing in my life, although I obviously must have had some.

END OF AN ERA

In August 1993 we were on board *Idolwood II* off Canada's Prince Edward Island when we finally decided to go public and float 30 per cent of Grundy Worldwide.

But the truth was, I knew I'd much rather sell the business. I didn't want to go public. I'd always been a sole trader and didn't really like the idea.

Earlier we'd briefed financial advisory and asset management firm Lazard to find us a buyer. We called it Mission Possible and a number of parties expressed interest, but none of them came to anything.

Lazards were instructed that unless they found a buyer by 17 January 1994 we would start down the IPO (Initial Public Offering) path.

Lazards beat the bushes around the world and it seems that Pearson TV in Britain at some time received a copy of the Information Memorandum for Mission Possible. However, since Anthony del Tufo, the Pearson's CFO, was never a big fan, they passed on the opportunity.

The January deadline came and passed and the IPO was moving down the usual path of such things. In a matter of weeks we would be listed on the New York Stock Exchange.

In January Greg Dyke became chairman and CEO of Pearson TV. Unlike del Tufo, Dyke thought Grundy and Thames Television, already a Pearson subsidiary, would make a great fit.

Dyke sent del Tufo to Monaco to go over figures with Sue McIntosh.

I recall showing him the valuation numbers on the IPO. He was not a big fan of the potential purchase and would never have gotten anywhere near the price we wanted were he not ordered to by Greg Dyke.

Sue McIntosh

The flotation being organised by Merrill Lynch valued Grundy Worldwide shares at between US$18 and US$20, raising a substantial amount for me and valuing the company at some hundreds of millions of dollars.

Ian Holmes and Tim Hughes were in New York for meetings. I said, 'I think Pearsons is going to buy us.'

They said, 'Not in a million years.' They just laughed at me.

I said, 'I want you to go to London and talk to Dyke.'

They said, 'Why? It's a waste of time.'

I said, 'I want you to go.' So, very, very reluctantly, they went.

At that meeting Greg Dyke confirmed his interest in our company and Ian and Tim went home to Australia.

We had decided to keep Pearsons honest by telling them we were still proceeding with the float, which meant almost inhuman hours were being worked by Kerry Wright and Sue McIntosh, backed up by our other financial whizzes like Ian Ousey.

I sent Kerry and Sue to London for talks with Pearsons to see whether a deal could be done. They met with Sarah Tingay, Pearson's director, legal and business affairs, and del Tufo on 20 March, but it didn't go well.

We all walked away from the table as there was absolutely no meeting of the minds. Both parties were intransigent on price.

SUE MCINTOSH

It was obvious now that if anything were going to happen, Dyke and I would have to sort things out. But there was no way I was going to him; he would have to come to me.

I suggested that Greg fly by Concorde to New York for a meeting to take place in a private room at Kennedy airport on Wednesday 22 March.

Present were Greg Dyke, Nancy Peretsman, an American merchant banker representing Greg Dyke, Dick Barovick, Joy and myself.

Joy, with tears in her eyes, explained that the company was our baby.

I was supposed to be a businessman yet I too was on the brink.

Dyke writes:

It took a while and towards the end I was saying, 'Look, if you're going to buy it, just buy it. We're running out of time'.

Greg said, 'I can't. I've got to wait for the board meeting', and I said, 'Can't you change the date?'

'No, I can't. They're a pretty stuffy lot.'

So it went right up to the deadline. It was very close. If it had taken any longer we would have been listed on the exchange and that would have been that.

The meeting at NY airport had taken four hours and Greg Dyke was able to return to London on Concorde the same day.

When Greg and I were informed of the stalemate we sent our teams back to the table.

That started another week of long hours for Kerry, Sue and Linklaters, our lawyers.

The meetings were held at Freshfields (Pearson's lawyers) at 65 Fleet Street, with no meeting finishing before the early hours of each morning and on one occasion at 4.30 am.

Why did del Tufo finally come round? Sarah Tingay told Sue privately that Dyke was a brand new chairman and CEO and Grundy was the first acquisition he wanted to make. She felt they had to let him have it.

Then it was time for Greg and myself to go over the final details.

We met in a room at the Dorchester Hotel on Park Lane, London. Joy, Geoff Hill, an Australian and my personal adviser, and our travelling assistant Robin Durst were there too. Dick Barovick was not. He was off in Edinburgh still plugging the IPO.

The race was really tight. Would we float or would we sell?

All along I had favoured the private sale over the public listing and the deal was finally signed at Freshfields late on the evening of Sunday 26 March 1995.

Dick Barovick was back from Edinburgh for that.

The streets were quiet as we were driven away from 65 Fleet Street.

It was over.

I had sold Grundy Worldwide, my life's work, to Pearsons for a bundle of money. I looked at Joy. Joy looked at me. We hugged.

Greg Dyke issued this statement.

'I don't want to throw away the Reg Grundy rulebook. He's the one who knows how to do it.'

I never heard from Greg Dyke again on a professional basis.

I had felt the new owners would have needed a hand for a while.

I was wrong.

Sue McIntosh reviewed the press release on 28 March—the day the deal was finally announced.

Joy and I retreated to a small village in Hampshire to get away from it all.

The next day, we bought copies of all the English papers.

The *Times*, owned by Rupert Murdoch, had given me a big splash on the front page.

I remembered the reception that Rupert Murdoch had held at the Wilshire hotel before the start of the 1984 Los Angeles Olympic games.

We were staying in our apartment at the Wilshire so it was easy for us to go down in the elevator and walk across the foyer to be greeted by Rupert, who took me around the room.

'This man's got Australia sewn up,' he kept saying.

Of course he meant television.

Maybe in one of our subsequent eight o'clock meetings in Rupert Murdoch's office at Fox just around the corner from Le Parc, our LA home, I should have proposed that he buy me out.

If Rupert had been interested, I reckon he would have wanted me to stick around.

I felt I never said what I wanted to say to him. We mostly talked about Australian art and I'd show him photos of some of our pictures. At one time he said, 'Oh, your Fred Williams is better than mine', or something like that. I never said, 'Why don't you have a look at buying me out and I'll stay on for 20 per cent?' I don't know why. I was somehow too embarrassed to say it to him. He was so huge and I was so small.

I was just too tentative. Yet throughout my life, I'd been anything but.

I wonder why he went on seeing me? Maybe he was waiting for me to open my mouth. It would have been very exciting if it had happened because I reckon he might have let me have a real whack.

I spent the rest of the following day calling senior Grundy executives in different parts of the world thanking each one for the part he or she had played in our success. Informing them that they would all receive special bonuses, some up to seven figures. I am proud of every single one of them. They were a special bunch and at the risk of sounding soppy, they meant a lot to me.

Joy phoned the family and told them.

At last all the calls were completed.

I had said goodbye to people who had become my close friends. Of course I would see them again, but it wouldn't be the same.

They would not be looking to me for direction any more. They had new leaders.

My feeling of excitement was changing to one of regret.

I had broken the connection.

Had I done the right thing?

Wolf Bauer, a senior executive of Bertelsmann, had once said to me, 'Why are you thinking about selling the thing you love?'

I didn't have an answer back then, and still don't.

Do I regret selling the company? You bet I do, but it was the only way to capitalise on a lifetime's work.

So what do you do after you sell your life?

Photography was to be part of the answer.

WHAT DO YOU DO AFTER YOU SELL YOUR LIFE?

Some years prior, in the early 1990s, Joy was doing a story for *Women's Weekly* after her second book, *My Zulu, Myself*, was published. We were in Los Angeles and so the 'shoot' was at our LA apartment.

As usual, I was working with my door closed.

And, as usual, the photographer asked Joy to ask me to pose for one shot with her. Which I always did.

I didn't know that the photographer Douglas Kirkland and his wife Françoise would become two of our closest friends.

Douglas is one of the world's great photographers and while I was selling my business in 1995, he was receiving a Lifetime Achievement Award from the American Motion Pictures Society of Operating Cameramen.

Joy wasn't aware of that when she said, 'Reg is an excellent wildlife photographer'.

Douglas turned to me.

'Why don't you drop by the house some time and bring your slides.'

I procrastinated for months but finally showed up at the Kirkland house in the Hollywood Hills.

On the wall was Judy Garland, a tear rolling down her cheek, Jack Nicholson holding a lit match between his teeth, the famous shot of John Lennon in camouflage gear and the topper—Marilyn Monroe naked under that sheet.

Douglas burst into the room.

'Sorry, Reg. Got tied up downtown. Did you bring your slides?'

I'm thinking, I'm not going to show this guy my pictures.

'Come on, Reg, let's do it.'

My slide box slipped from my hands and fell to the floor.

Meticulously, Douglas gathered the slides and led me into his workroom.

At the end of the presentation he turned to me and said, 'Reg, Joy is right. You are a great wildlife photographer'.

I didn't know whether to laugh or cry.

'There's a book in you. If you want, I'll help you get it done.'

It took a long time but at last *The Wildlife of Reg Grundy* became a reality.

These days, I'm pretty serious about wildlife photography and Chinni Mahadevan, our friend and curator of my library of images, is mounting exhibitions for me all over.

It all started in Bermuda in 1995—my very first visit to that beautiful island. All I saw was 13,000 slide images—which I sorted and catalogued for RG. Today we have about 150,000 images in our database. In the early days we used to develop the slides onboard the ships that RG and Joy had, and of course RG would be pacing around the dark room in the middle of the night to get a quick glimpse of the images. RG, as usual, has kept ahead in technology and has been shooting his subjects in digital format since its early days.

Now we have RG's wildlife images in exhibits around the world— Sydney, New York, Los Angeles, Bermuda to name a few! His work has had such an impact on people that an exhibit featuring just 'Longtails'— Bermudian tropic birds—was requested by the Government of Bermuda to be mounted to celebrate 400 years of the country being colonised.

CHINNI MAHADEVAN

I am perhaps at my happiest out in the wild with Joy by my side and a camera in my hand.

HOW CLOSE WERE YOU?

When people see my wildlife photographs the most common question is: 'How close were you?'

Sometimes I'm closer than I should be.

'Got to get the shot, y'know.'

But often, because I am using highly powerful lenses, I appear to be closer than I really am.

Nevertheless, I've had some interesting moments over the years.

Like that boomslang snake.

In South Africa on safari we stopped for coffee. I wandered over to a dam full of muddy water. On its bank was a bush. In the bush was a small green snake, quite beautiful.

Grahame Bateman, better known as Bat, was my assistant on all these adventures.

I moved in close and got a couple of shots. If I had wanted to, I could have reached out and touched the snake.

I didn't.

Simon Blackburn, the ranger, was walking towards me. 'Hope you got something. But I wouldn't advise you to ever do it again. That little green fella is a boomslang. If it bites you, you'll bleed from every orifice in your body, then die.'

I got a number of good shots of that snake and used one in my book, *The Wildlife of Reg Grundy*. The one I didn't use was probably the better shot, with the boomslang coiled to strike. Somehow I couldn't bring myself to feature it.

There's a shot in my book of a number of hippos in a river breaking the surface and blowing bubbles. It was a chanceful split-second frame of which I'm very proud.

I was standing beside the river with my boots almost touching the water. Simon was standing beside me with his rifle pointing down.

Why?

Because the river was infested with crocodiles and as I had a camera pressed to my face I needed someone to watch out for an attack.

Simon had a military background and was nearly always armed. Even jogging through the bush with Bat he carried a 9 mm Glock pistol in case they came across a hungry lion in search of afternoon tea.

In Ranthambore, India we travelled for days in a four-wheel-drive, searching for tigers. We introduced safaris to our friends Pam and Alan Boyd. Alan ran Grundy UK for years and produced many of our hits there. Alan has had a long successful career in light entertainment.

The Boyds accompanied us to India along with Chinni Mahadevan, who was born in Madras, and Grahame Bateman. One of the things we men did not quite understand was that the women seemed even more interested in viewing the jewellery in Jaipur on the final day of our adventure than in finding a tiger! I guess that's the difference between men and women.

We have photos of Joy and Pam standing by a mountain of luggage and photographic equipment taller than they were, when we left Jaipur airport in a sandstorm.

On our last day out looking for tigers, we moved along a narrow path on the side of a mountain and saw a massive female lying behind some bushes.

A stone's throw off the road.

Our normal set-up when shooting from a four-wheel-drive is with a tripod strapped on the horizontal bar, which is directly in front of me. Bat sets all this up on our arrival at a wildlife destination.

The lens attached to the camera body is mighty big—normally 600 millimetre or sometimes 1200 millimetre. The vehicle must face towards the subject; otherwise it's almost impossible for me to get behind the camera.

Now I found myself with the tiger at right angles to the vehicle and no way to change the position of the four-wheel-drive. My only resort was to lean forward across the bar and try to somehow get behind the lens.

I managed to capture one shot of this magnificent animal staring straight at me.

As I look up from my keyboard now I see a print of her looking down at me.

Churchill, Canada is often referred to as 'the Polar Bear Capital of the World'.

It's like nowhere else.

We travel in a Tundra Buggy, a large vehicle with huge wheels. There're usually four or five of us plus the guide.

On our first visit we were told that we must not lean out of the vehicle. And there is a good reason. A bear will stand up beside the vehicle and in order to do that it must launch itself up onto its hind legs.

It happened to me.

Within a second, its face was roughly level with mine. We were staring at one another.

I got the shot.

Getting close to black and brown bears has its moments too. I have photographs, taken by someone else, of me standing within touching distance of a black bear. My head is down. I am definitely avoiding eye contact.

Eventually the bear shuffled away. Phew!

We travelled on board our beautiful MV *Boadicea* to Katmai in Western Alaska and found an anchorage in Geographic Harbour. There was only one other boat there.

We watched from *Boadicea*'s deck as a tall man appeared to be going for a walk along the strand with two bears ahead of him like large dogs on leashes. To our astonishment he then lay on the pebble beach and encouraged the bears to come over to him.

Later that afternoon we met Lynn Rogers—the man who walks with bears. We walked to a slight bend in the river and settled ourselves at the edge of the stream full of salmon and bears. Together we photographed bears as they passed by.

Lynn was staying on the other boat anchored in the bay, and I was invited on board and saw a few of his delicate, inspiring images.

I returned the compliment. On board *Boadicea* he studied some of my shots. Strangely, he commented most on a photograph I had taken of a longtail, Bermuda's name for a tropicbird.

Lynn said, 'It's beautiful. You should enlarge it.'

In June 2009 I presented a show of longtails at a major art gallery in Bermuda to celebrate Bermuda's 400th year of settlement. Longtails are the favoured bird of Bermudians and my favourite too. The enlargement of that longtail Lynn liked was the feature picture in the exhibition.

Lynn Rogers invited me to Minnesota where he lives with the bears. Maybe sometime I'll make the trip.

At the end of one day in Alaska I left our group and walked over to the stream as a massive bear moved towards me. I waited to get a close-up as it went by.

The bear hesitated as it heard my shutter clicking.

Grahame had been trying to get to me but knew rapid movement could be dangerous.

The bear was within 2 metres of Reg when it stopped and turned its head, obviously attracted by the whirr and click of the motor drive. Reg stopped and slowly lowered the camera to his chin and was staring eye-to-eye with this huge 400 kilogram bear.

Both Reg and the bear were like statues. I was frozen to the spot, wondering what was going to happen next. I was hoping that Reg wouldn't shift his feet because he was standing among loose rocks and I was sure that if he tripped he would fall onto the bear. They were that close.

The bear was looking Reg up and down and seemed to be deciding its next move. A salmon leapt out of the water nearby and the bear jumped into the air, spun around, and started chasing the salmon back down the creek.

Reg walked over to me and said, 'That was amazing. I reckon that last lot of shots will be the best of the day'.

I said, 'Just as well, because they were almost the last shots you ever took.'

As we were walking away there was a short silence before Reg said, 'We don't have to mention any of this to Joy, do we?'

GRAHAME BATEMAN

The most frightening moment of my photographic adventures wasn't with a bear.

On a visit to Botswana we found ourselves surrounded by elephants. Hundreds of them.

Our ranger, Shane, in an open four-wheel-drive vehicle, was returning us to our camp on an island in the flooded Okavango Delta. As we rounded a bend we were confronted by a large female elephant standing in the middle of the track.

She started to trumpet, flap her ears, and stamp her feet. We came to a sliding stop on the track not far from her. Then she charged towards us. Shane smacked the bonnet of the vehicle but with little effect. He hurriedly crunched the gears and drove at full speed in reverse down the winding track with the elephant in pursuit.

Then we saw a young elephant off the side of the track. We had come between the mother and her child. That could be fatal. Once we were past the calf, the chase ended.

We sat silently and watched as hundreds of elephants crossed in front of and behind us, heading towards the water for their end of day drink and wash.

But it wasn't always the guy behind the lens who got the fright.

We were on a game drive in South Africa in an open vehicle when a male elephant approached us. Joy was seated in the highest spot in the vehicle, holding an umbrella over her head to shield her from the sun.

The elephant ambled over and swung his trunk up and pushed the umbrella. All Joy could do was be silent and motionless and push back.

I kept shooting.

After a while the elephant moved away. Great relief from Joy.

I got some excellent shots.

I believe I've accompanied Reg and Grahame on over 90 per cent of their wildlife adventures and when I'm in an overwhelming situation, like the day we could have been overturned by hippos in the stream or when the lioness appeared to take an unhealthy interest in me, sitting in the crouch position inches away, or when the wolf actually licked me on the throat, I imagine my two pet pigs, Sweet Face and Victoria, and my pet cattle Barnaby, Fleurette and Dorothy. Now they are the sort of wildlife I can handle.

JOY CHAMBERS-GRUNDY

So there are times in the wild that are dangerous. But sometimes the danger has nothing to do with animals.

A classic example was in the Kalahari Desert.

The perception is that the Kalahari is sand dunes and then more sand dunes. But that's only part of the experience. In the Southern Kalahari, thunderstorms, especially late in the year, are common.

One October, Joy and I, Chinni and his wife Zayra, and Grahame were in a four-wheel-drive with a ranger, heading into horizontal rain with lightning striking close by.

We were more than an hour away from the Tswalu Lodge.

We had stopped under a tree. Not the best place to be when there is lightning and blinding rain. The thunderclaps got closer together. The lightning was striking all around us. The ranger could not see to drive.

The storm stalled and after half an hour of incredible noise and lightning flashes, I said we should get out in the open and, in spite of the miserable and dangerous conditions, head back to base.

It was a wild drive back to the lodge. A bolt of lightning cut through the canvas roof above my head. We began to feel that at least one of us wouldn't make it.

At last we drove into the back entrance of the lodge where vehicles were parked. Through our heavy rain gear, we were all soaked to the skin. We ran through the kitchen to a relatively dry area.

Joy took her shoes off and poured water out of them as if from a jug.

Next day the rain had largely stopped but there were still flashes of lightning. I told Joy we would travel away from the storm. I got away with it. She came along.

The Kalahari may be a desert but sometimes there is torrential rain and storms. On another occasion the lightning struck the hut we were in and destroyed our computers.

In spite of this the Kalahari is always beautiful and the wildlife is marvellous, and Newton Walker who flies us from Upington to the lodge in his little aircraft is a terrific guy.

But our African adventures aren't all about taking pictures. There are also the people we meet.

We stayed overnight at Riley's Hotel in the frontier town of Maun before travelling to the Okavango Delta in Botswana.

Each new camp meant meeting a new guide. Getting to know him was important.

This one was special. He was a Kalahari Bushman and at first I was not impressed. He seemed to be moving away from the wildlife, not towards them. Sometimes I would call for him to stop because it took a moment or two for the vehicle to settle before I could get my shot.

And then the penny dropped.

I realised that he was herding the game rather than frightening the animals by driving directly at them.

'Belipe,' I said, 'maybe we should stop when you want to stop.'

Belipe looked at me and said one word.

'Yes.'

Soon I was to discover what a treasure he really was. He told us about his parents, who had slept in the open each night, hoping that a lion would not take them. We had had some great guides but Belipe was outstanding and on top of that was a wonderful human being.

Joy asked him one day if he enjoyed what he did. He hesitated.

'Sometimes okay. Best with people like you. Like now. Perfect.'

One day we went out in a flat bottom boat and saw hippos in the stream.

We kept away from them.

Belipe was drinking a coke. The weather was serene.

'You know, Belipe, when everything is just right, like now, we Australians say it is bonzer.'

Belipe smiled. 'Me Bonzer.'

And from then on he was 'Bonzer'.

'Bonzer, do you ever see any secretary birds around here?'

'You want to see 'em?'

I nodded.

Within twenty minutes we were watching two secretary birds in an open field.

'When they shake their heads it means they fly away.'

As if they had heard him, the birds shook their heads and took off.

Soon it was time for us to move on. Pictures were taken but we will always remember him, even without the photographs.

Outside Kruger Park the trackers who sat on the seat in front of the ranger were mostly Shangans and had been given first names such as July, January or whatever month in which they were born.

One had a more unusual name. Judas.

We always tipped them at the end of the stay and Joy said, 'Well, we know exactly how much to give Judas'.

I asked a new tracker where he was born, assuming it would be in one of the nearby villages.

He pointed and said, 'Up by the fence'.

The Shangans were marvellous people and we enjoyed being with them.

And then there were the Zulus.

It was the early 1990s: Joy was writing her saga, *My Zulu, Myself*, and we travelled to Zululand in Northern Natal for her to do research on the battlefields of the 1879 Anglo-Zulu War. It was there we met David Rattray, the most amazing raconteur we have ever encountered.

After hours of driving from Durban we arrived in darkness in a torrential downpour at the small lodge he and his wife, Nicky, ran at Fugitives Drift on the Buffalo River—no electricity and very remote. David, a good-looking man in his mid-thirties, and Nicky made the three of us welcome: Joy and I and Robbie Durst, our travelling assistant.

David took us to Rorke's Drift, made famous in the movie Zulu, *where a handful of British troops held off the 4000 Zulu warriors in 1879. After that we drove to Isandlwhana, the battlefield, with its numerous white cairns of stone dotted throughout.*

David had grown up with a Zulu friend from babyhood. They were like brothers. I was amazed, for this was so similar to the story I was writing in My Zulu, Myself.

JOY CHAMBERS-GRUNDY

As we finished breakfast on the morning we were to leave, David and Nicky, carrying their little toddler, entered with their Zulu staff—about fourteen men and women. They asked us to stand.

Reg and I and Robbie rose and they took our hands as we formed a circle around the room. David, Nicky and the Zulu people lifted their voices in song and swayed from side to side, singing traditional Zulu songs for us. It was one of the most moving moments we've ever experienced.

JOY CHAMBERS-GRUNDY

Almost twenty years passed and finally Joy and I had decided that on our next visit we would go to see David and Nicky. And then we read the news: David Rattray had been murdered in his lodge in Fugitives Drift; shot dead in front of Nicky—by Zulu robbers.

RIP David Rattray: raconteur and Zulu historian extraordinaire.

The success of a game drive depends on the ranger who is in charge. Some are outstanding, like Belipe and Simon.

And then, again in Botswana, there was Fox.

Some have stories to tell of their adventures on a drive, but I reckon this one tops them all.

We are in Botswana and Fox is talking.

I had an American couple on a drive once. It was their first time out in the bush and it was clear that the wife would have preferred to be back in a five star hotel reading a book.

We came across a big male lion standing in the middle of the track. We stopped the vehicle and I got out. The missus followed me. But fainted close to the lion.

I stood my ground as the big fella stepped right up to me and put his front paws on my shoulders.

I stared at him to prevent him from turning his attention to the woman.

It was over two hours before the lion dropped his paws and ambled away.

I carried the wife back to the vehicle and we returned to the lodge.

If I had not stood my ground the lion could have attacked me and then turned to my passengers.

That was Fox's story, just as he told it. If you believe him, you'd believe anything. He sure was a colourful tall story teller.

I'm not the only Grundy veteran with an interest in wildlife. Through a misunderstanding I was an hour late when I first met Ric Borns in London. He kindly accepted my apology. Ric became CEO of Grundy Australia and New Zealand for three years before I sold the business. We often talked about our mutual interest so it is fitting that he is now MD of the National Geographic Channel in Australia and finds a place in this chapter.

My adventures are not restricted to the wild but include a handful of those zoos where animals are given great freedom.

Belize for instance. Belize used to be called British Honduras and is a Central American country on the Caribbean coast.

Boadicea was anchored outside the reef.

On the shore, a vehicle stood by to take us to the Belize Zoo, which is located 50 kilometres west of Belize City. It sits on 34 hectares and houses more than a hundred animals indigenous to Belize. Many endangered.

Unlike most zoos in the world, the animals at the Belize Zoo, are not kept in cages or surrounded by bars or concrete bunkers, but rather, housed in large vegetated enclosures of mesh and wood.

I was privileged to be allowed to enter and photograph many of these animals close up.

National Geographic had been there the day before.

My regular visits are to fine zoos like Taronga Zoo in Sydney, Taronga Western Plains at Dubbo, Melbourne Zoo and the magnificent zoo in Singapore. The Chester Zoo in England is also excellent and the Apenheul Primate Park in Holland is amazing.

There will be more, but only when the standard is as good as at these zoos.

And do I continue to get too close in the wild?

Joy certainly thinks I do.

It had all started in 1952 when I first travelled into the veldt. When I put down a rifle and picked up a camera.

At first I didn't realise I had found a life that would capture me after the loss of Grundy Worldwide.

But I have.

Photographing animals, attempting to help endangered species and animals in need and well, yes, deficit financing books and exhibitions.

EVERY MAN HAS ONE

On 6 September 2003 Joy and I went to Cincinnati for me to have a full body MRI as a routine medical examination.

Odd place to go, you might think, but Cincinnati then had the most advanced MRI equipment in the country. So we were told.

The procedure took place under the football stadium, which was home to the Cincinnati Bengals, a fact confirmed by the vision of enormous men trotting by on their way to training.

We were told that I was in excellent health.

A few days later we returned home to Bermuda and on to London where Joy delivered the manuscript for her Second World War novel, *None but the Brave*.

We visited our London doctor Roger Hayward, who was a close friend. He checked my PSA level and found it to be slightly elevated.

'Reg, there's no real concern but next time you're in London, let's do an ultrasound.'

We both said in chorus, 'How about tomorrow?'

The ultrasound was done the following day—Friday 20 September at St John & St Elizabeth Hospital in St John's Wood. Results showed something not normal, so biopsies were taken immediately.

'Don't worry. I'll call you on the *Boadicea* as soon as I have some news.'

Two hours later we flew from Northolt RAF base to Nice and joined *Boadicea*.

The next day Roger called.

'Sorry to tell you, Reg, but the biopsy shows a virulent cancer of the prostate.'

For the first time ever I had the feeling that it could soon end.

I kept thinking about all the ups and downs over the years. Mostly ups, I suppose. Of a daughter I loved and lost. Of a wife who is the mainstay of my life. Of the friends who had passed on. Of the millions of people who had tragedy as their companion.

Keep throwing punches. These words kept playing over and over in my head.

So many people worse off than me.

What the hell. Get on with it.

A boatload of our friends were arriving the next day. It was too late to cancel.

What do we do? Tell them, or keep it to ourselves?

Joy wanted to hold back but we finally agreed that we should reveal our hand.

Joy's brother Jack and his wife Maria arrived first. They were devastated.

'Don't worry, we'll get on top of it. I'll be spending a fair bit of time on the Net before making a final decision. Just want to be sure I move in the right direction.'

The next day our other guests began to arrive and when they were all aboard we gave them the news.

I tried to reassure them.

'They've caught it in time. So let's get on with the cruise and enjoy ourselves.'

We sailed to Monaco, San Remo, Portofino and Antibes over the week.

I didn't see much of those beautiful places. I spent a lot of time researching the options. Of course I had many phone calls with Roger Hayward in London. He gave us the name of the world's leading prostate cancer surgeon, a name confirmed by other doctor friends in America and Australia.

It was unanimous. They all came up with the same name. 'He's the best in the world and he works at Johns Hopkins in Baltimore, USA.'

I immediately ordered his book, *How to Survive Prostate Cancer*.

Joy tells what happened next.

I had the London office find the appropriate phone number for me and taking into account the six-hour time difference I called Johns Hopkins.

I asked to speak to someone who could arrange an appointment with this world renowned professor of urology and surgeon of radical prostatectomy (I will call him Dr W.). I was put through to a woman in an office.

I explained the situation and the woman asked me how old my husband was.

I said, 'He's seventy-nine.'

Her reply was, 'Oh dear, Dr W. doesn't operate on anybody over sixty-five.'

I said, 'Really? Are you in his department?'

She sounded like a reasonable person as she replied, 'No, I just make appointments for him'.

'Look, I'm actually calling from a ship in the Mediterranean and I'd really like to speak to someone who works in his department if that's possible.'

'Can you hold on?'

'Yes, certainly.'

I must have looked very worried, for my brother Jack, sitting opposite me, shifted forward in his seat and asked, 'What's happening?'

'The booking lady said he doesn't operate on anybody over sixty-five. I can't believe it.'

I waited.

Jack says it was twenty-six minutes in all, during which period this same lady came back on the line three times and asked, 'Are you still happy to wait?'

I think because she knew I was overseas she was really trying to help me.

Each time I said I was happy to wait. This was my husband's life. I didn't care if I waited on the phone all day.

At last she came back and said, 'Oh, there's someone there now, I'll put you through'.

My pulse began to race. 'To whom am I speaking?'

My heavens! It was the man himself!

'Oh … Dr W., how do you do? My name is Joy Chambers-Grundy and I'm calling you from a yacht in the Mediterranean on behalf of my husband, Reg Grundy. He has been diagnosed with prostate

cancer at a hospital in London, last week.'

'I see. What is his PSA? And did he have a biopsy?'

I had learned an awful lot about the condition in a short time.

'Yes, 6.4 and he has a Gleason 8, but only in one stick of the six biopsies taken. We are prepared to come to America to see you. We could be there tomorrow.'

And then he said it. 'How old is he?'

'He's seventy-nine, but not the sort of seventy-nine you'll be imagining, Dr W. He is much younger in every way. He still runs businesses and is in his prime. He is probably more like a sixty-year-old.'

'I'm afraid I don't operate on anyone over sixty-five.'

I took a deep breath. 'Dr W., do you mean to tell me that if the President of the United States had prostate cancer and he was over sixty-five, you would not operate on him?'

Dead silence greeted this question. Seconds ticked by and my heart boomed in my chest.

When he spoke again his tone had altered. 'I could see you the week after next if that suits you?'

I had difficulty speaking but I got it out. 'Oh, that suits us all right, Dr W. Thank you so much.'

'Please wait on, Mrs Grundy, and I'll have my secretary take some details.'

I had done it. I had persuaded the great Dr W. to see my Reg!

Even though we had the Dr W. appointment, Reg's personality is such that during the rest of the time on Boadicea he continued to explore other avenues for treatment of prostate cancer. The centres he was attracted to were Loma Linda University and Cedars-Sinai Medical Center in California, as well as a place in Atlanta called Radiotherapy Centers of Georgia (RCOG).

JOY CHAMBERS-GRUNDY

I was intrigued by RCOG and the man who ran it, the founder Dr Frank Critz.

Our guests left the Boadicea in Antibes on Saturday 5 October.

On Monday we flew to London and on Tuesday we met with Roger Hayward at St John & St Elizabeth.

He was both amazed and delighted that Joy had secured the appointment with Dr W. but agreed that I should still explore the other options.

I was still intrigued with RCOG in Atlanta so Joy phoned them and made an appointment just a few days before we were due to see Dr W.

To take our minds off the situation, we decided to go to Las Vegas for the weekend with Grahame Bateman and Bobby Crystal. Our aircraft, a Boeing Business Jet, was waiting at Van Nuys Airport ready to fly us from LA to Las Vegas.

Steve Wynn, the owner of the Bellagio Hotel in Las Vegas, was at Van Nuys ahead of us and asked our crew if he could come on board as he was thinking of buying a new plane. The crew knew who he was and agreed on our behalf. He eventually bought a BBJ himself.

He left a message with the crew that he would like us to stay at his hotel, free of charge. Sure enough, when we landed in Las Vegas there was a big black limo ready to take us to the Bellagio.

We already had a reservation at the Venetian, so we politely declined his generous offer. We still haven't met Steve Wynn.

On Monday 14 October we flew from Las Vegas to Atlanta and the following day drove out to the suburb of Decatur to RCOG and met Dr Frank Critz.

RCOG is a one-storey sprawling building and the waiting room was full of middle-aged and older men. Some greeted one another as friends and as time passed Bobby Crystal and Grahame Bateman, who were with us, talked with a few of them.

'Who's the patient?' asked a man in a lumber jacket.

Bobby and Grahame pointed to me.

'You've come to the right place, sir,' he said, smiling at me.

'Ask anyone here. This is it.'

The men spoke of Dr Critz and his team as converts might of a newly found religion.

Eventually Joy, Grahame and I went in to meet Dr Frank Critz. He was a dapper man somewhere between fifty and sixty and he greeted us with a handshake. We seemed to bond almost immediately as I pointed to his jacket. 'Is that a Brioni?'

Frank nodded.

'So's mine.'

Frank spent a full hour with us and answered our questions in detail. He gave me a DVD explaining his treatment, ProstRcision: seed implants followed by radiation. No surgery.

He gave us statistics that clearly supported his method.

Joy told him we had an appointment to see Dr W. at Johns Hopkins. Of course he knew the surgeon well and was amazed that we had an appointment.

But we all felt very comfortable with Frank Critz.

At the end of the hour he wished us well and Joy asked him the question, 'If Reg decides to have your treatment, will you personally take care of my husband?'

'I will,' he replied.

Before we departed I had a CAT scan. We made no commitment to return and said we would get back to him when we had made our decision.

As we stepped into the limo Grahame made the point that at no time at RCOG had we been asked for one penny. We had spent an hour with the founder and felt comfortable with what had been explained to us. I'd had a CAT scan as well, all without charge.

At other medical institutions we had paid up front.

By now I had read Dr W's book, *How to Survive Prostate Cancer*, and I had studied all the literature and seen the DVD that Frank Critz had given us.

It was decision time.

The following day we flew to London.

During the flight I kept talking about what treatment I should have. We both hated the thought of surgery and all the side effects, the possibility of the cancer being outside the prostate and the inherent concerns of this form of treatment.

The more we read about Dr Critz's method, the more we liked it. Finally I decided that Dr Frank Critz and RCOG was the right way to go.

On reaching London Joy cancelled the appointment with Dr W. and wrote a letter to him, delivered by courier, explaining that we had decided to opt for Dr Frank Critz's ProstRcision—the seed implants followed by radiation.

Now we waited as 13 November, the date for my implant, came closer.

We were at the Atlanta Outpatient Surgery Center early. Frank Critz talked to me reassuringly. At last, I went in for my implant. About an hour and a half later Frank Critz and Dr Scott Miller, his assistant, came over to Joy. 'It was copybook. It went perfectly.'

Joy was in tears.

'Two of the seeds are gold,' Frank explained. He had inserted over 100 radioactive seeds into my prostate and in the coming weeks radiation would be aimed into these seeds to kill the cancer. The two gold seeds were to help control any inflammation.

It was early December when my radiation began and for seven weeks, five days a week, we went to RCOG in Decatur, Atlanta. I was measured for my exact treatment. I had three small tattoos marked on my body, one on my lower abdomen and one on each side of my upper thigh. The radioactive beams were aimed with precision on these positions.

Sometimes we stayed in hotels in Atlanta and other times, mostly weekends, we flew to *Boadicea*, which had crossed the Atlantic from her home in the Mediterranean and was berthed in the river in Savannah, Georgia, a half hour flight away. Joy was intrigued. Her father, as a young merchant seaman, had often sailed into Savannah.

During this time Joy flew to LA to be present while the cover illustration for *None but the Brave* was photographed by Douglas Kirkland.

While I was having treatment we got to know the people at RCOG— wonderful human beings who worked every day to save lives. I tried to wear a different pair of cufflinks every day. The girls always noticed and it became a standing joke: 'Let's see what you're wearing today?'

My thirty-five treatments ended on 22 January 2003. Of course there were minor side effects for a while. Some occurred at most inconvenient times.

In March we were in Los Angeles. I had an appointment at ABC, which had relocated out to Burbank.

Brian Frons, who had taken over from Lucy Johnson years before as head of NBC's daytime line-up, was now head of ABC daytime. Brian had bought *Scrabble* and *Time Machine* from me which, when added to *Sale of the Century*, meant we had three of the four daytime strips between ten and twelve each day on NBC.

So I knew him well.

During those years I pitched *Dangerous Women* to Brian but he'd shown little interest. The ironic thing was that Frons had rejected a show on which his wife Jeanette Guarneiri was to become assistant director.

Although Brian had passed on the project, I reckon there was much discussion about the show at night between husband Brian and wife Jeanette.

Fran Calderone, our unit manager, hired both Jeanette and Joe Behar, who had directed *Days of our Lives* for many years.

But that was then. Brian Frons had returned to America from where he'd been working in Europe to take over daytime at ABC. Maybe I could sell him that daytime strip I had up my sleeve.

Bob Crystal was with me and Greg Nathanson, who had been the programmer at KTLA, came along for the pitch.

Bob was driving.

We pulled up at the guard box and I was asked for identification papers.

I didn't have any.

I smiled at the guard. 'I never carry any papers, or credit cards or money, for that matter. Sorry.'

The guard stared at me then called up to Brian's office to ask him to come down and identify me. Brian didn't speak to me, just muttered to the guard, 'That's him', and turned on his heel.

It was a bad beginning.

At last we were waiting outside Brian's office.

'Sorry, guys, I've got to go to the loo. Where is it?'

I was given vague directions to a lower floor.

When I returned, Brian, his gorgeous assistant, Bob and Greg were waiting for me. My presentation went down like a lead balloon. Worst I'd ever done would be closer to the mark. What with the personal inconvenience I was having and the style of the show I was pitching I had lost before I started.

Brian wanted a human interest reality show and I was pitching a game show.

Wrong concept. Wrong day.

We got out of his office fast, said goodbye to Greg, who had his own car, and headed to the parking area below.

'Bob, I've got to go again.'

'Stand in front of the car and pee against the wall.'

I did.

On the way back to Beverly Hills, Bob had to pull to the side so that I could relieve myself behind a tree. I'd never had such a dreadful day.

But of course the incontinence ended as I recovered from the procedure.

Twice a year I fill in a form and send it to RCOG in Atlanta, as do all previous patients.

Currently, my PSA level is 0.01.

RCOG keeps detailed information on all the people who have been through the procedure. Frank Critz says the process is even better now than it was when I went through.

And of course it was natural that Frank would become one of our close friends.

How else can you thank a man for saving your life?

BOADICEA

I sold Grundy Worldwide to the Pearson Group in 1995 and found myself wondering what to do next. I had been in media since 1947, some forty-eight years, and had had little time for anything else except boating, which had been a helpful adjunct to my main interest. Joy and I had entertained many show business people, from writers, directors and producers to celebrities and businessmen.

So it was natural that we would again turn to boating to help make up for the loss of my empire.

What if we were to build a superyacht? How much might it cost? How long would it be before we could actually be on board?

We were soon to find out.

With the help of experts we started our quest. There were many meetings. One that stands out in my mind was with a department of P&O in London. There were Joy and I and our yacht captain, our good friend, Robert Peel (yes, related to the man who began the first police force in London—the peelers).

We met in what we imagined might sometimes be used for a boardroom.

It was decided that if we went ahead, our masterpiece would be some 70.4 metres long and we wanted it to have plenty of beam. In spite of the tut-tutting in the room, all three of us kept to our view that she should be 14 metres wide. Three metres wider than the experts had recommended.

And the three things that we insisted on were stability, stability, stability. Joy was even more emphatic than I, and the discussion got heated as the experts discussed ways to make the boat almost impervious to the winds and water movements.

'Maybe we could have telescopic legs that extend to the sea bed.'

Sarcasm, was it? Possibly.

Finally one of the experts directed one more question to Joy.

'Wouldn't you be better to build a house?' She just grinned.

In spite of everything we decided to move forward with the build. Like all major enterprises the project had to have a code name. The men in the room were looking at each other for inspiration.

Joy suggested *Boadicea* after the warrior queen of the Iceni people of Norfolk in eastern Britain who fought the Romans. Everyone in the room nodded in agreement.

As time went by the name *Boadicea* became the name of the build, not just the code name.

British designer Terence Disdale was hired—a choice we were never to regret. Dutch shipbuilder AMELS was commissioned to build her.

A few crew members of *Idolwood II* moved to Makkum in Friesland, Holland to work on the build. Captain Robert Peel took up residence to oversee the build and he had a lot of fights on our behalf. And in the final six months Chris Russell, who was to become *Boadicea*'s final captain, and Chinni Mahadevan who was our head of the interior, became part of the supervising team. These three men remain great friends of Joy's and mine.

Planning started in late 1996. The build took three years.

While it was being built Joy and I travelled to Holland on a regular basis to see the *Boadicea* in her various stages. Robert always picked us up in Amsterdam and drove us north to Makkum. The first time was simply to view the hull—the massive steel structure—and as it grew and developed we became more excited.

I remember one stage when the superstructure had been added and Reg and I were standing on the deck outside the bridge. It was winter and the yacht was being built inside a massive shed. Reg pointed over the endless scaffolding to a vessel's bow in the distance. 'Who's yacht is that?' he asked, thinking another must be being built in the same shed.

'That's yours,' Robert replied.

JOY CHAMBERS-GRUNDY

Between 1996 and 1999 there were many problems, many changes, many reasons to regret the decision to build her.

REG GRUNDY

But when, in May 1999 in St Lucia in the Caribbean, we anchored off the twin Pitons, primeval peaks that towered more than 600 metres above us, all that was forgotten.

It was time to christen her. Long ago, *Boadicea* had become not the code word for the build but the name of our new superyacht.

Captain Bob Peel did a superb job in attaching *Boadicea* to the end of a flimsy jetty for the christening ceremony. A steel band were standing by as the new and old guests mingled, waiting for the show to commence. Our dear little sheltie Calpurnia was there, wearing a glorious lavender bow.

The band made a valiant effort to play 'Waltzing Matilda'. It didn't sound quite the same as it had that night back in 1952 when I had called the Carruthers–Toweel world title fight. This was the Caribbean's unique version of Australia's unofficial national anthem.

The wind was sweeping across the jetty. The rain came belting down upon us. The crew was on hand with umbrellas as Joy and I, feeling a little uncomfortable, stood on the wooden podium which had been erected for my welcoming speech and Joy's ceremonial smashing of a bottle of champagne across the bow.

There was silence as the beribboned bottle hit the stem and bounced back. Joy was getting desperate as she swung the bottle for the fourth time before it finally smashed, sending a foaming stream of champagne sliding down the bow and into the tropical water.

As we moved away, the podium blew off the dock.

We were wet but happy as we walked up the gangway onto *Boadicea*. In the Brisbane lounge we gathered around the TV for the video replay. There was more laughter and cheering as we watched the champagne bottle at last explode on the bow.

Next morning the *Boadicea* moved out into the waters of the Caribbean. It had been a wonderful twenty-four hours.

Over the years we travelled as far south as New Zealand and as far north as Anchorage and the Hubbard Glacier in Alaska. We sailed up old father Thames and through Tower Bridge as it opened for us to tie up beside HMS *Belfast*, which had seen action on D-Day.

We circumnavigated the British Isles and off the Orkney Isles we cut the engines as we passed over the watery grave of Lord Kitchener, who appears prominently in Joy's book, *Vale Valhalla*.

But the most moving moment of all was when we came through Sydney Heads and sailed down the harbour and under the Sydney Harbour Bridge.

Australians have a reputation for chopping down tall poppies and I suppose I had become one. But then, and over the next few days, people waved and called out from their small boats: 'Good on you, Reg, you deserve it!' and 'Swap you for me sixteen-footer'. Laughs, catcalls and cheers greeted me from ordinary Australians who reckoned I was okay. Maybe some of them knew that I'd received a pound a week at my first job and had never forgotten those days.

And on a later visit with *Boadicea*, while alongside at Garden Island, I picked up one of the dailies and saw a cartoon which showed a little guy standing on a pier holding a pad and pencil and looking up at an exaggeratedly high foredeck of *Boadicea* with a captain peering over the side.

The captain is calling out, 'Mr Grundy wants you to know he owns a bloody big boat'.

The reporter asks, 'Anything else?'

Captain replies, 'No, he's a recluse!'

We bought the original by cartoonist Rod Clement and it hangs in our NSW country property where Doug Graham, our marvellous manager and friend, takes care of everything including Joy's pet animals.

By the way, I'm not much of a recluse these days.

We have some very interesting neighbours down there in the country including good pal Alan Jones and we entertain each other with hearty dinners when we can. Of course, Alan and I as the Southern Highlanders entertain the guests with a few songs.

We don't get paid, but we are thinking of passing round the hat ... one of these days!

THE ONES THAT GOT AWAY

Overall I've had a fortunate life.

But it hasn't all been smooth.

Sometimes I created bumps by making the wrong decision.

The list is long, but here are a few.

After the success of *Prisoner: Cell Block H* in America the phone started to ring. CBS had managed to get hold of a copy of the show and it soon got around that it was 'the hottest tape in the building'.

CBS indicated that they might finance an American pilot.

I turned them down.

I decided to go into syndication and worry about a US network version later. Syndicators were approaching me for the distribution rights. There was big money to be made.

Viacom, who had an enormous distribution arm, even made mock-ups of the press and radio campaign they would run.

I turned Viacom down.

Telepictures, a newly formed distribution company, said they would get behind *Prisoner: Cell Block H* for six months to the exclusion of all other product.

I turned them down.

I chose Len Firestone who had a small and successful distribution company. I reckoned I'd be able to control him. It would have been far better to go with Viacom with its power in the marketplace, or to have taken a chance and worked with CBS.

But CBS still had its eye on me and agreed to look at any drama concepts we might have before the upcoming season started.

Instead of offering one or two developed concepts I sent them about twenty single-paragraph ideas. All were rejected.

In desperation, I suggested that a prison show where male guards worked in a woman's prison might work.

We got a script deal.

Reg Watson wrote the script. I interfered. CBS passed.

And that was that.

I sat in Brandon Tartikoff's office one afternoon and pitched a few ideas.

One was a Western to be shot in Australia. Title, *Brimstone*.

Brandon looked at me and said, 'Westerns are out of fashion'.

I was surprised.

I'm sure he had said he'd be interested in a Western.

I put the sample script back in my briefcase and pitched three more concepts, each of which was received with indifference.

I had one left.

'Brandon, we all know how successful *Love Boat* was. So how about a *Love Boat* featuring teenagers?'

Brandon's face lit up.

'That's not a bad idea. Funny, but my mother is the entertainment director on a cruise ship.'

'We could use her as our technical adviser.'

Brandon was smiling

'Good idea.'

And here's the stub-your-toe part.

I didn't ask him for his mother's phone number. I didn't follow up in any way. I threw away the chance to make a TV movie which could have become a prime time series on NBC.

And there's more.

Some years after selling my production companies I previewed an English quiz show. I just knew it would be a hit. I showed it to Bob Noah, who agreed.

My lawyer, Kerry Wright, knew Paul Smith the producer well. We had taken a couple of his concepts and remade them in other countries.

We approached Paul for the American rights. Paul Smith upped the ante.

'Reg, if you think the format's so hot, why don't you buy the company?'

Paul Smith said he'd sell 50 per cent for £4 million.

'That's as cheap as it will ever get.'

I passed.

The show was *Who Wants to Be a Millionaire*.

Well, you can't do everything!

ON 4 AUGUST

It's 4 August 2010, which means I am now eighty-six.

Of course it's not good news. Simply reminds me that I'm getting closer to the finishing line.

But I am not, I repeat, am not a year older; I am simply one day older than I was yesterday. And when you look at it that way, everyone without exception is a day older unless they died yesterday, and then they are not a day older and never will be.

Within the next hour or so the people around me will converge. Maggie, my secretary, will be smiling as she steps forward with the cake with, hopefully, one candle which I will blow out in a matter-of-fact manner and then watch the glorious procedure of giving everyone a slice.

I don't like cake, except carrot cake, and because two of our best friends, Quinton and Vicki Edness, had dinner at our place a couple of days ago I have a new carrot cake which Vicki brought with her and presented lovingly to me.

'Here it is, Reg, your very own carrot cake. I know how much you love it.' She was right.

But I still have only small slices, even though she is probably the best carrot cake maker in the whole wide world.

I said to Joy early this morning, 'Hey, we've got Vicki's cake we haven't cut. Call Maggie and stop her buying a new one with all the add-ons. We'll eat the carrot cake'.

So that's what will happen in an hour or so.

We'll probably have it in the kitchen as we usually do. Calliope, our little princess, our sheltie dog, will get a piece and the handful of us will all have a munch.

Hopefully there'll be a limit on the candles.

Someone will take a few happy snaps. I'll try to create a few slightly better ones. Family and friends and people in our offices like Jo Cullen

Cronshaw, who runs Monaco for us, and Elaine Bower, Naomi Barham, Fiona Newman, Louise Syder, John and Tracey in London and Shirley in Brisbane, great people, who've all been with us forever, will send messages by phone and email.

Everyone will tell me how remarkable I am.

'You don't look eighty-six, RG.'

'You look so young.'

I'll remind myself that I ain't what I used to be. Joy thinks we should tell everybody from now on that birthdays are to be ignored; perhaps next year we'll do that!

Anyway, I'll hint to everyone that the ceremony is over and that we can all get on with our work.

But first, there's something I'd rather do.

Our property wraps around an inlet, creating a saltwater lagoon. And across the lagoon, there's a craggy 'cliff' in which resides a baby longtail, an elegant tropicbird.

I'll just pop out and see if he's ready to fly out of that crevice in the rocks where he was born. To fly upwards and upwards until he can see the ocean where he will live for the next two or three years until he flies back to that crevice with a girlfriend and the whole process will start all over again.

He hatched weeks ago and he's in his hole in the cliff right now.

Sometimes we go over to visit Longford, the name Derek Smith, our maintenance man, came up with and the name we have given him without, I must confess, his permission. We use aquabikes so as not to disturb him while I attempt to photograph him. It's tough because he hides inside the cliff face.

I wonder where he'll be for the next two years?

Joy just walked in and reminds me.

'Sweetie, he'll live out there in the middle of the North Atlantic.'

And where am I?

Well, in our Bermuda home where we spend most of our time.

One of our assistants, Neil Freestone, and I are on duty each morning at 6.30 with still and video cameras to watch for our longtail to emerge.

At 11.30 today Neil calls us. Longford has moved closer to the opening in the rock. Joy and I hurry out onto the patio overlooking the water and grab our cameras. Longford is taking his first tentative peek at the world outside.

Today or over the next few days, he will sally forth and make his first attempt to fly.

The tiny cave in which he has been living stops him from trying out his wings, which means he must leap into the unknown and hope that he can control his flight and fly upwards towards the sun until he can see the ocean and fly towards it.

If he fails, he will fall into our saltwater lagoon and we will pluck him out and dry him down. Or take him to a higher spot, maybe on the verandah outside our bedroom, and help him fly away.

Today there will be more emails and phone calls and tonight we will go to a nearby beach restaurant for a meal with our two closest advisers, who are here for a couple of days: Sue McIntosh and Kerry Wright, who have been with us since the world began.

We have a board meeting today and tomorrow and, along with Joy and me, Sue and Kerry comprise the board. Neil, who is from London, and Maggie Moore, who was born in Ireland, will join us for dinner. We're a cosmopolitan lot.

Tomorrow there will be meetings in our library. Business as usual.

It's already the day after my birthday and I am resigned to the fact that I am eighty-six.

No time to remember it. Too much happening.

This morning when I got out of bed I walked out onto the balcony and looked down and saw Neil standing beside a tripod that was carrying a massive 800 mm telescopic lens while beside it, propped up on another tripod, was my wife's little camcorder.

Every morning we meet and wait. After an hour or so, I leave. Neil stays on.

Joy and I come when he calls.

We know that one day very soon Longford will take a deep breath and tumble out of the cliff, hoping to fly away.

I've taken thousands of shots of these beautiful birds. But I have never seen a baby longtail leaving its nest. Nor have the vast majority of people.

Chinni, who is the curator of my photographic collection, returns tomorrow. He and Derek and I had been keeping an eye on this baby until he went away and Neil flew in from London to take over.

Everyone tells me to take it easy. What else is an 'old man' supposed to do? But that's not my way. I want to be on the spot when Longford flies out.

But there's a problem. Those meetings.

My dilemma? How to be in two places at once.

Neil will call me if there's any action.

So I spend the day running through the house to get to the viewing point. Sometimes all four of us are heading for the door.

What is more important?

The lousy financial reports, courtesy of the worldwide depression, or our little friend Longford?

At last the meeting is over. It's nearly four o'clock. Sue and Kerry have just left.

Neil calls. It looks like Longford is about to take off. Joy and I run outside.

The moment comes. He struggles out of the hole in the cliff and, flapping his wings, falls straight down into the lagoon.

We have been warned that we may have to rescue him.

No need for that.

He is struggling in the water but slowly moving himself forward. Joy shouts and Neil jumps on an aquabike and follows Longford out through the rocky entrance of the lagoon into the harbour, in case he becomes waterlogged.

But Longford gathers up his strength and finally lifts himself and flies away. Up, up into the blue sky he goes—a small dark dot.

We are all a bit misty-eyed and Joy whispers in my ear, 'Must fly. Goodbye'.

The sign-off I had used at the end of my *Wheel of Fortune* show so long ago.

Longford will live out there in the Sargasso Sea, never touching land for two or three years, and then return to this same hole in the cliff in our magical saltwater lagoon.

Joy and I kiss and hug one another and wave.

I hope I'll be here waiting for you, Longford.

APPENDIX

Honours awarded to Reg Grundy

1982 The Television Society of Australia's Colin Bednall Award, for his outstanding contribution to the television industry.

1983 The Order of the British Empire, for his services to Australian television.

1993 *TV Week* Hall of Fame Gold Logie, for his lifetime services to Australian television.

1996 International Emmy—the Founder's Award, for individuals distinguished by their creative achievements, whose work is recognised throughout the world, crossing cultural boundaries to touch our common humanity.

1999 The Lifetime Achievement Award from the Variety Club of New South Wales.

2003 The Golden Nymph Award, received from Prince Albert at the Monte Carlo Television Festival for his concept of 'parochial internationalism' and the contribution that he has made to local and international television production. The Prince proclaimed that the world should recognise him.

2004 Honorary Doctorate from the prestigious University of Queensland, Australia. Conferred by the Chancellor Sir Llew Edwards.

2008 Companion of the Order of Australia (AC), Australia's highest honour in the Queen's Birthday Honours, for services to the entertainment and television industry in depicting national cultural identity, to the promotion of Australia internationally and to the community through philanthropic contributions to a range of organisations. Bestowed by Major General Michael Jeffery, Governor-General of Australia.

2010 A Lifetime Achievement Award from FRAPA (Format Recognition and Protection Association) to be presented in Cannes, France, on 6 October by Ute Biernat, FRAPA Chairman.

TV theme credits

DRAMAS

Boney (Frank Strangio)

Chopper Squad (Mike Perjanik)

Class of '74 (Brian Cadd)

Dangerous Women (Ray Ellis)

Embassy (Peter Sullivan)

Escape of the Artful Dodger (Peter Dasent)

Glenview High (Mike Perjanik)

Goede Tijden, Slechte Tijden (Good Times, Bad Times) (H. van Eijck/ B. van der Veer)—The Netherlands

Mission Top Secret (Ian Davidson)

Madre y Hijo (Mother & Son) (Alejandro Gaete Aguirre)—Chile

Neighbours (Tony Hatch/Jackie Trent)

One Way Ticket (Nerida Tyson-Chew)

Other Side of Paradise, The (Martin Armiger)

Pirates Island (Mike Harvey)

Possession (Mike Harvey)

Prisoner (Allan Caswell)

Professor Poopsnagle's Steam Zeppelin (Bob Young)

Restless Years, The (Mike Perjanik)

Richmond Hill (Ashley Irwin)

Runaway Island (Bob Young)

Secret Valley (Marie Cowan/David Phillips/arranged: Bob Young)

Sons and Daughters (Peter Pinne/Don Battye)

Starting Out (Mike Harvey/Kay Parker)

Tanamera—Lion of Singapore (Mario Millo)

Taurus Rising (Garry McDonald/Laurie Stone)

Waterloo Station (Tony Hatch)

Young Doctors, The (Brian King)

GAME SHOWS

Blankety Blanks (Jack Grimsley)

Blind Date (Jack Grimsley)

Celebrity Game (Jack Grimsley)

Concentration (Jack Grimsley)

Family Feud (Jack Grimsley)

It's a Knockout (Rick Turk)

Man-O-Man (Alejandro Gaete Aguirre)—South America

Matchmates (Peter Best)

New Price Is Right, The (Jack Grimsley)

Perfect Match (Rick Turk)

Sale of the Century (Jack Grimsley)

Wheel of Fortune (Jack Grimsley)

MOVIES

ABBA: The Movie (Benny Andersson/ Stig Anderson/Björn Ulvaeus)

Barry McKenzie Holds His Own (Peter Best)

TELEMOVIES

Alternative, The (Bob Young)

Is Anybody There? (Bob Young)

Night Nurse, The (Peter Clarke/James Sloggett)

Plunge into Darkness (Peter Clarke/ James Sloggett)

Special Place, A (Peter Pinne/Don
    Battye)
Two-Way Mirror (pilot) (Geoff Harvey)
    (same tune as *The Sullivans*)

Grundy productions

$100,000 Moneymakers 1982

$200,000 Question 1987

$7,000 Question 1971

7 Million Dollar Fugitive 1981

A Special Place 1980

ABBA: Down Under 1976

ABBA: The Movie 1977

All at Sea 1976

Ampol Big Game 1964

Ampol Stamp Quiz 1964

Anything Can Happen 1972

Australia's Most Wanted 1989–1995

Barry McKenzie Holds His Own 1974

Beat the Odds 1971–1972

Beato Tra Le Donne 1994—Italy

Bellamy 1980

Big Challenge 1971

Billion Dollar Baby (comedy pilot) 1976

Blankety Blanks 1976–1979

Blind Date 1967–1970

Boney 1990–1991

Case for the Defence 1975

Casino 10 1975–1976

Celebrity Family Feud 1990–1991

Celebrity Game 1969

Celebrity Game Challenge 1976

Celebrity Squares 1975

Celebrity Squares 1993—UK

Celebrity Tattletales 1979–1980

Chopper Squad 1977–1979

Class of '74 1974

Class of '75 1975

Concentration 1960–1967

Confessions of Ronald Biggs 1977

Crossfire 1987–1988

Dai Pai (Card Sharks) 1982—Hong Kong

Dai Sou But (Sale of the Century) 1982—
    Hong Kong

Dangerous Women 1991—USA

Demolition 1978

Desafio Familiar (Family Feud)
    1993—Chile

Elles I Ells (Man-O-Man) 1993—Spain

Embassy 1990–1992

Emergency Line 1972

ESP and All That 1971

Everybody's Talking 1969

Famili Seratus 1995—Indonesia

Family Feud 1977–1984

Family Feud 1989–1995

Family Game 1967

First Impression 1964

Ford Superquiz 1981

Funny You Should Ask 1972–1974

Gambit 1972 & 1974

Generation Gap 1969

Get the Message 1967

Glenview High 1977–1979

Goede Tijden, Slechte Tijden
    (Good Times, Bad Times)
    1990—Netherlands

Going for Gold 1987—UK

Gone to Ground 1976

Great Temptation 1971–1974

Guessing Game 1966–1967

Gute Zeiten, Schlechte Zeiten (Good Times, Bad Times) 1992—Germany

Have a Go Show 1980–1981

Heartline 1970

High Adventure 1984

High Rollers 1975

Hopp oder Top (Sale of the Century) 1990–1993—Germany

Hot Streak 1985—USA

Hotline 1970

How Do They Do That? 1993—UK

Hypnotism and All That 1971

I've Got a Secret 1965–1974

Ideal Fun Day 1970

Image of Death 1978

In Town Tonight 1969

Is Anybody There? 1975

Island Trader 1982

It's a Knockout 1985–1987

Jackson High 1976

Jeder gegen Jeden 1997—Germany

Jeopardy 1990—UK

Jeopardy 1992—NZ

Junior Moneymakers 1972

Kevin Arnett's World of the Supernatural 1977

Keynotes 1989—UK

Killers of the Great Barrier Reef 1979

Kinder Ruck Zuck (Junior Hot Streak) 1991–1992—Germany

King's Men 1975

Kricket 1995—India

La Venta del Siglo (Sale of the Century) 1995—Paraguay

Le Jeu (The Main Event) 1992–1993 France

Lucky Seven 1970

Madre y Hijo (Mother & Son) 1995—Chile

Mama's Gone a-Hunting 1976

Marriage Game 1966–1969

Martin St James 1971

Match Game 1969

Match Mates 1981–1982

Matchmates 1983–1986—Brunei

Missing Link 1969

Mission Top Secret (telemovie) 1991

Mission Top Secret 1992

Moneymakers 1971

Name That Tune 1975

National Star Quest 1978–1979

Neighbours 1985—present

Newlywed Game 1968

Numbers Game 1967

One in a Million 1975

Password 1972–1973

Penthouse Club 1972–1974

Perfect Match 1984–1989

Perfect Match 1990—NZ

Personality Squares 1967–1969

Play Your Cards Right 1984–1985

Play Your Hunch 1969–1974

Plunge into Darkness 1977

Poor Fella Me 1973

Possession 1984–1985

Pot Luck 1987

Pot of Gold 1975–1978

Pot of Gold 1993—UK

Press Your Luck 1987–1988

Press Your Luck 1991–1992—UK

Pretty Petrol (comedy pilot) 1983

Prisoner: Cell Block H 1979–1986

Professor Poopsnagle's Steam Zeppelin
1985–1986

Punishment 1980

Que le Meilleur Gagne (Everybody's
Equal) 1991–1995—France

Questionario Millionario (Going for
Gold) 1991–1992—Spain

Questions pour un Champion (Going for
Gold) 1988–1995—France

Rap Klap (Hot Streak)
1990–1991—Belgium

Return to the Good Old Days 1977

Richmond Hill 1987–1988

Ron Cadee Show 1970

Roses Bloom Twice 1978

Ruck Zuck (Hot Streak)
1989–1995—Germany

Runaway Island (children's) 1981–1984

Sale of the Century 1980–1995

Sale of the Century 1983–1989—USA

Sale of the Century 1989–1991—UK

Sale of the Century 1989–1993—NZ

Say When 1962–1964

Scattergories 1993—USA

Scrabble 1984–1990—USA

Scrabble 1993—USA

Second Chance 1977

Second Guess 1987

Secret Valley (children's) 1979

Shortland Street 1992–1995—NZ

Showdown 1968

Sky Star Search 1989–1990—UK

Small Talk 1994—UK

Sons and Daughters 1981–1987

Spending Spree 1971

Split Personality 1967

Split Second 1972–1973

Starting Out 1982–1983

Super Seven 1976

Superquiz 1989

Tanamera—Lion of Singapore 1988

Taurus Rising 1982

Tell the Truth 1971

Temptation 1970–1974

The Alternative 1976

The Better Sex 1978

The Celebrity Game 1975–1976

The Death Train 1978

The Main Event 1993—UK

The Martins & McCoys (pilot) 1974

The New Price Is Right 1989

The Newman Shame 1978

The Nightnurse 1977

The Other Side of Paradise 1991

The Phantom Horsemen 1990

The Price Is Right 1973–1974

The Restless Years 1977–1981

The Rogue Stallion 1990

The Scalp Merchant 1978

The Young Doctors 1976–1988

Three on a Match 1972

Tic Tac Dough 1960–1962

Time Machine 1985—USA

Tonight Show 1967–1968

Travelling Out West 1972

Two-Way Mirror (pilot) 1974

Txandaka (Kids Are Funny Too)
    1991—Spain

Un Posto al Sole (A Place in the Sun)
    1995—Italy

Unter Uns 1994–1995—Germany

Until Tomorrow 1975

Verbotene Liebe 1994–1995—Germany

Waterloo Station 1982–1983

What Do You Know? 1970

Wheel of Fortune 1959–1995

Women's World 1969

Wreck of The Batavia 1973

You've Got to Be Joking 1970–1971

INDEX

Noah, Bob 77, 190, 240, 241, 266–9, 274,
    277, 278, 344
None but the Brave 330, 336
Norton, Ezra 31
Number 96 141, 143

O

Oakley, John 199
O'Brien, Frances 138, 261
O'Callaghan, Gary 39, 40, 41–2
O'Grady, John (Jog) 53–6, 58, 61–4, 71–2,
    76–9, 89, 97, 98, 159, 195, 208, 308
O'Keefe, Johnny 91–2
Olympic Games 1956 59, 271
Ousey, Ian 313

P

Pace, Johnny 193
Packer, Clyde 289–91
Packer, Kerry 152, 153, 154, 161, 176,
    178–9, 287, 289, 290–4, 295–6
Packer, Sir Frank 79, 124, 287, 290, 291
Page, Tim 180
Palmer, Skip 228
panel games 107, 114–15
parochial internationalism 303–4, 306–7
Parramatta Hour 41
Party Line 278, 279, 280
Patrick, Vic 32–5, 37
Pearce, Guy 256
Pearson TV (UK) 312–13, 315
Peel, Robert 339, 340, 341
Peretsman, Nancy 313
Perfect Match 263
Phillips, Godfrey 204
Phillips, Margaret 16
phone calls, broadcasting of 62–3
Pick-a-Box 62, 68, 123, 128
Pike, Jerry 172–3, 175
Pinne, Peter 9, 205
Play Your Hunch 115
Plumb, Gwen 180, 219–20
Poor Fella Me 199
Possession 294
Powell, Lola 66–7, 71, 85, 109
Powell, Michael 113

Powell, Tom 27
Powers, Narelle 94
Preston, Mike 193
Price Is Right 275–6
Prisoner 151, 189, 201–6, 221, 247, 261,
    263, 305
    Prisoner: Cell Block H 206–9, 244, 248,
    343
Punishment 151, 244–6

Q

Qantas 43, 46, 49–50
Questions pour un Champion 300–4
Quinn, Anthony 135
Quintex 260
quiz shows 76–9, 80, 131

R

race calling 282–3, 288
radio stations
    2BS Bathurst 281, 282
    2CH Sydney 53–4, 59–60, 64, 271, 308
    2DU Dubbo 281
    2GB Sydney 32
    2GZ Orange 22–3, 24
    2KY Sydney 23–4, 45, 101
    2SM Sydney 24–5, 29, 32, 36, 40, 43, 51,
        63, 126, 281, 308
    2UE Sydney 41, 63
    2UW Sydney 32
    NBC radio (US) 59
radio talkback 126
Radio with Pictures 79
Radiotherapy Centers of Georgia (RCOG)
    333–6, 338
Rafferty, Chips 113
Ramsay, Gordon 173–5
Rand Stadium 48–50
'Rathmore' 118–19
Rattray, David 326
Rattray, Nicky 326
Read, Jack 30–1
Reagan, Nancy 136
Reg Grundy Enterprises 71–2, 81, 88, 93, 289
    logo 87
Reg Grundy Productions 240, 241, 270

TCN's new daytime quiz show Everybody's Talking is being produced at station's studios by Reg Grundy Enterprises. Pictured during production are, from left, compere Philip Brady, Terry Dear (guest panelist), panelists Joy Chambers and Ron Cadee and producer Reg Grundy.

SEVEN KEYS

R... GRU...

Australia's ace sp...

...en to 2CH Monday to Friday for THESE B...
... radio programmes designed for YOU, th...

• 9.15 p.m. BOXING DESCRI...
• 9.00 p.m. SPORTSMAN IN THE...
• 9.00 p.m. STUMP THE SPORTS...
•, 9.00...
9.00 p...

...se BIG s...
l compere...

The scene at Sydney Stadium when Darwin k...d Patrick. Radio commentator Reg Grundy is inter-viewing Darwin while McQuillan watches anxiously as ambulance men attend the prostrate Patrick.

2CH FOR THE DAVIS CUP

DAVIS CUP

UNINTERRUPTED DESCRIPTION!

2CH brings YOU every exciting moment of the DAVIS CUP described by REG GRUNDY and DINNY PAILS.

Hear the singles described from 1.00 p.m. Monday and Wednesday and the doubles on Tuesday from 1.45 p.m.

DAVIS CUP
2CH—MON., TUES., WED.

Presented by ...AIRWAYS LTD.

RUGB
Match
REG.

Associate
80 minute...

...r a fast and accurate...
...urday afternoon and...
...sunday night and com...